The Transfer of Ideas

The Transfer of Ideas: Historical Essays

Edited by *C. D. W. Goodwin*

and *I. B. Holley, Jr.*

The South Atlantic Quarterly
Durham, N. C. 1968

Library of Congress Catalogue Card Number 68-26691
© 1968 Duke University Press

Printed in the United States of America

Preface

Given the problem: How are ideas transferred across national or cultural boundaries?, the sponsors of this symposium cast about for a suitable frame of reference around which to structure the work of the participants. But a suitable model, even one formulated in the most general terms, proved impossible to find. There is certainly no dearth of scholarship on the theory of communication; the difficulty is of quite another order. The transfer of ideas is under study at so many different levels and in so many different ways that no single approach has yet emerged. The guidance which may be gained from the literature on communication in moving toward a theory of idea transfer we suggest briefly at the end of the book.

The sponsors of the symposium hoped that by imposing no preconceived scheme upon the participating scholars they would encourage a diversity not only in subject matter but in approach. This, they expected, would lead the participants to a fuller appreciation of the need for some sort of model to give order and meaning to their collective investigations. The lively discussions generated by the extended sessions of the symposium proved far more effective in identifying problems than in harmonizing them into an abstract model. Nonetheless, a number of useful ideas of general significance did emerge.

For the editors of this book to summarize or use conclusions as a basis for hazarding a generalized theory of the transfer of ideas is impractical in this brief introduction. It may be helpful, however, to point out some of the concerns which occupied these scholars. A major question which faced all participants was, what are the factors which affect the speed at which ideas flow and what are the principal vectors? When the authors examined this question, they found their attention drawn first to conditions in the place of origin and in the place of reception. In the country where an idea began its journey, at least two factors seemed to be critical. For an idea to travel effectively across national and cultural borders, it must have been developed thoroughly and presented convincingly to the domestic audience. A clear contrast can be observed in these studies between the slow exportation from Germany during an era of modern communications of the embryonic technology of shell architecture, and the speedy diffusion at a much earlier date of reformist thought as expounded eloquently by Martin Luther. A second condition in the country of origin which affects the transfer process is the relationship between the idea itself and the personal welfare of those who were carriers of the idea. It is striking that emigrants from old countries invariably brought certain sets of ideas with them to new environments as essential parts of their baggage. The Common Law of Great Britain, the notion of laissez faire, and principles of administrative justice, all flowed effectively between nations because the interests of their carriers were linked closely with the transfer.

The degree of similarity of social, economic, and political conditions—and especially of language—in the countries of origin and reception also has appeared to be critical in the flow of ideas. Legal and religious thought moved comparatively easily within the relatively homogeneous Western world. Economic ideas spread quickly from their place of birth in Great Britain, even though they underwent substantial adaptations in their new environments. Such a minor disparity between the countries of origin and reception as a difference in the working relationship of architects and engineers was a significant factor in the slow transfer of construction techniques.

The character of the mechanism for transferring ideas was of major interest in these studies. Where large groups of people took ideas with them from an old country to a new one, as in the case of immigrants to the American West or to Jamaica, the human beings themselves were the most significant carriers. When the Protestant message was carried across Europe with reformist zeal, the human element also was vital. When the transfer process came through a reading of literature in translation or through the casual interchange of individuals, as in the movement of economic ideas to Spain and shell architecture to the United States, the transfer mechanism was less reliable and effective. The one-way character of most idea vectors was marked; there is relatively little evidence in any of these studies of an important reverse flow of innovative thought. British society derived few gains from the legal precedents of the American frontier or from the economic ideas of their colonies and southern European neighbors.

Distinctive changes in important ideas during the actual process of transfer were revealed in most of these studies. Some changes were merely expedient for the carriers, as in the passage of architectural thought. In some instances, ideas were transformed in preparation for transfer, notably during the Reformation. Because the "big" simplistic idea often travels best, subtleties and qualifications were removed from systems of thought as they were made ready for export. The whole framework of social-science thought moved from a basic descriptive orientation in old countries to a prescriptive outlook in new ones. For example, market analysis, whether of free price determination or of collective bargaining, began in its European home as an attempt to explain existing sets of phenomena. In new countries these economic ideas were used to guide the building of new economic systems. It was significant that often the move from a descriptive to a prescriptive foundation came unconsciously and without recognition of the specific time and place for which the principles originally had been formulated.

From these studies, it is not yet possible to suggest a generalized explanation for the transfer of ideas. Nor is it possible to give an exhaustive list of the factors which condition the flows. It can be hoped, however, that by focusing a group of case studies upon this vital question, new insights have been gained and a basis has been laid both for further specialized research and perhaps for the tentative formulation of significant theory in the field of intercultural communication.

*   *   *

The papers contained in this collection are products of a symposium held at Duke University during 1966. A brief recounting of how this symposium came to be held may help the reader to understand the articles which grew out of it. The original idea arose in an interdisciplinary faculty committee formed to en-

courage research related to the history and transfer of ideas between or among nations. Widespread contemporary interest in what
has come to be called modernization, especially the movement to
and adoption of Western ways and means by the newly emergent
nations of the non-Western world, seemed to give a special relevance and even urgency to this question.

Because no entirely satisfactory explanatory model for the
transfer of ideas exists, the committee decided to bring together
case studies of the transfer process over a wide range of times and
places, from which it was hoped a useful paradigm might ultimate-
ly be derived. This pattern of procedure was dictated at least in
some measure by the desire of the organizers to make the fullest
possible use of scholars already on the Duke campus. It seemed
highly desirable to attract participants whose current research projects bore in one way or another upon the problem in hand; and
this approach avoided that tendency toward artificiality which is
so often evident when scholars are invited to write papers on a
theme set by an extraneous group of conference organizers. By encouraging the presentation of papers drawn from the scholar's
ongoing research, the diversion of energies was minimized and
the author's enthusiasm for the task was heightened; the range and
catholicity of the studies gave special interest to the results.

In approaching potential participants, the committee took as
its point of departure a single question: in the author's particular
subject for research, what were the problems encountered in the
transfer of ideas across cultural boundaries? Authors then were
left free to deal with their research materials as they saw fit. As it
turned out, some focused on one part of an incident of transfer,
some on another part, and some on the complete process.

In order to achieve the maximum impact and effectiveness for
the symposium, the committee laid out a three-part program extending over six months. The sequence of events was as follows:
for the first phase, in the spring of 1966, two distinguished scholars
were brought to the Duke campus to present addresses which
sparked discussions on the theme selected for the symposium. The
first such visitor was Professor Emeritus F. S. C. Northrop of Yale
University, who delivered a public lecture on the topic "Intercultural Transfer of Ideas: East Meets West." Professor Northrop
spent two days on the campus holding discussions with various

members of the symposium group. The second distinguished visitor was the late Professor Moses Hadas of Columbia University, who spoke on "Cultural Diffusion: The Hellenistic Melting Pot." Professor Hadas also spent two days in discussions on campus.

The second phase of the program came during the early summer of 1966 when the faculty members involved in the symposium were invited to join a weekly luncheon meeting with a group of graduate students, most of whom were beginning work on a dissertation related to the theme of the symposium. At each weekly meeting, one student presented a brief account of his project for general criticism and discussion, with a special focus on implications of the paper for the mobility of ideas in an intercultural context.

The third and final phase of the symposium came in the Autumn of 1966, when faculty members offered papers for discussion at a series of three dinner meetings. The papers collected here, all of which are historical in nature, were with one exception drawn from these sessions. The paper by Mr. Paul Echols, presented during the summer, was judged to be sufficiently meritorious to be worthy of inclusion.

The interdisciplinary faculty committee that originally conceived the plan for the symposium included John H. Hallowell, professor of political science; Lionel Stevenson, James B. Duke Professor of English; I. B. Holley, Jr., professor of history; and Craufurd D. W. Goodwin, chairman, associate professor of economics. The detailed work of planning was carried on by Goodwin and Holley working in conjunction with Seymour Mauskopf, assistant professor of history, who co-ordinated arrangements. Financial support was provided by the Duke University Committee on the History and Comparative Study of Ideas with funds granted by the Ford Foundation. The views expressed by contributors to this volume are, however, exclusively their own.

The symposium is reprinted from the *South Atlantic Quarterly* for Spring, 1968.

C. D. W. G.

I. B. H.

Contents

The Development of Shell Architecture in the United States,
1932-1962: An Examination of the Transfer of a
Structural Idea   *Paul Clinton Echols*   3

The Transmission of English Law to the Frontier
of America   *W. B. Hamilton*   43

The Spread of the Protestant Reformation of the Sixteenth
Century: A Historical Case Study in the Transfer
of Ideas   *Hans J. Hillerbrand*   65

German Socialist and Russian Soviets: The Transfer
of Workers' Councils from Russia to Germany
in 1918   *John Raphael Staude*   87

English Economic Thought in Spain, 1776-1848
Robert S. Smith   106

Economic Ideas in the Development of Jamaica:
Colonial Reception of Social Thought
Craufurd D. W. Goodwin   138

Toward a Theory of the Intercultural Transfer of Ideas
C. D. W. Goodwin and *I. B. Holley, Jr.*   170

The Transfer of Ideas

The Development of Shell Architecture in the United States, 1932-1962

An Examination of the Transfer of a Structural Idea

Paul Clinton Echols

Mid-century America has witnessed the rapid evolution of a new method of building with reinforced concrete based upon a European structural development—the principle of the thin shell. Pioneered in the 1920's by French and German civil engineers, shell design soon spread throughout Europe, being applied to a wide variety of building types ranging from market halls and factories to planetariums and sports arenas. By 1932, when the shell was introduced in the United States, its advantages already had been amply demonstrated through ten years of experimentation in Europe. Yet American engineers tended to view the shell merely in terms of a new technique of roof construction rather than as a revolutionary concept of space enclosure. Shell buildings erected in this country during the thirties and forties displayed little breadth of imagination, lagging behind European structures both in numbers and in quality. American architects did not begin exploiting the structural and aesthetic possibilities of shell design until the late fifties.

The failure of American builders to capitalize initially upon a significant technological innovation in an age dependent on applied technology and rapid communications for its survival raises a number of questions concerning the means of the transfer of ideas from one environment to another. It has been said that the evolu-

MR. ECHOLS graduated magna cum laude from Duke University, where an earlier version of his research on shell architecture won a prize in the undergraduate honors seminar in history. He is now working toward a doctorate in musicology at New York University with a Woodrow Wilson Scholarship.

tion of a new form is determined essentially by two causes: new needs and new possibilities.[1] The establishment of shell design as a technique of erecting wide-span roofs may well have been dependent upon the mechanics of supply and demand, of new possibilities and new needs. However, its evolution as an "idea" from a technique in the hands of civil engineers to a broadly based form of architectural expression involved a far more complex interaction of factors.

In attempting to isolate those factors that impeded—or, conversely, fostered—concrete shell development in this country, such material considerations as economic feasibility, competition with other structural systems, and the suitability of the shell to current building types come first to mind. They were certainly foremost in the minds of the engineers concerned with developing shell design. But behind these considerations stood equally important, though less tangible, factors such as the impact of contemporary architectural style on shell design, professional and public receptivity to new ideas in building, and the influence of technical and historical precedent. The growth of the shell as a technique was dependent primarily upon the material considerations; but the evolution of the shell as an idea can be understood only by examining the more basic factors that in turn conditioned the environment in which the shell took root.

I

The shell was developed in Europe as a solution to the problem of spanning large interior spaces economically with a minimum of materials and supporting columns. The spectacular halls and pavilions of the great nineteenth-century expositions were built, for the most part, of iron and steel. But the early pioneers of reinforced concrete construction discovered that a concrete mix, strengthened with a network of steel mesh or rods, combined the plasticity and compressive strength of concrete with the tensile pliancy of steel to produce a material emminently suited to spanning large areas. As the plastic nature of reinforced concrete became better understood, its use evolved from the early imitations of wooden or steel post-and-beam construction to vaults and flat, monolithic slabs.

---

[1] Jacques Barzun, "The Architect and the Aspirations of His Day," *Four Great Makers of Modern Architecture* (New York, 1963), p. 7.

The breakthrough of reinforced concrete to a position where it could realistically compete with structural steel in spanning large areas was accomplished in the early decades of this century by a small number of brilliant engineers, among them François Hennebique and Eugène Freyssinet in France, and Robert Maillart in Switzerland.[2] European architects, led by such men as Auguste Perret and Tony Garnier in France, and Hans Poelzig and Max Berg in Germany, experimented with reinforced concrete in the design of different types of vaults, roof slabs, and domes. And such renowned figures as Erich Mendelsohn and Le Corbusier began searching for an "aesthetic" of reinforced concrete, for new ways of using this material.[3]

The chief obstacle to the use of reinforced concrete in vaults and wide spans, however, was that the weight of the concrete increased proportionally with the width of the span, necessitating the use of thick ribs or other devices for support. Methods had to be devised that would reduce the amount of concrete to make its use in wide spans more economically attractive.

With the erection of a series of airship hangars in 1916 and 1920-1921, the French engineer Freyssinet developed a system of roof construction employing parabolic arches that greatly reduced the thickness of reinforced concrete roofs. The hangars, at Orly, used free-standing reinforced concrete arches bridged together by a thin, corrugated concrete skin.[4] Freyssinet's methods were quickly taken up in Germany and adapted to the design of a number of large halls and auditoriums, thereby receiving the name of *Hallenbau* construction. During the twenties this system spread throughout most of Europe.[5]

[2] See *Encyclopaedia of Modern Architecture*, ed. Gerd Hatje (London, 1963), pp. 109-111, 181-183; A. A. Raafat, *Reinforced Concrete in Architecture* (New York, 1958), pp. 29-30, 75-79; and Max Bill, *Robert Maillart* (Zurich, 1949; 3rd ed., 1962), for biographical surveys of these engineers.

[3] See Peter Collins, *Concrete: The Vision of a New Architecture* (London, 1959), pp. 19-76, and Henry-Russell Hitchcock, *Architecture: Nineteenth and Twentieth Centuries* (Baltimore, 1958), pp. 307-319, for the development of reinforced concrete in architecture during the nineteenth century.

[4] P. Morton Shand, "Steel and Concrete: A Historical Survey," *Architectural Review*, LXXII (Nov., 1932), 178. See also Jürgen Joedicke, *A History of Modern Architecture* (New York, 1959), pp. 138-140, for a description of the *Hallenbau* system and illustrations of buildings.

[5] Arnold Whittick, *European Architecture in the Twentieth Century* (2 vols.; London, 1953), II, 161-162; Joedicke, *Modern Architecture*, p. 139.

The *Hallenbau* system was the immediate forerunner of the structural shell. Its chief advantage was that the strength of the roof derived not from the thickness of the concrete but from the rigidity produced by the corrugated folds of the thin concrete skin, resulting in a great reduction of the amount of concrete needed. The transition from the *Hallenbau* system to the shell was effected by extending the principle of rigidity from a corrugated skin to curved, monolithic slabs such as domes and barrels.

The credit for the first true shell building belongs to two German engineers, Walter Bauersfield of the optical firm of Carl Zeiss, and Franz Dischinger of the engineering and contracting firm of Dyckerhoff and Widmann.[6] As developed by these two men and others who followed, the shell may be defined as a thin, curved, continuous membrane or skin capable of sustaining stresses and loads through the rigidity of its curved shape rather than by the thickness or strength of the materials. The structural properties of the thin shell are akin to those of the sea shell and the eggshell in which great strength is derived solely from their curved shapes, which resist bending. Parallel to its use in building, the shell principle has long been applied in part or in whole under the name of "monocoque" construction to shipbuilding, automobile and airplane manufacture.[7]

Because of its ready availability and economy, concrete has remained the principal material employed for shell construction. In recent years, however, shell builders have made increasing use of other materials, chiefly laminated plywood and steel plates. Both

[6] Though the work of Bauersfield and Dischinger can be considered the first systematic exploitation of the shell and generated most of the future developments in shell design, there were still earlier shell or shell-like buildings. The Catalan architect, Antonio Gaudí, constructed plaster models of hyperbolic paraboloidal forms and actually constructed a scalloped shell to cover a school in 1909. He most probably did not use any systematic mathematical analysis, however, relying instead upon model testing and his own engineering intuition in his work with shells. In the United States, at the turn of the century, there were any number of brick or concrete silos, cisterns, and similar structures built on the shell principle through intuition rather than by mathematical calculation. Charles S. Whitney lists a number of shell buildings built before 1922 (the earliest dating from 1910) in "Reinforced Concrete for Thin-Shell Structures," American Concrete Institute *Proceedings*, XLIX (Feb., 1953), 524-528. All of these shells that I have been able to identify must, however, be considered as more properly of the *Hallenbau* type rather than true shells.

[7] For a more technical definition of shells, see Hatje, *Encyclopaedia*, p. 257, and Leonard Michaels, *Contemporary Structure in Architecture* (New York, 1950), pp. 102-103.

I. DOMES

II FOLDED PLATE

III BARRELS

LONG

SHORT

IV CONOIDS

V SCALLOPS

VI HYPERBOLIC PARABOLOIDS

SADDLE

UMBRELLA

VII FREE FORMS

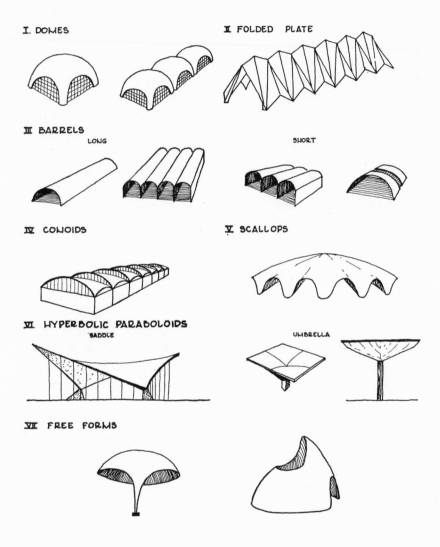

materials are particularly adaptable to certain shell forms, such as
hyperbolic paraboloids and folded plates, and they do not require
elaborate scaffolding, as is the case with reinforced concrete, to
be erected into place.[8]

The forms possible with shell construction are numerous and
have been classified most frequently by their type of curvature or
mathematical derivation. Shell construction was first applied to traditional geometrical forms such as domes and barrels. Two types
of barrels were commonly used: short barrels, in which the length
is approximately equal to the width; and long barrels, in which the
length is significantly greater than the width. The principle was then
extended to more complex forms: conoids; scallops; and hyperbolic
paraboloids, either saddle or umbrella shaped. Because of its unique
configuration the hyperbolic paraboloid does not require the use of
warped boards or steel plates for supporting formwork, making it
one of the most economical shell types to erect. In recent years
there has been some growth of non-symmetrical free forms, which
are more difficult and expensive to compute than standard geometrical ones.[9]

The shell was one of the most complex and technically advanced developments in the field of reinforced concrete design. In
contrast to the relative simplicity of steel-frame statics, shell design
required a detailed knowledge of the plastic properties of concrete
and an understanding of the complex structural behavior of curved
membranes. Precise mathematical formulae had to be derived in
order to analyze to an exacting degree the compressive and tensile
stresses operating on a shell form.[10]

The complexities of the design process were equaled by those
of the actual construction. An intricate system of wooden or metal
formwork had to be erected in the exact shape of the shell over

[8] See Daniel H. Brown, "Plywood Shell Structures," and Arthur H. Nilson,
"Light Gage Steel Shell Roofs," *World Conference on Shell Structures: Proceedings* (Washington, D. C., 1964), pp. 109-116, 117-126. This volume contains
a number of papers dealing with the application of various materials to shell
construction.

[9] For illustrations and descriptions of different shell types the definitive work
to date is J. Joedicke, *Shell Architecture* (New York, 1963). See pp. 20-28 for
definitions, and pp. 175-176 for diagrams of free-form shells.

[10] See A. L. Bouma, "On Approximate Methods of Shell Analysis: A General Survey," *World Conference on Shell Structures*, pp. 475-486, for an historical
survey and brief descriptions of methods of shell analysis.

which the concrete was to be cast, necessitating in most cases the use of warped boards to fit the curvature. The casting of the shell itself called for a large labor force, and the cost of such labor, coupled with that of the preliminary design and formwork, could amount to a staggering percentage of the total cost of the entire building.[11] Despite such technical difficulties, shells were ideal for roofing large, open spaces for a number of reasons: the absence of obstructing interior supports or columns, minimal maintenance costs, a high degree of fire resistance, and minimal amounts of materials needed for the shell. In contrast to traditional masonry or wooden roofs, shell thicknesses generally ranged from four inches to one and three-quarter inches.

The earliest solutions to the problems of design and construction of shells were worked out by Bauersfield and Dischinger in the building of a number of planetariums for the Zeiss firm in Jena, Germany. The firm had perfected a planetarium projector and scheduled the first unit for installation in the Deutsches Museum at Munich. The apparatus was to be placed in a hemispherical room, and the firm needed a similar domed structure built immediately and cheaply for testing purposes. In 1922 Dischinger and Bauersfield completed their first concrete shell structure, fifty-two feet in diameter, on the roof of one of the factory buildings at Jena.[12] Patents were subsequently taken out by Zeiss and Dyckerhoff and Widmann for the method of design and steel reinforcement of the shell developed by the two engineers. The method became known as the Zeiss-Dywidag or Z-D system.[13]

With the construction of a market hall at Frankfurt-am-Main in 1927, the Z-D system was further extended to cover the design of barrel shells. The new development, however, did not spread unchallenged. Skeptical authorities requested a model test of the

[11] The problems of erecting formwork for shell casting are analyzed by Anton Tedesko, "Construction Plant for Shell Structures Should be Carefully Co-ordinated," *Civil Engineering*, XXIII (Feb., 1953), 44-49.

[12] Joedicke, *Shell Architecture*, pp. 281-283. Reprint of a paper given by Bauersfield in Berlin, Dec. 12, 1942.

[13] A complete analysis and thorough discussion of the Z-D system is found in H. J. Krause and Franz Dischinger, *Dachbauten: Kragdächer, Schalen- und Rippencuppeln-Bearbeitet* (4th ed.; Berlin, 1928). This work is reviewed by A. Floris, "Domes and Self-Supporting Arches," *Engineering News-Record*, CII (Feb. 21, 1929), 321-322. Incidentally, this is the first reference found by this writer to shell design in an American publication.

Frankfurt hall before approving the construction of so important a building. The test proved so successful that the model took up to 50 per cent more than the planned load.[14]

The earliest steps in the introduction of more sophisticated shell forms were made in France by F. Aimond and Bernard Lafaille in their work with hyperbolic paraboloidal forms. During the early thirties, both men published papers setting out methods for the calculation of this type of shell. In Italy, at the same time, the engineer, Giorgio Baroni, built a number of small storage sheds for the Alfa Romeo factory at Milan using simple hyperbolic paraboloidal saddle roofs.[15]

By 1932, when the shell was introduced in the United States, much of the groundwork for the calculation and construction of shells had been laid. Cylindrical, octagonal, and barrel shells had been applied to a variety of utilitarian building types: market halls, garages, indoor swimming pools, power plants, and warehouses.[16] The firm of Dyckerhoff and Widmann sent one of its engineers, Anton Tedesko, to the United States to negotiate the rights to the Z-D patents. Both the rights and the services of Tedesko were acquired by the engineering company of Roberts and Schaefer in Chicago.[17] In 1934 the first shell building in this country was erected, a small barrel-roofed dairy barn for one of the exhibits at the Chicago Century of Progress Exposition.[18] A year later the Roberts and Schaefer Company designed the hemispherical shell dome of the Hayden Planetarium in New York, the first permanent large-scale shell in the United States.

During the thirties Roberts and Schaefer, largely by virtue of its patent rights, retained an almost complete monopoly on shell design. The depression, of course, had severely inhibited building

[14] K. Hajnal-Kónyi, "Shell Concrete Construction," *Architect's Year Book*, No. 2 (London, 1947), pp. 175-176.

[15] Eduardo F. Catalano, "Structures of Warped Surfaces," *Student Publication of the School of Design* (North Carolina State), X, No. 1 (1960), 2.

[16] See Charles S. Whitney, A.C.I. *Proceedings*, XLIX (Feb., 1953), 524-528, for a fairly comprehensive listing of the important shell buildings erected in the United States and Europe up to 1953; and Whittick, *European Architecture*, II, 160-168, for a survey of European shell development up to the thirties.

[17] "Thin Concrete Shells for Domes and Barrel-Vault Roofs," *Engineering News-Record*, CVIII (April 14, 1932), 538.

[18] "Concrete Shell Roof Used on World's Fair Building," *ibid.*, CXII (June 14, 1934), 775-776.

1. PLANETARIUM: JENA, GERMANY
W. BAUERSFIELD; DYCKERHOFF & WIDMANN
1925   DOME

2. MARKET HALL: ALGECIRAS, SPAIN
EDUARDO TORROJA
1934   DOME

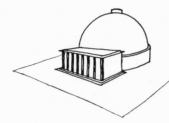

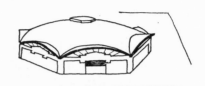

4. ST. LOUIS-LAMBERT AIRPORT TERMINAL: ST LOUIS, MO.
HELLMUTH, YAMASAKI & LEINWEBER;
ROBERTS & SCHAEFER, ENGINEERS
1956.   CROSS BARRELS

3. ALABAMA LIVESTOCK COLISEUM: MONTGOMERY, ALA.
AMMANN & WHITNEY, ENGINEERS
1950   BARREL

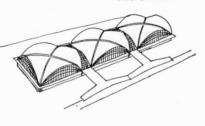

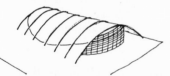

5. T.W.A. TERMINAL: KENNEDY INTERNATIONAL AIRPORT, N.Y.
EERO SAARINEN
1962   FREE FORM

6. WARM MINERAL SPRINGS INN: VENICE, FLORIDA
VICTOR LUNDY
1958   HYPERBOLIC PARABOLOID-UMBRELLA

construction, and the company had few competitors in the unex-
plored, relatively new field of shell building. Architectural firms
employing shell construction contracted the actual shell design to
Roberts and Schaefer or to one of its allied firms. Other engineering firms were drawn into shell design during the forties, largely
because of increased military construction (hangars, warehouses,
etc.). The variety of shell types remained disappointingly limited,
however, domes and barrels continuing as the standard forms. More
imaginative design and the use of more exotic forms, such as hyperbolic paraboloids, did not begin until well into the fifties.[19]

The initial delay in exploiting the potentialities of the structural shell had not gone unnoticed. In 1935 an editorial in the *Engineering News-Record* criticized American engineers for failing
to make use of new structural ideas and methods:

The thin-shell concrete dome has received even less of a welcome, the
planetarium roof in New York being the first example except for a small
cowbarn at the Century of Progress Exhibition in Chicago. Its advantages nevertheless are plainly demonstrable, and it may have a bright
future before it in American structural practice. The important point is
that engineers in this country should let none of these European developments escape their notice. Structural thinking is bound by no national
ties.[20]

The editorial went on to point out that the shell dome had been
used in Europe for over a decade but was still extremely rare in this
country.

Almost twenty-five years later practically identical complaints
continued to appear. In a 1954 article on thin shells for *Architectural Record*, engineer and educator Mario Salvadori, himself one
of the prime contributors to shell development in the United States,

[19] See Hajnal-Kónyi, "Shell Concrete Construction," pp. 175-193, for an
evaluation of European and American shell construction up to 1947. I find no
mention of any hyperbolic paraboloidal shells or similar warped forms being built
in the United States until the fifties; however, Prof. Salvadori of Columbia University indicated in a letter (Oct. 1, 1966) to me that he recalls seeing
some photographs of a hyperbolic paraboloid built by a student at Columbia to
roof his parents' home *ca.* 1945. I am particularly grateful to Prof. Mario Salvadori and Mr. Boyd Anderson of Ammann and Whitney, consulting engineers,
for their generous co-operation in answering numerous questions on the development of shells, and to Prof. I. B. Holley of Duke University who originally
suggested this field of research to me.
[20] "New Structural Forms," CXV (July 25, 1935), 130-131.

noted that "the wide possibilities of thin shells have been only slightly tapped, particularly in the United States."[21] Many engineers, architects, and critics echoed Salvadori's comments on the lack of progress in shell design. Numerous reasons were cited to explain the delay, most of them having to do with economic problems. An early article on shells, which appeared in *Architectural Forum*, pointed out that European engineers, faced with chronic shortages of structural steel, turned to shell concrete as an inexpensive means of construction, but their American counterparts, provided with a plentiful and far more inexpensive supply of materials, had much less incentive to design simply for economy of building material. The article summed up: "It is the economic situation which for years has held the U.S. behind other nations in the development of highly refined designs in shell concrete."[22] Lawrence Lessing, a consultant to the *Forum*, brought forward other reasons for the delay, citing the high labor costs involved in erecting elaborate framework for shells, the lack of consistent concrete research in American institutions, and the outdated nature of most building codes, which often contained excessive restrictions on reinforced concrete construction in general.[23]

Despite the apparent consensus of many on the importance of the technical and economical obstacles to shell development, some viewed the problem of delay in a different light. The great Mexican shell builder, Félix Candela, in an article for the 1952 *Proceedings* of the American Concrete Institute, saw the principal reason for the limited progress made in shell design in this country in "the reluctance of owners to accept any change in the conventional type of roof, and chiefly in the general impression held by the average practicing engineer that the design of a shell is a highly scientific problem requiring specialized knowledge."[24]

John Burchard and Albert Bush-Brown, in their detailed study of American architecture, added yet another view:

[21] Mario G. Salvadori, "Thin Shells: Part I," *Architectural Record*, CXVI (July, 1954), 174.
[22] "Shell Concrete for Spanning Large Areas," *Architectural Forum*, XCI (Dec., 1949), 104-105.
[23] Lawrence Lessing, "The Rise of Shells," *ibid.*, CIX (July, 1958), 109.
[24] Felix Candela and Eric C. Molke, "Discussion on Candela's 'Simple Concrete Shell Structures,'" A.C.I. *Proceedings*, XLVIII (Dec., 1952), 332.

The usual explanation, that high labor costs and low steel costs prevented our exercises in concrete, ignores the fact that Americans have purchased anything they really wanted; the truth is that until recently Americans did not understand concrete well enough to design in it and did not want the forms enough to wish to study the methods.[25]

Still others saw the delay of shell development as a result of a lack of co-ordination between engineers—with a technical outlook—and architects—concerned principally with aesthetic considerations. Theodor Rohdenburg, professor of architecture at Columbia University, briefly summarized the danger of a breakdown in communications between the two professions: "This divorce of architectural form and expression from the structure within, coupled with the ever increasing complexities of the science of construction in steel and reinforced concrete, considerably curtailed the architect's hitherto comprehensive sphere of control."[26]

Many observers, concerned over the technical and economic obstacles to shell development in the United States, rightly pointed out that its success in Europe was the result of a completely different set of circumstances.[27] The formula of new needs and new possibilities that appeared to work so well for shell construction in Europe became bogged down in a host of complications, not all of which were sufficiently understood in this country. How prepared were architects and engineers to take up shell building? Was there a definite place for shell construction in the United States? What was the condition of reinforced concrete research and technology, upon which depended the rapid implementation of the shell principle? In looking back to the state of the building arts in this country parallel to European developments during the first third of the century, it may be possible to find the causes for an environment unfavorable to new structural ideas and to discover how the early difficulties of shell construction were finally overcome.

[25] *The Architecture of America: A Social and Cultural History* (Boston, 1961), p. 468.

[26] Theodor K. Rohdenburg, *A History of the School of Architecture, Columbia University* (New York, 1954), p. 18.

[27] Among articles citing technical problems of shell design and construction may be mentioned D. Briggs and G. Modsen, "Building for Economy with the Hyperbolic Paraboloid," *A.C.I. Proceedings*, LVII (Oct., 1960), 373-383; Milo S. Katchum, "Economic Factors in Shell Roof Construction," *World Conference on Shell Structures*, pp. 97-102; and Antone Tedesko, "Construction Aspects of Thin-Shell Structures," *A.C.I. Proceedings*, XLIX (Feb., 1953), 505-520.

II

At the opening of the twentieth century, American concrete technology was struggling to catch up with the advances made by Europeans. The development of Portland Cement, an English achievement, had been an important step forward in the creation of a very strong, consistent cementing agent capable of binding together the mixture of sand, water, and stone gravel that made up concrete.[28] Until 1900, almost three quarters of the Portland Cement consumed in the United States was imported from Europe. After the turn of the century the cement industry in this country underwent a period of tremendous growth. The United States remained behind Europe, however, in the development of high early-strength cements and in the use of the rotary kiln, an advance over older kilns that more than tripled the daily production of cement.[29]

Concrete research and experimentation with different types of reinforcing methods gradually pulled abreast of European work. From the last decades of the nineteenth century onward increasing numbers of patents were given to American engineers and inventors for applications of reinforcing techniques in concrete construction.[30] In 1903 the first engineering experiment station was established at the University of Illinois; the following year a second research center was set up at Iowa State College (now University).[31] The National Association of Cement Users, later to become the American Concrete Institute (A.C.I.), was founded in 1905. In 1916 the Portland Cement Association was established. Both institutions, made possible through financial support from the cement industry and other private concerns, undertook a major portion of the research on concrete and cement during the first third of the century.[32]

As a result of the increasing attention paid to the possibilities of reinforced concrete construction, a number of American build-

[28] A short survey of English and French developments in Portland Cement is found in Jasper O. Draffin, "A Brief History of Lime, Cement, Concrete, and Reinforced Concrete," *Bulletin* of the Engineering Experiment Station, University of Illinois, XL (June 29, 1943).

[29] *Ibid.*, p. 29.

[30] Carl W. Condit, *American Building Art: The Nineteenth Century* (New York, 1960), pp. 231-240.

[31] James G. McGivern, *First Hundred Years of Engineering Education in the United States* (Spokane, Wash., 1960), p. 158.

[32] W. A. Maples and P. E. Wilde, "A Story of Progress: Fifty Years of the American Concrete Institute," *A.C.I. Proceedings*, L (Feb., 1954), 410-425.

ers began to adapt the new material to the construction of grain elevators, warehouses, and other similar utilitarian buildings.[33] The mass-production techniques of such industrial concerns as the Ford and Packard Motor Companies required wide-span interiors free of columns to accommodate huge assembly lines and to provide space needed for the rapid retooling of machinery. The use of reinforced concrete to meet these requirements was pioneered by two men in particular, Ernest L. Ransome and Albert Kahn.[34] Their factories, constructed with utilitarian necessities rather than exterior beauty in mind, were nonetheless strikingly handsome. They were among the first examples in the United States of the use of plain surfaces and long, horizontal lines on the exterior of a building that gave meaning to the structural core of reinforced concrete.[35]

The work of Kahn and Ransome gave name to an emerging industrial architecture in the first decade of the new century, the Factory Style. This new trend in American industrial architecture, far removed from the popularly accepted styles of "polite" architecture of the day, did not escape the notice of the contemporary Functionalist movement in European architecture. Le Corbusier, the leading French exponent of Modern Architecture, was moved to say: "Thus we have the American grain elevators and factories, the magnificent first fruits of the new age. The American engineers overwhelm with their calculations our expiring architecture."[36]

American reinforced concrete building, despite so auspicious a birth, was beset with serious problems. There were large numbers of failures in concrete construction and many cases of malpractice involving concrete during the early years of the century.[37] Ernest Ransome complained in 1912 of the frequent practice on the part

[33] See Carl W. Condit, *American Building Art: The Twentieth Century* (New York, 1961), pp. 151-177, for a survey of concrete construction methods in the United States from the turn of the century.

[34] Ada Louise Huxtable, "Concrete Technology in U.S.A.: Historical Survey," *Progressive Architecture*, XLI (Oct., 1960), 147-149. See also by the same author, "The Work of Ernest L. Ransome," *ibid.*, XXXVIII (Sept., 1957), 139-142; and George Nelson, *Industrial Architecture of Albert Kahn, Inc.* (New York, 1939).

[35] See Ada Louise Huxtable, "Factory for Packard Motor Car Co.—1905," *Progressive Architecture*, XXXVIII (Oct., 1957), 121-122; and Albert Kahn, Inc., *Industrial and Commercial Buildings* (Detroit, 1937), *passim*, for illustrations of some of the major projects of Ransome and Kahn.

[36] *Towards a New Architecture* (1st ed., 1927; New York, 1946), p. 33.

[37] Huxtable, "Concrete Technology in U.S.A.," p. 149. See also Thomas McKaig, *Building Failures: Case Studies in Construction and Design* (New York, 1962), pp. 13-46.

of contractors of rubbing cement mortar into exposed building surfaces, forming a thin finishing layer which soon peeled and cracked:
"There is hardly any locality where samples of this work may not
be found, showing the disgraceful results obtained."[38] As efforts to
attain maximum spans in factories increased, reinforced concrete
was left behind in favor of structural steel. Concrete technology
could not keep up with burgeoning industrial demands and cheap
structural steel.[39] Imaginative and economical design in reinforced
concrete was further stymied by rigid and sometimes backward procedures specified by the building codes of American cities.

Specifications regarding reinforced concrete construction of
various types were first incorporated in building codes during the
early years of the century. Considering the relative newness of the
material at that time, it is not surprising that many of the codes
tended to discriminate against it. As late as 1926, a writer for *Concrete* magazine noted that: "Because of the shortage of general
knowledge of the material, concrete was hedged about with pre-
cautionary safety factors that actually proved to be excessive, and
in many cases which were the result of arbitrary selection rather
than of scientific determination."[40]

While concrete technology suffered through its birth pains and
engineers studied new uses for reinforced concrete, American architecture, in the throes of a period of stylistic eclecticism, concerned itself with other goals. The Chicago Exposition of 1893
marked the triumphant entry of Neo-Classic style, its pompous
echoes of Imperial Rome an appropriate reflection of the burgeoning national consciousness and imperialistic mood of the nation.[41]
Neo-Classicism, while predominant at the turn of the century, was
accompanied by an active disinterment of other historical styles—
Gothic, Renaissance, Romanesque—and an occasional excursion
into the more exotic fields of Aztec, Assyrian, and Egyptian architecture.

[38] Quoted in Huxtable, "Concrete Technology in U.S.A.," p. 149.

[39] Nelson, *Industrial Architecture of Albert Kahn*, p. 11.

[40] "Reinforced Concrete and the Building Codes," *Concrete*, XXIX (Sept., 1926), 37.

[41] See Montgomery Schuyler, "Last Words About the World's Fair," *Architectural Record*, III (Jan.-March, 1894), 271-301, for a penetrating analysis of
the architectural significance of the Chicago Exposition. Burchard and Bush-
Brown, of all sources consulted, have the most to say on the "Imperial" aspects
of early twentieth-century architecture; see pp. 220-222, 273-275, 295.

The demands of eclecticism for faithful reinterpretations of previous styles did not, however, preclude the use of contemporary developments in steel and reinforced concrete. The work of Louis Sullivan and his contemporaries of the Chicago School produced great strides forward in the use of the structural steel skeleton in skyscraper construction.[42] The functional and aesthetic theories developed by Sullivan in his quest for an appropriate architectural expression of the skyscraper were largely ignored by his contemporaries. Yet his technological innovations attained a wide circulation. Steel and concrete were the sinews of many of the most important buildings erected in the United States during the first third of the century; however, the outer clothing was generally of masonry or plaster in the appropriate Gothic, Neo-Classic, or Renaissance style. Decorative flying buttresses and Gothic tracery effectively covered over the steel cages of such buildings as the Woolworth Tower (1913) in New York and the Chicago *Tribune* Building (1925).

Despite the increasing use of reinforced concrete in building construction, the struggle to find a new concrete aesthetic commensurate with the unique potentialities of the material was taken up not by the architectural profession but by the industrial builders of the Factory Style. The split between architect and engineer over the development of new structural processes had been evident in the United States since the nineteenth century.[43] In 1894, Montgomery Schuyler, one of America's foremost architectural critics, noted:

The architect resents the engineer as a barbarian; the engineer makes light of the architect as a dilettante. It is difficult to deny that each is largely in the right. The artistic insensibility of the modern engineer is not more fatal to architectural progress than the artistic irrelevancy of the modern architect. In general, engineering is at least progressive, while architecture is at most stationary.[44]

[42] Carl W. Condit, *The Chicago School of Architecture* (Chicago, 1964); Mark L. Peisch, *The Chicago School of Architecture: Early Followers of Sullivan and Wright* (New York, 1964).

[43] James M. Fitch, *American Building: The Forces that Shape It* (New York, 1948), pp. 62-78. See also, by the same author, *Architecture and the Esthetics of Plenty* (New York, 1961), pp. 229-240, for a survey of the gap between the two professions in the twentieth century.

[44] "Modern Architecture," *Architectural Record*, IV (July-Sept., 1894), 13. This and other important writings by Schuyler are collected in *American Architecture and Other Writings*, ed. William H. Jordy and Ralph Coe (2 vols.; Cambridge, Mass., 1961).

While "barbarian" engineers such as Ransome attempted to develop an aesthetic approach to reinforced concrete construction, American architects of the early twentieth century seemed to do little to disabuse themselves of Schuyler's indictment. The general attitude seemed to be that engineering problems were no concern of theirs. A. O. Elzner, the architect of one of the earliest reinforced concrete skyscrapers, the Ingalls Building in Cincinnati (1902), stated the architects' case: "The principles of concrete-steel are rapidly coming to be fairly well understood, especially so by the structural engineers; for, after all, it is primarily an engineering problem."[45] Few architects followed the example set by Frank Lloyd Wright in his extensive use of reinforced concrete slabs and bold treatment of exposed concrete on the exterior walls of the Unity Temple in Oak Park, Illinois (1906).[46] And few architects seemed to be aware of what their European contemporaries were doing with reinforced concrete. When American architects did use concrete for exterior walls and surfaces, it was frequently cast so as to look like carved stone. Buildings such as the Mayan Theater in Los Angeles and Grauman's Chinese Theater in Hollywood were bizarre examples of the extremes to which concrete was employed for ornamental purposes as a cheap substitute for carved masonry.[47]

Undoubtedly the reluctance of architects to develop new ways of using concrete as a surface material and to experiment with the structural possibilities of reinforced concrete was partially owing to the prevailing feeling during the first quarter of the century that concrete was somehow not fit for "polite" architecture and was better left to industrial and utilitarian building. The many early failures in reinforced concrete construction and the general lack of experience in working with concrete were also serious obstacles to the acceptance of the material as worthy of architectural consideration.[48] Yet American architects, by failing to take up the

[45] "The First Concrete Skyscraper," *Architectural Record*, XV (June, 1904), 533.

[46] "Unity Temple became the first concrete monolith in the world—that is to say—the first building complete as monolithic architecture in the wooden forms in which it was cast." Frank Lloyd Wright, *The Future of Architecture* (New York, 1953), p. 195.

[47] Raafat, *Reinforced Concrete in Architecture*, pp. 35-39.

[48] See n. 37, above. I can find no sources that specify architects' objections to reinforced concrete in architectural design. Secondary works, especially Burchard and Bush-Brown, pp. 342-343, 410-411, allude to the unconcern of American architects for the use of concrete.

challenge of new structural innovations, and by failing to evolve an
imaginative and tasteful expression of reinforced concrete, risked
being left behind altogether in the development of still more advanced structural ideas. If older generations of architects were inexperienced in working with reinforced concrete, it became, then,
the responsibility of educational institutions to train a new generation adept at handling the material and aware of its structural possibilities. A glance at architectural training during the early years
of the century, especially in regard to the teaching of design and
structural theory, may give an idea of how well or how poorly the
task was accomplished.

American architectural training during the final years of the
nineteenth century gradually became oriented toward the French
system of education as set forth by the Paris École des Beaux Arts.[49]
In 1893 a group of American alumni of the École founded the Society of Beaux Arts Architects, with the aim of promoting "the
principles of taste required at the École," encouraging American
students to enroll there, and creating a national school of architecture modeled after the École.[50] The society did not attain its goal
of creating a national school, but it succeeded in exercising considerable influence on the architectural schools of the day, particularly in the teaching of design.

Design was the mainstay of architectural curriculum in most
schools and was co-ordinated with courses in architectural history,
theory, and drawing. The study of construction also was included
in the regular curriculum but was generally taught completely in-
dependently of design, and in some schools it was the responsibility
of the engineering department.[51] During the first decade of this century the curriculum of the architectural school at the University of
Pennsylvania included "Orders and Elements" first year, freehand
drawing second year, and "Historic Ornament" and water color
drawing third year. As against these offerings, courses in building
construction were given one hour a week during the third and fourth

[49] Schuyler, "Schools of Architecture and the Paris School," *American Architecture*, II, 575-578. The most detailed study of the Beaux Arts influence in the
United States is James P. Noffsinger, *The Influence of the École des Beaux Arts
on the Architects of the United States* (Washington, D. C., 1955).

[50] Arthur C. Weatherhead, *The History of Collegiate Education in Architecture in the United States* (Los Angeles, 1941), p. 77.

[51] *Ibid.*, pp. 159-160.

years.[52] At Columbia University a fourth-year elective was offered in architectural engineering, consisting of a series of practical problems in wood, brick, stone, and iron. There was no mention of reinforced concrete design and construction in any of the specifications courses taught at Columbia; nor was there any mention of any courses in structural theory.[53] The types of courses at Columbia and Pennsylvania were typical of those offered in architectural schools across the nation.

The alienation of the aesthetic and formalistic approach taught in design courses from an engineering or structural viewpoint was intensified by the growing influence of Beaux Arts principles. In 1916 the Society of Beaux Arts Architects created the Beaux Arts Institute of Design (B.A.I.D.) to administer nationwide architectural design competitions.[54] By the twenties almost all schools of architecture were participating to one degree or another in the B.A.I.D. design program, which was closely modeled after that of the Paris École. The emphasis of the B.A.I.D. competitions was upon design in traditional styles rather than upon structural solutions to design problems. The student's knowledge of archeology and of architectural history was often more important than his grasp of structural principles.[55] Design problems set forth by the B.A.I.D. stressed a monumental and formal treatment of the project. Typical projects included "A Private Art Museum," "A Palace for a Retired Monarch," "A Large Restaurant in the Environs of a City," and "The Monumental Treatment of the Lower End of Manhattan Island."[56]

The B.A.I.D. design competitions suffered from many of the same abuses as the École: medals and prestige became the chief goals rather than creative design; promising students were too often

[52] Percy C. Stuart, "Architectural Schools in the U.S.—University of Pennsylvania," *Architectural Record*, X (Feb., 1901), 324-330.

[53] Percy C. Stuart, "Architectural Schools in the U.S.—Columbia University," *ibid.*, X (July, 1900), 15-16.

[54] Turpin C. Bannister, ed., *Evolution and Achievement*, Vol. I of *The Architect at Mid-Century* (2 vols.; New York, 1954), p. 101. See also Carl Feiss, "Out of School," *Progressive Architecture*, XXXI (Jan., 1950), 116 ff., for a first-hand account of B.A.I.D. methods.

[55] Rohdenburg, *History of the School of Architecture, Columbia*, p. 29.

[56] John F. Harbeson's *The Study of Architectural Design* (New York, 1927) contains many illustrations and plans of Beaux Arts projects. See especially the chapter on the "Grand Plan," pp. 201-215, for insight into the Beaux Arts concepts of monumental planning.

"assisted" on their projects by teachers and instructors; and many schools, by participating passively in a centralized program, abdicated their own responsibility to determine the best methods of teaching design to meet individual or special needs.[57] The École at its best taught principles of architectural composition rather than strict adherence to any particular style. Many of its graduates, such as Anatole de Baudot, Perret, and Garnier, went on to become innovators in the development of new materials—glass, steel, and reinforced concrete. Many of the American École-trained architects, however—men such as McKim and Burnham—attempted to force their own stylistic preferences upon American architecture and architectural training. By doing so they probably did much to give the Beaux Arts methods of design training a bad reputation among the younger architects of the Modern Movement.[58]

After World War I, Beaux Arts methods began to suffer a gradual decline in prestige and influence when several schools, following the lead of the University of Oregon, began to experiment with new methods of instruction.[59] Advances in steel technology already had begun to create an appreciable effect on architectural curricula. Massachusetts Institute of Technology, in response to the demands for graduates trained in methods of steel construction, had gradually increased the number and content of courses in steel design and construction from 1900 onwards. The school eventually added courses in reinforced construction.[60] The demand for men trained in reinforced concrete principles was slight compared with steel; yet concrete technology, while still lagging behind the tremendous upsurge in steel research, was coming of age.

By 1925 the cement industry had so improved in quantity and quality of production that the United States was exporting more than a million barrels annually to Latin America.[61] Three years later, America's first high early-strength cement was introduced

[57] Bannister, *Evolution and Achievement*, p. 101.

[58] See statement by Burnham quoted in Schuyler, "Last Words About the World's Fair," *American Architecture*, II, 557-558; also see Wayne Andrews, *Architecture, Ambition and Americans* (New York, 1964), pp. 184-197, for a critical assessment of the work and influence of McKim, Mead, and White.

[59] Weatherhead, *History of Collegiate Education in Architecture*, pp. 193-198.

[60] Caroline Shillaber, *M.I.T., School of Architecture and Planning, 1861-1961: A Hundred Year Chronicle* (Cambridge, Mass., 1963), pp. 40, 48-49.

[61] B. W. Bagely, "Cement," *Mineral Resources of the U.S.* (Part II, 1925), pp. 259, 274-275.

when the Lone Star Cement Company began production under the brand name of "Incor."[62] The advantage of high early-strength cement, first developed by French chemists in 1913, was that it took only twenty-four hours or so to form a tight bond up to full strength; earlier cements had taken as much as a week or longer.[63] As a result of the improvements made in cement production, the American Concrete Institute began setting up standards for cement-water ratios in concrete mixing. These recommendations, along with those for reinforced concrete design itself, were used by many cities as the basis for their own building code requirements in concrete construction. In 1928 the A.C.I. helped publish one of the first general handbooks in the United States on reinforced concrete design.[64]

Engineering education in the twenties profited from the research conducted by such organizations as the A.C.I. and the experimental stations being set up at various institutions, but it suffered from several important drawbacks. The Beaux Arts methods of architectural training, whatever their weaknesses in curriculum, emphasized design training at the hands of practicing architects; but engineering training was largely in the hands of educators with little experience in the field.[65] While American architectural schools retained close ties with their European counterparts by importing French design critics and École-trained architects to preside over their design programs, engineering institutions in the United States were more isolated from European trends and were not nearly as professionally oriented as the great technical schools of Germany and France.[66] Engineers and critics were later to point out the provincial aspects of professional training in this country during the first third of the century. One of the more serious shortcomings was the lack of foreign treatises or English translations of important European technical works.[67] Arthur J. Boase, an engineering con-

[62] "Twenty Years of Progress in High Early-Strength Cement Concrete," *Concrete*, LVI (June, 1948), 5-6.

[63] Draffin, "Brief History," p. 29.

[64] *Handbook of Reinforced Concrete Design*, published jointly by the A.C.I., the Portland Cement Association, the Concrete Reinforcing Steel Association, and the Rail Steel Bar Association.

[65] McGivern, *First Hundred Years of Engineering Education*, p. 61.

[66] *Ibid.*

[67] Mario Salvadori, of the Columbia University School of Engineering, and Boyd Anderson, senior partner of Ammann and Whitney, in questionnaires com-

sultant for the Portland Cement Association, pointed out the deficiencies of American engineers compared with their Latin American counterparts after visiting Brazil and Argentina in 1944:

The South American engineer has one very great and noticeable advantage over his brother engineer in the United States. He is less provincial. His knowledge of foreign languages is far superior. Most of the men . . . could speak French and German in addition to Spanish or Portuguese. . . . A surprising number can speak English.[68]

American architectural institutions, while keeping in close contact with the established European academies and schools of architecture, remained for the most part uninfluenced by the rise of the Modern Movement in Europe during the twenties. The work of Gropius, Mies van der Rohe, Le Corbusier, and other seminal figures in the development of twentieth-century architecture was little known in this country until the thirties.[69]

The lack of integration of design courses with those in construction methods persisted in architectural education throughout the twenties and early thirties. Arthur C. Weatherhead, in his comprehensive study of architectural education in the United States, noted that construction courses most often stressed practical application and detail, and neglected broader principles of structural theory.[70] The place of structural knowledge in architectural design at this time is perhaps most strikingly illustrated by an astonishing incident which occurred at Columbia University:

On one occasion an eminent New York architect who visited the school to lecture to the students explained to them that in planning a building, if the "poché" pattern (the pattern of black and white defining solids and voids on a plan drawing) was in scale and looked well, the structural supports in the building would be adequate.[71]

---

pleted for this author, both confirmed the lack of any manuals on shell design (other than articles in journals) in this country prior to the late forties. McGivern, p. 61, points out that many American engineers had to learn either French or German to be able to read technical works.

[68] Arthur J. Boase, "South American Building Is Challenging," *Engineering News-Record*, CXXXIII (Oct. 19, 1944), 126.

[69] The first major exposition of European modern architecture in the United States was the International Exhibit of Modern Architecture at New York's Museum of Modern Art in the spring of 1932. See Henry-Russell Hitchcock and Philip Johnson, *The International Style: Architecture Since 1922* (New York, 1932).

[70] Weatherhead, *History of Collegiate Education in Architecture*, pp. 158-160.

[71] Rohdenburg, *History of the School of Architecture, Columbia*, p. 29.

The Beaux Arts system in the United States, with its emphasis on formalistic, often grandiose planning and design, functioned at its best in the grandly laid out fairs and exhibitions of the early twentieth century. But it proved inadequate to handle the increasingly complex problems of modern planning and design in which it was incumbent upon the architect to maintain a grasp of all facets of a project. Ignorance of engineering and structural problems could easily result in the architect's losing control of a project to the structural engineer, the air-conditioning specialist, the interior decorator, or the contractor. In reverse, the architect could very well negate the specialists' skills if he lacked a thorough grounding in the principles, if not the fine points, of their crafts.

III

Against a confused and varied background shell building took root in the United States. It was a background of stylistic eclecticism in architecture, of architectural training dominated by French Beaux Arts traditions, of a breakdown in communication between architect and engineer, and of a concrete technology largely separated from the mainstream of architecture. Influencing these circumstances in turn was a severe, world-wide economic depression.

Once the shell had been demonstrated as a viable technique of roof construction, its success depended on the ability of civil engineers to master technical difficulties and develop practical uses for it. And equally important, engineers had to create structures with a genuine aesthetic appeal.

The early shell builders concentrated on the solution of technical problems, which presented themselves almost immediately with the construction in 1934 of the first permanent shell building in the United States: New York's Hayden Planetarium. The type of formwork for shells most commonly used in Europe at that time was a self-supporting network of prefabricated, V-shaped, rolled-steel units. In an article for *Engineering News-Record*, R. L. Bertin, one of the construction engineers for the building, pointed out that specialized machines for making the steel units were not available in this country. A complex formwork of wooden ribs, pipes, and cork insulating boards had to be devised instead.[72]

[72] R. L. Bertin, "Centering for Planetarium Shell Dome," *Engineering News-*

The shell engineers of Roberts and Schaefer, to counter the problem in the thirties of high costs for formwork and labor, concentrated almost exclusively on barrel and half-barrel shells, which permitted the use of traveling formwork mounted on rails. Using high early-strength cements, the shell could then be cast section by section, each taking only a few days to complete. Many of these early barrels required rib stiffeners, cast integrally with the shell, to maintain curvature and stability.[73] Unfortunately their use marred the effect of a single, continuous surface. To facilitate the moving of formwork and to create a smooth surface on the inside, the ribs were often placed on the exterior. When placed over the shell the ribs helped create the impression of heaviness and bulkiness found in such buildings as the Hershey Sports Arena (1937) and the Ardmore Skating Rink (1938), both in Pennsylvania, and most of the hangars built for the Army and Navy during World War II.

The early barrels and domes erected in the thirties later came under criticism for being rather clumsy compromises between true structural shells—ideally constructed with no stiffening or supporting ribs—and mere vaults, held up in the main by arch rather than true shell action.[74] Certainly the early American shells were no match for the contemporary work of the Spanish engineer, Eduardo Torroja, or the Italian, Pier Luigi Nervi, whose light, graceful shells far outstripped their American counterparts in beauty of form and lean structural efficiency. Torroja's ribless double-barreled vault for the Recoletos arena in Madrid (1935) stood as one of the great engineering feats of the twentieth century. Nervi's experiments with new structural concepts in reinforced concrete resulted in an extension of the shell principle to cover pre-cast elements locked together to produce a roof consisting of not one monolithic shell but a mosaic of small shell-like blocs rigidly connected by ribbing. His Municipal Stadium in Florence (1930-1932)

Record, CXV (July 25, 1935), 108; see also, by the same author, "Construction Features of the Zeiss-Dywidag Dome for the Hayden Planetarium," A.C.I. *Proceedings*, XXXI (May-June, 1935), for a more technical discussion of the construction problems.

[73] See Raafat, *Reinforced Concrete in Architecture*, pp. 141-151, for a discussion of barrel shell construction.

[74] See G. A. Oravas, "Thin Shells: Engineering Fitness and Architectural Form," Part I, *Architectural Record*, CXXVII (March, 1960), 216-221; Part II, *ibid.* (April, 1960), 246-250; and Lessing, "The Rise of Shells," pp. 107-111.

and his hangars for the Italian Air Force in 1935-1938 and 1940-1943 were brilliant demonstrations of his new structural concepts.[75]

The work of Nervi and Torroja, exemplifying as it did the almost perfect mating of aesthetics with structural engineering, might have provided American builders with models worthy of emulation. Unfortunately, neither their buildings nor their writings became widely known and appreciated in this country until after World War II. Language interposed an immediate barrier, and the political unrest and subsequent rise of Fascism in both Italy and Spain made for poor communications with the United States. Torroja remained in Spain during the troubled thirties and forties and was a reticent man by nature. Nervi, though far more gregarious a person, did not attain international prominence as a builder and educator until after the war.[76]

American engineers, though generally unaware of the work of Nervi and Torroja, nevertheless benefited by the growth of technical literature on shell design and theory. European research on shells produced a substantial number of papers and books, many written by the German shell pioneers, Dischinger, Bauersfield, and Finsterwalder.[77] Translations were rare, however, and the ponderous German prose of many of the papers was a formidable obstacle toward better understanding of current German and Swiss work.

The majority of the early articles in the United States on shells appeared in the *Proceedings* of the American Concrete Institute and in the publications of the American Society of Civil Engineers. Most of these were either of a general, descriptive nature or dealt with constructional aspects of shells. As shell research expanded during the thirties and forties, more analytical and theoretical papers began to appear. The three chief engineers of Roberts and

[75] For discussion of Torroja's work see his book, *The Structures of Eduardo Torroja* (New York, 1958), esp. pp. 23-28; for Nervi, see his *Aesthetics and Technology in Building* (Cambridge, Mass., 1965), pp. 98-103.

[76] Salvadori, in a statement to the author (Oct. 1, 1966), said that he became acquainted with the work of Nervi and Torroja around 1950. I can find no reference to any visit made by either Nervi or Torroja to this country before the fifties (although both came to the United States a number of times after 1950). Nervi's work, in particular, must have quickly gained widespread admiration and publicity after 1950 as he was made an honorary member of the American Institute of Architects in 1956.

[77] Detailed bibliographies of the writings of Dischinger, Bauersfield, and other important European shell builders are listed in Joedicke, *Shell Architecture*, pp. 291-298.

Schaefer, Anton Tedesko, J. Kalinka, and Eric C. Molke, wrote numbers of articles, traveled extensively, and lectured on shells to a growing audience.[78] In 1940 the first book on shells written in the United States appeared: *Theory of Plates and Shells*, by Stephen Timoshenko, professor of technical and applied mechanics at Stanford University.[79]

Increased research in the larger fields of cement and reinforced concrete technology resulted in a gradual liberalization of building codes. The United States, in contrast to most European and Latin American countries, had no uniform, national code, but rather a bewildering variety of statutes on state, county, and city levels. There was little standardization across the nation regarding items such as cement-water ratios in concrete, the size and weight of columns, beams, and slabs, or test determinations of the strength of particular mixtures of concrete.[80] Engineers, aside from having to operate under dozens of different requirements, faced the fact that many codes, aside from detailing numerous safety specifications for arch, girder, and slab construction, also rigidly defined design procedures themselves for reinforced concrete. In Northern states, to provide for snow loads and strong wind action, heavier roof thicknesses and, at times, stiffening ribs were required. In most states, fire regulations specified more than the practical minimum roof thicknesses. Although the Mexican national code permitted a minimum roof thickness of only one centimeter, American codes generally required a basic minimum of twice that width.[81]

Thanks to many of the reforms of building codes during the thirties, engineers were freed from the unenviable tasks of coping with a multitude of different and conflicting specifications and of conforming to rigid frameworks of code requirements in attempting economical and efficient design. One of the prime contributors to reform was the American Concrete Institute, which published in 1936 a uniform set of specifications for reinforced concrete con-

[78] For articles by these and other United States shell builders, see Joedicke, *ibid.*, also the *55-Year Index: 1905-1959* of the A.C.I., ed. Robert G. Wiedyke (Detroit, 1960); and M. P. Levy, "Thin Shells: Some Basic References for Architects and Engineers," *Architectural Record*, CXXV (June, 1959), 224-225.

[79] New York: McGraw Hill.

[80] "Reinforced Concrete and the Building Codes," p. 37.

[81] Candela and Molke, "Discussion on Candela's 'Simple Concrete Shell Structures,' " p. 332.

struction. Their requirements, very liberal in comparison with earlier codes, were incorporated into the revised Chicago Building Code of 1937 and later became the principal guidelines for most reinforced concrete specifications in the United States.[82] In 1941 the A.C.I. added to its recommendations a section requiring flat concrete slabs to be designed according to more advanced frame analysis methods, a newer system of determining loads and stresses on concrete slabs by mathematical calculations. This same principle had been in effect in Brazil and in many European countries at least ten years earlier.[83]

During the thirties much of the work in shell design and experimentation had been carried out by Kalinka, Molke, and Tedesko of Roberts and Schaefer, and Timoshenko at Stanford, all European-born and -educated.[84] They were joined in the forties by still more European emigrés and other American engineers as the exclusive monopoly of Roberts and Schaefer in shell design was broken. The Z-D methods applied only to domes, barrels, and certain kinds of cantilevered or "butterfly" shells. Increasing sophistication in concrete reinforcing methods and shell analysis gradually outdated the early Z-D processes. Timoshenko's book (1940) set out methods for the calculation of shell forms. In the forties, Robert S. Whitney, senior partner in the firm of Ammann and Whitney, developed his own design methods.[85] During World War II the

[82] "Chicago Building Code Advances," *Engineering News-Record*, CIXX (Sept. 23, 1937), 512-513.

[83] Boase, "South American Building Is Challenging," p. 124. For further comparisons of United States and Latin American engineering methods, see also, by the same author, "Building Codes Explain the Slenderness of South American Structures," *ibid.*, CXXXIV (April 19, 1945), 68-77; and "Brazilian Concrete Building Design Compared with U.S. Practice," *ibid.*, CXXXIV (June 28, 1945), 80-88. Boase raises the interesting point that Latin American shell design was possibly given an initial lead over that in the United States because many contracting and engineering firms in both Brazil and Argentina were formed by Germans and Italians who brought reinforced concrete innovations with them from Europe.

[84] *Who's Who in Engineering* (1959), Tedesko, p. 2433; *Who's Who in America* (1964-1965), Timoshenko, p. 2013. Neither Kalinka nor Molke appear in the above sources, but Salvadori, in a letter to the author (Oct. 1, 1966), has verified their European origin.

[85] Boyd Anderson, in a letter to the author (June 14, 1967), stated of Whitney's design methods: "This was all privileged information at this time and was not published. The main interest was barrel vault roofs with flexible stiffening systems." Many of Whitney's calculations were incorporated into a design manual for shell construction published in 1953. See n. 96, below.

Z-D patents were seized by the Alien Property Custodian, and the system became open to general use.[86]

While a small group of engineers laying the foundations of shell design and construction, a revolution was overtaking American architectural education. Precipitated by the rise of Nazism, a small galaxy of brilliant European architects and designers, the foremost leaders of the Modern Movement in the German-speaking countries, emigrated to the United States. They included Walter Gropius, Mies van der Rohe, Moholy-Nagy, Marcel Breuer, and Josef Albers, all of whom had been associated with the famed German school of design and building art, the *Bauhaus*.

The *Bauhaus*, organized by Gropius, was a descendant of the nineteenth-century German schools of applied arts. Many of the German pioneers of reinforced concrete design had received their training in these schools, separated from the mainstream of eclectic architecture enshrined in the state academies of design. From 1897 onward many of these institutions were reorganized under men who supported the views and ideals of the Modern Movement.[87] Gropius and his German contemporaries were heirs to this applied arts tradition, and they carried their message to the United States.

In 1937 Harvard University installed Gropius as head of the graduate division of architectural studies. The same year, Chicago's Institute of Design appointed Moholy-Nagy as head. In 1938 the Illinois Institute of Technology called Mies van der Rohe to chair the department of architecture. In 1940 North Carolina's famed experimental school, Black Mountain College, hired Josef Albers; and in 1944 M.I.T. called Gyorgy Kepes, a pupil of Moholy-Nagy, to take charge of the visual design courses. These men rapidly reoriented the curriculum in design and architecture at their respective institutions.[88] The primary emphasis was placed on a close integration of structural concepts with design. Students were to solve architectural problems using modern materials—glass, steel, and concrete—and contemporary structural concepts.

[86] "New Ways with Concrete," *Fortune*, XLIV (Aug., 1951), 114.

[87] For a declaration by Gropius of the aims of the *Bauhaus*, see Herbert Bayer, Walter and Ise Gropius, *Bauhaus* (New York, 1938), pp. 22-31. See also Walter Gropius, *The New Architecture and the Bauhaus*, trans. P. Morton Shand (Cambridge, Mass., 1965).

[88] Bannister, *Evolution and Achievement*, pp. 106-107; and C. L. V. Meeks, "Architectural Education in America," *Architect's Year Book*, No. 2 (London, 1947), pp. 124-127.

The rapid installation of the German modernists as heads of some of the most prestigious schools of design and architecture in the United States effectively ended Beaux Arts hegemony over American architecture. The Beaux Arts system had been on the decline since the twenties, and the influx of German educators, by undercutting its influence on the schools, ensured its demise. A new generation of architects was trained in the light of new structural ideas and modern machine technology. Among the outstanding members of this generation were Eero Saarinen, who studied at Yale; Minoru Yamasaki, at the University of Washington; Eliot Noyes, Ieoh M. Pei, John Johansen, and Victor Lundy, all of whom studied under Gropius at Harvard; and Hugh Stubbins, who assisted Gropius in the graduate program of the architectural school.[89] It was this generation, coming into prominence in the late fifties, that took up the challenge of shell design in architecture.

World War II seems to have been a major turning point in shell development. Wartime steel restrictions proved a boon for reinforced concrete construction of all types.[90] Both Roberts and Schaefer and Ammann and Whitney received numerous commissions for shell hangars and other military installations; and the stepped-up pace brought in more engineering firms to the field of shell design. Postwar prosperity ensured a continuing boom in building construction. The demand for auditoriums, sports arenas, and coliseums provided numerous commissions for shell roofs.

Increased mechanization and standardization of formwork during the forties was responsible not only for cheaper costs but for shorter construction timetables.[91] The shell for the Alabama State Coliseum in Montgomery, designed by Ammann and Whitney in 1949, was completed so quickly with movable formwork that the entire structure took only five hundred days to build as compared with a projected 750 for a steel structure.[92] For their design of the

[89] Biographical data drawn from Ian McMallum, *Architecture, U.S.A.* (New York, 1959), and *American Architects Directory*, ed. George S. Koyl, sponsored by the American Institute of Architects (2nd ed.; New York, 1962).

[90] See Arthur J. Boase, "Concrete Building Design Trend Shaped by Clear Space Needs," *Engineering News-Record*, CXXXV (Oct. 18, 1945), 138. Boase states: "It took a war to popularize shell roof structures." Boyd Anderson feels the turning point began about 1940 "with the growth of the aircraft industry."

[91] "Large Concrete Warehouses Built with Moving Falsework," *ibid.*, CXXXVI (April 24, 1941), 53-54.

[92] "Shell Concrete for Spanning Large Areas," *Architectural Forum*, XCI (Dec., 1949), 106.

University of Wisconsin Field House (1949-1950) Ammann and Whitney published cost estimates of $238,572 for the shell barrel vault as compared with $252,816 for a steel-arched truss, demonstrating that shell concrete could indeed have an edge over steel economically as well as in terms of quicker construction times.[93]

Principles of shell design also were introduced into classrooms. Mario Salvadori, having begun shell design in Italy, where he was born and raised, initiated a course in shell statics at Columbia in 1948. In 1955 Salvadori became associated with Paul Weidlinger, another European, who had studied reinforced concrete design at the Swiss Polytechnic Institute. Weidlinger and Salvadori became one of the principal firms engaged in shell design during the fifties.[94] Both men wrote numerous articles and gave many lectures on shells.

One of the signs marking the coming of age of American concrete technology was the opening in 1950 of the Portland Cement Association's Structural Concrete Laboratory in Skokie, Illinois. This major research center, together with others at institutions such as the University of California at Berkeley, North Carolina State College, Purdue, and Columbia, provided testing grounds for new work in mathematical and scale-model analysis of shell design, methods of construction, and applications of new forms.[95] In 1952 a committee of the American Society of Civil Engineers, under the leadership of Salvadori and Whitney, published a manual on the design of cylindrical shell roofs. The first of its kind in the United States, the manual was made widely available with the intention of presenting simplified design procedures to all engineers interested in shell construction.[96]

Until the early fifties, the only shell forms that continued to be exploited to any degree were domes and barrels. Ammann and Whitney's Field House for the University of Wisconsin received an

[93] *Ibid.*

[94] *Who's Who in Engineering* (1959), Salvadori, p. 2138, Weidlinger, p. 2613.

[95] Condit, *American Building Art: The Twentieth Century*, p. 191. See also "Plastic Forms for Shells," *Architectural Forum*, CXIII (Aug., 1960), 124; T. Y. Lin, "Revolution in Concrete," *ibid.*, CXIV (May, 1961), 121-127; and Bernard P. Spring and Donald Canby, "Concrete, the Material That Can Do Almost Anything," *ibid.*, CXVII (Sept., 1962), 78-96, for brief surveys of research in concrete during the fifties.

[96] *Manual #31: Design of Cylindrical Concrete Shell Roofs* (New York, 1952).

award from the Concrete Reinforcing Steel Institute for excellence in design.[97] But no shell building in this country had yet received national or international acclamation for its structural innovations or beauty of form.

Salvadori's statement of 1954 that "the possibilities of thin shells have only been slightly tapped" is easily verified by the somewhat painful contrast of American efforts with European buildings. Europe gave rise to a group of true "master builders" on the order of Maillart, Nervi, and Torroja, most of whom combined the functions of both architect and engineer, sometimes including even that of contractor. Maillart's Swiss Cement Hall, Torroja's Algeciras Market, and Nervi's exhibition halls in Turin, all built during the thirties and forties, had yet no equals in this country. American engineers were criticized not only for failing to experiment with more advanced forms such as hyperbolic paraboloids but also for their timidity in handling simple domes and barrels.

American engineers, faced with economic problems differing greatly from those of Europe, were concerned primarily with getting costs down to where shell concrete could compete with steel rather than building beautiful structures. It is somewhat ironic, however, that the engineers, in their efforts to develop shell construction, overlooked the immense publicity value that could have been derived from shells with an authentic aesthetic appeal. Economic considerations, however real and valid, do not wholly account for the undeniable beauty of many of the European shells. Nor do they explain the total understanding of both structural and aesthetic potentialities of shells that Nervi, Torroja, and Maillart displayed.

The United States by mid-century had yet to produce a shell builder of the caliber of a Nervi or a Torroja. The small number of shell pioneers to that date was composed for the most part of engineers trained in Europe. None of the prominent architects of the day, Wright, Lescaze, Walker, Neutra, Belluschi, had yet shown any interest in shell design.

Architectural interest in shell design began in the early fifties. One of the first to experiment with shell forms was the Argentinian

[97] "Shell Concrete for Spanning Large Areas," p. 106.

architect, Eduardo Catalano, who was appointed professor of architecture at North Carolina State in 1952. His work with hyperbolic paraboloidal forms at the school culminated in 1955 with the construction of this type of roof for his home in Raleigh.[98] Catalano's work with hyperbolic paraboloids was the earliest of its kind in this country. His work was largely overshadowed, however, by that of the great Mexican shell builder, Félix Candela.

Candela, of Spanish birth, began shell design in the late forties and soon concentrated his greatest efforts on developing hyperbolic paraboloidal forms.[99] After 1950 he became world renowned as the foremost exponent of this special form and equally famous for his insistence upon the importance of intuitive skill in shell building. His first article for an American periodical appeared in a 1951 issue of the American Concrete Institute *Proceedings*. Throughout the fifties he wrote extensively for American engineering and architectural journals and made numerous visits to this country to lecture on shells.[100]

The work of Candela, along with that of Nervi and Torroja, was featured from about 1950 onward not only in architectural and engineering journals but also in such mass circulation magazines as *Time* and *Life*.[101] Nervi's book, *Structures*, and Torroja's *Philosophy of Structures* were translated and became available in the United States toward the end of the decade.[102] Along with the increased attention given to the work of foreign shell builders, American journals began publicizing imaginative shell design by native engineers and architects. The Universal Atlas Cement Company

[98] "A New Way to Span Space," *ibid.*, CIII (Nov., 1955), 171-177. For descriptions of research done at North Carolina State, see also Eduardo Catalano, "Two Warped Surfaces," *Student Publication* (North Carolina State), V (No. 1, 1955), 2-17; and, by the same author, "Structures of Warped Surfaces," *ibid.*, X (No. 1, 1960), 2-6. See also n. 19, above.

[99] See Colin Faber, *Candela: The Shell Builder* (New York, 1963), pp. 12-15, 30-32, for an account of Candela's early experiments with shells.

[100] Candela, "Simple Concrete Shell Structures," A.C.I. *Proceedings*, XLVIII (Dec., 1951), 321-331. An earlier paper submitted by Candela was rejected as "argumentative" (Faber, *Candela*, p. 13).

[101] Bibliography on Candela in Faber, *Candela*, pp. 236-239. For articles on Nervi, see Ada Louise Huxtable, *Pier Luigi Nervi* (New York, 1960), pp. 119-122. See also "Spectacular Shapes in Concrete," *Life*, April 18, 1960; and "Felix Candela: Architect on Shells," *Time*, Sept. 8, 1958, both articles on Candela. For Nervi, see "Poetry in Concrete," *Time*, Nov. 11, 1957. The bibliography on Torroja is much smaller. See Torroja, *The Structures of Eduardo Torroja*.

[102] *Philosophy of Structures*, trans. J. J. and Milos Polivka (Los Angeles, 1958); *Structures*, trans. Guiseppina and Mario Salvadori (New York, 1956)

sponsored a number of shell concrete projects in consumer magazine advertisements during 1956 and 1957.[103]

An increasing interest in structural concepts of design was reflected not only in the new attention given to the work of Nervi, Candela, and Torroja, but also in the prominence given to the teaching of structural theory in American architectural schools. Courses in "Historic Ornament" had given way to courses in "Principles of Design and Planning in Reinforced Concrete," and in "Analysis of Aesthetic Qualities and Structural Capabilities of Architectural Materials."[104] In 1954 the first American conference on thin concrete shells took place at M.I.T. Some 450 architects, engineers, and teachers met to discuss the problems of shell design and construction. Among the principal topics discussed were methods of using concrete more efficiently in shells, and the lighting and acoustical problems of shell buildings; but most interest centered on an examination "of highly functional and expressive shapes where structure and enclosure are one."[105]

The preoccupation with structural concepts was accompanied by increased attempts at mechanization and prefabrication in shell construction. Engineers began prefabricating shells as a whole on the ground or at a nearby plant and then raising them into place by means of mechanical jacks, borrowing from lift-slab techniques originally designed to raise concrete slabs in multi-story buildings.[106] Another method of shell construction was developed that eliminated the necessity for lifting the shell into place. A raised mound of earth was shaped in the configuration of the shell type desired. The shell was then cast over the mound, and after hardening, the earth was removed leaving the shell roof in place. The Albuquerque Civic

[103] The company's series of designs was widely publicized, and several of the shell designs were reprinted in articles. See "Shell Concrete with a Flair," *Architectural Forum*, CV (Aug., 1956), 152-157; "Two New Shapes in Concrete," *ibid.*, CV (Nov., 1956), 125-127; and "Tomorrow's Airport," *Progressive Architecture*, XXXVIII (Dec., 1957), 108-110.

[104] Rohdenburg, *History of the School of Architecture, Columbia*, p. 55.

[105] "Shell Concrete Today," *Architectural Forum*, CI (Aug., 1954), 157.

[106] See Joedicke, *Shell Architecture*, pp. 146-151, for an explanation and photos of lift-slab techniques in shell construction; and James H. Marsh III,. "Construction of Thin Shell Structures by the 'Lift-Shape' Process," *World Conference on Shell Structures*, 447-452, for an economical variation of the lift-slab process, whereby the reinforcing armature is laid on the ground and then lifted and warped into place. Concrete is then applied.

Center, completed in 1955, was the first large-scale realization of this novel method.[107]

The increased use of prestressing, whereby concrete was strengthened using steel rods held in tension, from 1955 onward allowed for more frequent use of lift-slab techniques without the danger of the shell cracking or bending unduly under strain during the lifting process.[108] The Air Foam method, developed in 1941 by Wallace Neff, a West Coast architect, came into practical use during the mid-forties. This method consisted of inflating a neo-phrene nylon balloon, shaped to the form of the shell desired; the balloon was then covered with a type of plastic "sheet" over which concrete was sprayed. After the balloon was deflated, the plastic "sheet," left in place, acted as insulation.[109]

The firm establishment of a shell architecture in the United States, if a definite date can be assigned, was signaled by the completion of the St. Louis-Lambert Airport Terminal in 1956. The designer, Minoru Yamasaki of the Detroit firm of Leinweber, Yamasaki, and Hellmuth, was the first of the new generation of architects to design a truly monumental shell structure. His building, roofed by three adjoining shell cross vaults, was given the American Institute of Architects' First Award for that year. Although still heavy-looking in comparison with the graceful shells of Candela, the building was hailed by the institute as being among "the first of the dramatic new thin-shell structures in the United States."[110]

[107] Walter E. Riley, "Shell Construction: A New Approach," A.C.I. *Proceedings*, LVII (April, 1961), 1361-1371; see also Joedicke, *Shell Architecture*, 106-107, for photos of the Albuquerque Center.

[108] Lawrence Lessing, "Prestressed Concrete: The Big Stretch," *Architectural Forum*, CX (March, 1959), 143. See also T. Y. Lin, "Revolution in Concrete," Part I, *ibid.*, CXIV (May, 1961), 121-127; Part II, *ibid.*, CXIV (June, 1961), 116-122, for a brief review of the development of prestressing in the United States.

[109] See "Balloon Houses Designed for Defense Workers," *Life*, Dec. 1, 1941, pp. 34-35, for a description of the first application of Neff's method; and Joedicke, *Shell Architecture*, pp. 137-139, for photos of the construction process. Neff's method initially received wide publicity but dropped out of sight in favor of more traditional methods until the late fifties. In 1967 an Italian architect, Dante Bini, brought to the United States a more sophisticated version of the Neff method, which eliminated the need for scaffolding by casting the concrete over a vinyl sheet laid out on the ground and then blowing it up into position with air compressors. See "Concrete Shell Inflated in Test," New York *Times*, May 17, 1967, Sec. II, p. 1.

[110] Wolf von Eckhardt, ed., *Mid-Century Architecture in America: Honor Awards of the American Institute of Architects, 1949-1961* (Baltimore, 1961),

Increasing numbers of architects began to take keen interest in shell design after 1956. Eero Saarinen designed the dome-shaped Kresge Auditorium for M.I.T. that same year, and followed it with the free form of the Trans-World Airlines Terminal at Idlewild (John F. Kennedy) International Airport in 1961. Both shell structures received widespread publicity. I. M. Pei roofed the May Company Department Store entrance hall in Denver, Colorado (1957-1958) with the largest hyperbolic paraboloid in the country to date. Eliot Noyes and John Johanson, both graduates of Harvard along with Pei, began experimenting with the application of the Air Foam method to housing projects and schools. Noyes built a small summer house at Hobe Sound, Florida, to demonstrate the economy of the technique.[111] While much of the most adventurous work in shell design was being done by this new generation of architects, older, more established firms such as Harrison and Abramovitz also began using shells on occasion for solutions to architectural problems.[112]

The monumental shell buildings of the late fifties, such as Saarinen's Kresge Auditorium, dramatized the ability of the shell principle to generate a new class of exotic structural forms. The structure of a building, traditionally a supporting framework covered over with an architectural veneer, now transmuted itself into a visually predominant position. This emancipation of the structural framework was one of the key accomplishments of the European Functionalist movement of the twenties and thirties. The shell

---

p. 70; see also Anton Tedesko, "The St. Louis Air Terminal Shells," *World Conference on Shell Structures*, pp. 469-474.

[111] Cranston Jones's *Architecture: Today and Tomorrow* (New York, 1961) contains photos and descriptions of all of these shell buildings. The bibliography on the shell buildings of these architects is quite extensive, particularly as to periodicals. Among the most valuable articles are "Shaping a Two-Acre Sculpture," *Architectural Forum*, CXIII (Aug., 1960), 119-122 (TWA Terminal); "Three Critics Discuss M.I.T.'s New Buildings," *ibid.*, CIV (March, 1956), 156 ff. (Kresge Auditorium); Anton Tedesko, "Shell at Denver: Hyperbolic Paraboloidal Structure of Wide Span," A.C.I. *Journal*, LVII (Oct., 1960), 403-412 (May Company Store); "Sculpting with Sprayed Concrete," *Architectural Forum*, CXI (Oct., 1959), 167-168 (Johansen's shell designs). See also Joedicke, *Shell Architecture*, pp. 137-139, for a description and photos of the Hobe Sound house.

[112] "University of Illinois Spectacular," *Architectural Record*, CXXXIV (July, 1963), 111-116. See also "Beethoven and Basketball: Tallahassee Civic Auditorium," *Architectural Forum*, CVII (March, 1957), 114-115, for shell design by Walter Gropius and The Architects Collaborative.

was correspondingly transformed from a roofing solution into a crustacean merger of supports, walls, and roof all in one.

The realization by American architects of the structural possibilities of the shell led in turn to an exploitation of its expressive qualities.[113] Saarinen and Yamasaki both used shells for their air terminals to evoke an impression of flight. Yamasaki's building was greeted as a "symbol of flight," as a "Grand Central Station of the Air."[114] Architect Victor Lundy used hyperbolic paraboloidal umbrella roofs in his Warm Mineral Springs Inn at Venice, Florida (1958), to suggest "white palms" in an attempt at reflecting the surrounding vegetation.[115] His highly romantic and expressive use of shell forms found justification in his statement: "I want my buildings to be exuberant, not safe, lovely cubular things. Creative architecture comes out of the individual, not out of group design."[116]

The expressionistic tendency of many shell buildings of the late fifties and early sixties, however, came under criticism from various quarters. Paradoxically, chief among the critics was Candela, himself a prime source of inspiration for much of the newfound expressionism in American shell design. In deploring the "expressionistic" traits of many American shell buildings Candela asserted that functional necessity rather than any preconceived ideas should dictate a structural form.[117] Torroja and Nervi were equally adamant in their belief that structure should never become an end in itself any more than should stylistic purity. According to Nervi, a solution must "satisfy the needs for which it was built, and must achieve the maximum result with the minimum means."[118]

Reasons for the rise of expressionism in shell building—and, for that matter, in much of contemporary architecture as a whole— can no doubt be found in the postwar affluence of the United States. As one critic stated, in a new twist of the old aphorism: "Com-

[113] See Museum of Modern Art, *Four New Buildings: Architecture and Imagery* (Museum of Modern Art *Bulletin*, XXVI, No. 2, 1959). A good exposition of the relationship of architectural expression to structure is found in *Structure in Art and Science*, ed. Gyorgy Kepes (New York, 1965). See especially the essays by Eduard F. Sekler, Pier Luigi Nervi, and Buckminster Fuller.

[114] B. L. Pickens, "Proud Architecture and the Spirit of St. Louis," *Architectural Record*, CIXX (April, 1956), 197; "New Thinking on Airport Terminals," *Architectural Forum*, XCVII (Nov., 1952), 135.

[115] Jones, *Architecture: Today and Tomorrow*, pp. 174, 179.

[116] *Ibid.*, p. 175.

[117] Faber, *Candela*, p. 10.

[118] Nervi, *Aesthetics and Technology in Building*, p. 2.

modity and Firmness were taken for granted, and attention was focused on Delight."[119] The rigid, straight-line character of the early Functionalist movement relaxed considerably after the battle against eclecticism had been won. Younger architects, freed from the necessity of maintaining the ideological stance of functional chastity taken by their elders, could indulge in a search for freer forms and could explore new uses of the curve. Whether or not contemporary architecture was headed for a new "Baroque" phase, as some have maintained, the fact remains that the shell principle provided an ample opportunity for exploitation of curved surfaces.[120]

Many observers pointed out that the practical uses of the shell were limited to single-story, wide-span structures. While the shell found its most logical employment in the spanning of large, open halls, auditoriums, and similar building types, there have been recent attempts beginning in the late fifties at developing other uses. I. M. Pei, in co-operation with engineers Anton Tedesko and Giorgo Baroni of Roberts and Schaefer, designed a hyperboloidal office tower, 1,400 feet high, that would theoretically make possible a savings of 33 per cent in steel compared with more conventional solutions.[121] Marcel Breuer, in his design for St. John's Abbey at Collegeville, Minnesota (1961), employed paraboloidal side walls to support a corrugated, folded-plate type of roof.[122] Recent structural conventions, the Third National Structural Conference held at Chicago in 1957 and the World Conference on Shell Structures held at San Francisco in 1962, concentrated on the further evolution of the shell principle. While the Chicago conference paid considerable attention to the problems of cost and preparing public opinion to accept new designs and materials, it is indicative of fu-

[119] John Dixon, *Architectural Design Preview, U.S.A.* (New York, 1962), p. 10.

[120] For discussion of "Baroque" aspects of contemporary architecture, see G. Habasque, "L'architecture actuelle s'orient-telle vers un nouveau baroque?" *L'Oeil*, XCIX (March, 1963), 24-37; T. H. Creighton, "The New Sensualism," *Progressive Architecture*, XL (Sept., 1959), 141-147; this article is continued in the following October issue, pp. 180-187. For imaginative and utopian designs in shell building, see Ulrich Conrads and Hans Sperlich, *The Architecture of Fantasy*, trans. and ed. C. C. Collins and George Collins (New York, 1962), pp. 70-73, 80-82, 120-121.

[121] Joedicke, *Shell Architecture*, pp. 202-203.

[122] "Three New Projects: Marcel Breuer," *Architectural Record*, CXXXI (March, 1962), 121-136. See also Whitney S. Stoddard, *Adventure in Architecture: Building the New St. Johns* (New York, 1958).

ture trends in shell building that the San Francisco conference also emphasized the increased use of prestressing in construction and the use of model analogues and computer analysis in shell design.[123]

By the early sixties there was enough demand for shell structures so that design procedures and construction methods could at last be assembly-line produced. The lesson of mass production, learned so readily by the engineers who developed the steel frame skyscraper, at last took hold in the field of shell concrete.[124] The intensive use of standardization and prefabrication of conventional formwork and scaffolding played as much of a role in the fight for economy in shell building as did the more novel construction methods developed in the fifties.[125]

Conclusion

The establishment of a shell architecture in the United States was the result of a confluence of many factors besides those of a technological or economic nature. The resolution of technical difficulties was largely achieved through a parallel development of a firm foundation in concrete and cement research, the reform of building codes, and the improvement of construction techniques. The growth of the shell idea, however, was contingent upon the full realization of its vast potential by the engineers who began working with shell construction in the thirties and forties. The spark needed to capitalize on the technical gains and to foster the spread of shell building was provided by increased publicity, a growing appreciation for the work of the European shell pioneers, and the demand for building types—sports arenas, halls, factories, and civic centers—for which shell roofs were ideal solutions. The

[123] For details of the Chicago conference, see "Creative Trends in Structural Design Studied," *Civil Engineering*, XXVIII (Feb., 1958), 97. The important papers of the San Francisco conference have been published in the *World Conference on Shell Structures: Proceedings*. See especially the papers on construction methods and computers.

[124] See *Architectural Forum, Building, U.S.A.* (New York, 1957), especially the chapters on the contractor, the labor force, and the manufacturer for a survey of the development of mass production methods in American building.

[125] Boyd Anderson, in commenting in a questionnaire on the development of more economical shell buildings, stated: "We started with a shell for efficiency in materials; broke down elements of installation cost; then redesigned the shell to reduce the most important elements of cost (reduced size and repetitive use of costly elements). . . . We added the benefit of our experience to new contractors in the field. Multitudes of little details made the total workable."

degree to which these interacting factors influenced the course of shell development, however, was determined by the rise of a new generation of architects in the fifties—a product of a new school of architectural thought—which turned to the use of the shell principle in search of new forms of expression.

The United States did not produce a group of structural giants on the order of Nervi, Torroja, or Candela, who were able singly to control the aesthetic, technological, and constructional aspects of building. This universality in combining functions was achieved in the United States only by close teamwork between architect, engineer, and contractor. The reform of architectural education in the thirties provided in large part the tools needed by architects to develop intelligent and effective leadership in shell design. Under *Bauhaus* methods of education, students were encouraged to develop structural and technological perception, to study the engineering aspects of design, and to use modern materials—glass, steel, and concrete—according to the intrinsic nature of each. Without such tools the architect could not bridge the schism separating architecture from engineering. And without architectural leadership the shell would have remained a structural technique entirely in the hands of the engineers.

The transfer of the shell was a vastly more complex process than simply the realization of new needs and new possibilities. The transfer could not be achieved by applying European solutions to the problems of creating an efficient and beautiful shell architecture in this country. Despite all of the advantages it had demonstrated in Europe, shell construction had to overcome a native building tradition based on wood and steel and a host of unfavorable circumstances. Beyond all of the technical and economic factors, the full realization of the shell principle began to take effect only when many of these circumstances—stylistic eclecticism, Beaux Arts methods of training, the lack of teamwork between architect and engineer—were overturned.

Shell architecture, in its technical complexity, may well prove to be but an advance guard of still newer structural concepts and building techniques in which the close integration of architectural and engineering functions is an absolute necessity. The initiative must come, as it eventually did in shell design, from the architect. In the words of Mario Salvadori: "It is mainly up to the architect to bridge the gap. . . . The architect is the leader of the construction team; the engineer is just one of its members."[126]

The dynamism of shell architecture resulted from the bridging of the gap. That the architects did so was not the result of an economic necessity, of a sudden need that developed. What Europe pioneered through economic necessity came about in this country by choice. In the absence of such a necessity, the development of a shell architecture hinged on changes in habit and attitude. It was the change in the concept of architectural function and aesthetics that made it possible for shell architecture in the United States to become a reality.

[126] Mario Salvadori and Robert Heller, *Structure in Architecture* (New York, 1964), p. 8.

The Transmission of English Law to the Frontier of America

W. B. Hamilton

Frederick Jackson Turner, in his vague, eloquent, and poetic search for an answer to a question at least as old as Crèvecoeur—What then is the American, this new man?—rebelled against the myth that traced American institutions back to the Teutonic tribes in the north European forests and proclaimed, without bothering with evidence, that Americans' "most fundamental traits, their institutions, even their ideals were shaped by interaction between the wilderness and themselves. . . . The evolution of American political institutions was dependent on the advance of the frontier [a word Turner defined variously at divers times] . . . and in all America we can study the process by which in a new land social customs form and crystallize into law."[1] "The peculiarity of American institutions is the fact that they have been compelled to adapt themselves to the changes of an expanding people—to the changes involved in crossing a continent, in winning a wilderness, and in developing at each area of this progress out of the primitive economic and political conditions of the frontier into the complexity of city life. . . . This perennial rebirth, this fluidity of American life, this expansion westward with its new opportunities, its continuous touch with the simplicity of primitive society, furnish the forces dominating American character."[2] "The men of the 'Western World'

MR. HAMILTON, who teaches English history at Duke, was editor of The Transfer of Institutions (Durham, 1964).

[1] Quotations by Francis S. Philbrick, The Rise of the West, 1754-1830 (New York, 1965), p. 367, from "The West and American Ideals," Washington Historical Quarterly, V, 245, 289; "The Significance of the Frontier in American History" (1938), p. 213; and Turner, "Middle Western Pioneer Democracy," Minnesota Historical Bulletin, III (Aug., 1920), 400.

[2] "Significance," in The Early Writings . . . with an Introduction by Fulmer Mood (Madison, 1938), pp. 186-187.

turned their backs upon the Atlantic Ocean, and with a grim energy and self-reliance began to build up a society free from the dominance of ancient forms."[3]

These are enough fragments (out of context, but fair enough) for our purpose to suggest (as far as institutions are concerned) the "Turner thesis," for a long time the leading model for the study of American institutions and character. Stephen Vincent Benét, in *John Brown's Body*, another eloquent and poetic hymn to Americanism, put it succinctly:

> And Thames and all the rivers of the kings
> Ran into Mississippi and were drowned.[4]

Turner's nebulous generalizations gave rise to an enormous literature, pro and con.[5] He probably suffered as much at the hands of his disciples as he did at those of his detractors. A recent severe critic, Francis S. Philbrick, a law professor who has studied the Old Northwest for fifty years, is amusing on the writings of the disciples. After wading through their efforts, he concludes that the Turner thesis has been buried under a heap of miscellaneous rubbish so people would not know it is dead: "Sometimes, on the old frontier, when it was necessary to bury a member of a hunting party, his comrades sought to prevent profanation of the body by burying it beneath the campfire site, then strewing matter over that which they thought would make impossible any suspicion of a burial."[6]

We do not, in this paper, have to test all the features of the

[3] Turner, "Contributions of the West to American Democracy," reprinted in *The Turner Thesis . . .* (Problems in American Civilization; Boston, 1956), pp. 24-25.

[4] And again:
> "They tried to fit you with an English song
> And clip your speech into the English tale.
> But, even from the first, the words went wrong,
> The catbird pecked away the nightingale."

Both quotations from 1930 edition (Garden City, N. Y.: Doubleday, Doran and Co.), p. 4.

[5] Keys to it may be found in Ray Allen Billington, *The American Frontier* (Service Center for Teachers of History, American Historical Association; Washington, 1958); Robert E. Riegel, "American Frontier Theory," *Journal of World History*, III, No. 2 (1956), 356-380, *inter alia*. A bibliography of Turner's printed writings begins at p. 233 of *Early Writings*. William Coleman explored the origins of some of Turner's mythology in "Science and Symbol in the Turner Frontier Hypothesis," *American Historical Review*, LXII (Oct., 1966), 22-49.

[6] *Rise of the West*, p. 386.

model—democracy, self-reliance, individualism, inventiveness, safe-ty-valve for the poor in the East, and so on, although it would be fun to see how the presence of the marches of Wales and Scotland or of the royal forests induced in England the democracy of the manorial court and the City of Westminster, of the seventeenth-century Levellers and republicans, and of the eighteenth-century re-formers; the notable individualism of the cockney on the frontiers of Cheapside or the eccentricity of the landed gentry; or the inventiveness and drive of the Watts, the Boultons, the Arkwrights, and the Wedgwoods. Or for that matter, à la Walter Prescott Webb, how those things were brought on in England by the presence of the world frontier after 1492.

We shall content ourselves with a modest empirical survey of law on the old frontiers of America, in the farthest reaches of the American empire in the Old Northwest and the Old Southwest, from the source nearly to the mouth of the Mississippi River, into which poured the law of Westminster Hall on the Thames. Was it drowned? Was the law of Wayne County in the North and the Natchez District in the South shaped by environment or was it imported? Did the frontier devise its own law for a new world, or did it receive it perforce by example and precept from the Old World or from the Eastern seaboard? Did the law suffer a sea change in transit?

Are we discussing the transmission of ideas or that of institutions? The laws of England during the seventeenth and eighteenth centuries, when America was being settled, were several: (1) the common law, which at the outset was the king's law, invading and consuming feudal law partly by force, largely because it sold through the writ shop a more sensible mode of settling disputes—the hall-mark of the king's law was the petty jury. In the hands of the king's judges it gradually grew into an adaptable body of procedures that could embrace the new issues of a commercial age. It became an institution because it developed fixed machinery of which we will mention only the central courts, sitting at Westminster, of Exche-quer, Common Pleas, and King's Bench; the circuit or assize courts; and the local field representatives of the king, the justices of the peace, gathered into the Court of Quarter Sessions. It acquired not only specialized personnel and specialized functions, or procedures, but specialized records and precedents, and those became institutionalized. As it did so, the common law became an important idea, or set of ideas. It became increasingly independent of the king, for one thing, and the very embodiment of the medieval idea of a rule of law. At the hands of the Edward Cokes, judges and reporters, it grew to represent the defense of the people, through the rule of law and the use of the jury (the Palladium of our Liberties), against tyranny. This fact was merged, in the generation of Americans of whom we write, into a mythology that gave the common law a special sanctity. Thomas Jefferson shared with Judge Thomas Rodney in the Mississippi Territory a myth that ran somewhat like this: The Saxons developed the common law in its purity. Alfred the lawgiver wrote it down, King Edward the Confessor refined it. Came the aristocratical, feudal Normans, who tried to subvert it, and indeed succeeded in encrusting it here and there with undemocratic law, which one has to watch out for. Magna Carta restored the ancient luster (what did the myth-makers do with the feudal barons?), and Coke, the Petition of Right, and the Bill of Rights once more furbished it up in the seventeenth century. It was good law for republicans and libertarians.[7] This was not unanimous opinion during the post-Revolutionary period, but it prevailed. So we deal with both an institution and concepts. The common law also involved procedures that might be classed as techniques, which likewise had to be transported, e.g., the forms starting an action (the original writ was no longer used), which in turn governed the formulae for the remaining forms and for the written pleadings. Such techniques could be gotten from form books, easily transmissible, just as were the ubiquitous carpenter's manuals so influential in architectural design and its detail. (The tricks of oral pleading and advocacy had to be learned.) The lower rank of judges had manuals to go by, such as numberless editions of Burn's *Justice of the Peace*. These could be imported, or assembled locally as *The Magistrate's Assistant*, etc.

There were also these other main bodies of English law: (2) Statutes, which Americans sharply differentiated from common

[7] For the history that the Revolutionary generation lived on, see H. Trevor Colbourn, *The Lamp of Experience* (Chapel Hill, 1965). Rodney's version is in his charge to the grand juries, spring circuit, 1808, and in *In re Clerk of the Supreme Court*, Dec., 1808, printed in W. B. Hamilton, *Anglo-American Law on the Frontier* (Durham, 1953), pp. 335-336, 435-436. I am indebted to the Duke University Press for permission to quote liberally from that book.

law, although the latter had been shaped in part by statutes, or had absorbed old ones, such as the land legislation of Edward I, and statutes were concealed in its procedural forms. (3) Equity, another body of king's law, arising from petitions to him being handed over to the chancellor. Equity is usually distinguished from law by its willingness to order specific performance and to look behind a formal document for fraud and forgery. Vague and shapeless in the Middle Ages, by our time it had its formal court, it had rigidified, it followed its own precedents, and its decrees were embalmed in a number of volumes of reports and digests. The more enthusiastic of the common law mythologists frowned upon it as a prerogative court: It did not use a jury. The chancery court was abolished briefly during the English Civil War and Interregnum, and it was anathema to most of the New England states. (4) A branch of chancery business, inherited from the church, probate and orphans, had of course to be adopted in some form everywhere. (5) Admiralty, which was suspect to every loyal, smuggling Revolutionary, but somehow necessary wherever seagoing ships could sail. (6) Custom, not to be construed vaguely, but consisting of local law stubbornly held to by some town or county in England, such as the custom of Kent in the inheritance of estates. Some of this was incorporated from time to time by some judge to whom it appealed into the common law, even at late dates. Some of it was imported into America in the heads of immigrants, but without a statute or a body of citable cases behind it, it was a perishable commodity. (7) The law merchant, an international law. It was to be found in the civilians, and lay outside the common law until the second half of the eighteenth century except so far as actions of case (fourteenth century and beyond) had been able to ingest it.

English law, since it was not a dead thing, graven on tablets of stone, was growing and changing in the seventeenth and eighteenth centuries. This statement may seem to the reader a simple-minded truism, but it needs to be constantly kept in mind when one is studying its transmission abroad. The law was one thing when the settler landed at Jamestown and Plymouth Rock. It was quite another when the newly independent states extended their government to the Mississippi in the 1780's. The factory back home produced new articles of export, more and more modern, varied, and sophisticated. The reports and digests in which the products were described multiplied prolifically. The Americans had in the early seventeenth century made do with what little they had brought with them, or had bravely said they would repudiate all the old ways of a godless monarchy and manufacture their own, maybe out of the Bible and Puritan tracts, making a new start in a brave new world.

This proved hard to do in a court in which its advocates could not produce an American casebook, while their adversaries could cite Coke or Croke, or when the judge happened to have been a magistrate in an English county and had his experience and a manual stashed away. It became even more difficult as the reports multiplied in England and arrived on every ship, and as the English produced their great documents of liberty in the struggle with the king. There are differences of opinion among legal historians upon the extent to which English law was received in the seventeenth century,[8] but there is substantial agreement that in the eighteenth century the authority of English law asserted, or reasserted, itself, especially strongly in the Southern colonies. Richard B. Morris uses the epithet "reaction" in writing of this abandonment, if that is what it was, of the trend toward formation of an American law.[9]

Then, in the period immediately following the Revolution there was a widespread attack upon English common law, compounded of Anglophobia, democratic antiformalism, Francophilia, patriotism, and the spirit of reform. There were efforts to prohibit by statute the citation of cases decided in English courts after 1776 (New Jersey, Delaware, Pennsylvania, Kentucky, New Hampshire, for example), or even after the date on which the state had first been settled as a colony.[10] Maybe so; we have not studied the reports for the seaboard, but our good guess would be that Burrow (in spite of Lord Mansfield's Toryism) and Durnford and East (K.B., 1785-1800, also cited as Term Reports) kept arriving on the docks and the lawyers kept citing them. As for the civilians, they might play around with them, but few could read them and they would be difficult to apply.

Let us now pack our saddle bags and set out across the moun-

[8] See Francis R. Aumann, *The Changing American Legal System: Some Selected Phases* (Columbus, Ohio, 1940), chap. i.

[9] *Studies in the History of American Law* (New York, 1930), pp. 62-68.

[10] Aumann, *Changing American Legal System*, pp. 79-86.

tains. What shall we put in them? At the time of the establishment of American colonial rule in the West there was not one single fully developed volume of American law reports; so we pack up Coke, Blackstone, and company. They would be needed, for the Northwest Ordinance of 1787 provided for judges who should have common law jurisdiction and guaranteed to the inhabitants the benefits of habeas corpus, trial by jury, and "judicial proceedings according to the course of common law."[11] Not content with this, the governor and judges of the Northwest Territory a few years later (acting as a legislature) adopted a Virginia statute of 1776 which declared that the common law of England *and* all the English statutes of a general nature passed before the 4th of James I, excepting three Tudor enactments on usury, were in force.[12] Indiana Territory not only inherited the laws of the Northwest Territory, but re-enacted the Act just described, in 1807.[13] In Illinois, when it became separate, "questions regarding the adoption of the common law were never seriously mooted."[14] Nor were they in Mississippi Territory, established in 1798 on the general lines of the Northwest Ordinance.[15] There was no effort to chop off the citation of the common law at any given time, so that all the advances of the late eighteenth century were available to the courts, including Lord Mansfield's reforms, which included bodily taking over into the common law the most important cases of mercantile law. True it is that the judge who has left reports, Thomas Rodney, once pronounced that Mississippi was governed by the common law as it stood at the time of the Revolution, but he meant this to say that certain changes in the common law with regard to the testamentary disposition of personality which had occurred after the settlement of America were ruling law in his court.[16] He did not intend the statement to be a limitation.

[11] Purest text of the Ordinance is in *The Territorial Papers of the United States*, ed. Clarence E. Carter (in progress, Washington, 1934—), II, *The Territory Northwest of the River Ohio, 1787-1803* (Washington, 1934), pp. 203-204. Confirmed, with barely enough change to make it fit the circumstances, by Act of Congress, Aug. 7, 1789, 1 Stat. 50-53.

[12] *The Laws of the Northwest Territory*, ed. Theodore Calvin Pease, *Collections* of the Illinois State Historical Library, XVII (Springfield, 1925), 253.

[13] *The Laws of Indiana Territory, 1801-1809*, ed. Francis S. Philbrick, *Collections* of the Illinois State Historical Library, XXI (Springfield, 1930), 323.

[14] *Ibid.*, p. cii.

[15] Act of April 7, 1798, in *Territorial Papers of the U. S.*, V, 18.

[16] *Vousden* v. *Exrs. of Vousden*, 1808, Supreme Court. Hamilton, *Anglo-American Law on the Frontier*, pp. 383-385 at 385.

In Ohio, on the other hand, where common law had been declared ruling by the Northwest Territorial act, by the Constitution
of 1802, and by an Act of 1805, the legislature repealed early in
1806 so much of the Act "as declared the common law of England . . . to be in force." The courts of that state, after one decision *contra*, seeing that there had already been enough criminal
law enacted to constitute a code, interpreted this statute as saying
that criminal law did not obtain, but that such other common law
as was applicable in Ohio "has been and is followed by our courts,
and may be said to constitute a part of the common law of
Ohio. . . ."[17] In Michigan Territory, Judge A. B. Woodward, who
could adduce a three-and-a-half page list of authorities on the law
relating to Sunday,[18] said of the common law: "The United States
of America derive So much of their government and jurisprudence
from the Celebrated and potent island on the western Coast of
Europe . . . that it is difficult, even at this day [1809], to decide
ordinary Cases, without a reference to the laws and policy of
Britain."[19]

One cannot get a real view of the reading of the lawyers, or an
idea of what was permitted to be cited in court, without reports.
They are scarce for the frontier in our period. We have edited
Judge Thomas Rodney's notes for the Mississippi Territory; appar-
ently the earliest reports Professor William Wirt Blume found in
Michigan were those for 1819-1820, in the Supreme Court, by
Doty. The courts there had certainly not cut off citations of English
cases at the Revolution. Durnford and East, H. Blackstone (C.P.,
1788-1796), and Chitty on Pleading (1808) alongside Croke
(Eliz., Jac., and Car.); Coke; Buller's, Selwyn's, Espinasse's, and
Peake's Nisi Prius; Comyns' Digest; Hawkins' Pleas of the Crown;
Tidd's Practice; Latch's K.B.; W. Blackstone; *et. al.*, were cited.
By that late in the day American reports had begun to proliferate,
and they share the honors; we find intermingled with the English
citations Dallas (U.S.), Mass. T. R., Call (Va.), Hall's *American*

[17] William T. Utter, "Ohio and the English Common Law," *Mississippi Valley
Historical Review*, XVI (Dec., 1929), 321-333. Last quotation is as late as 1853,
2 Ohio State Reports 387, quoted at p. 332.
[18] *Transactions of the Supreme Court of the Territory of Michigan, 1814-1829*,
ed. W. W. Blume (2 vols.; Ann Arbor, 1939), I, 445-448.
[19] *Transactions of the Supreme Court of the Territory of Michigan, 1805-1814*,
ed. W. W. Blume (2 vols.; Ann Arbor, 1935), I, xxxix ff.

Law Journal, Washington, Coxe (N. J.), Cranch (U.S.), Caines (N. Y.), Johns (N. Y.), Hening and Mumford (Va.), Day (Conn.), and Tyng's Mass. R., not to belabor the list.[20]

The earlier lawyers and judges were likewise bookish people, in both the Northwest and Southwest.[21] Blume, after examining the evidence, scornfully refutes an absurd statement by one of Turner's disciples that the frontiersmen made up their own law. They were good and orthodox pleaders:

> Turning finally to the records of the Court of Common Pleas of Wayne County (1796-1805) [about as far out as the frontier ran at the time] we find almost no evidence of the informality often supposed to be a characteristic of frontier justice. Instead, we find a strict compliance with applicable statutes, and, where the procedure was not governed by statute, with the English common law. English law books were available and trained lawyers practiced before the court. English forms, including the various pleading fictions, were closely followed. Of the many pleadings listed in the Appendix, infra, only two are listed as "informal."[22]

In Indiana and Illinois, Professor Philbrick thought the records showed evidence of both bad and good pleading, the lawyers being too ignorant to be technical or fine in the points of law, on the one hand, and a form book being easily copied, on the other. And yet, in a rare comment on an actual case, he says that on a motion in an Indiana court in 1809, the judges produced a "careful" argument, following such English authorities as Hale P.C., Ld. Raymond, Strange, and Foster.[23] He did not find the sophistication in forms of action[24] that Blume did or that we did in the Mississippi colony.

The Natchez District in the latter, as a matter of fact, does not fit the stereotype of a frontier. It was rather a commercial community given to agreements in pursuit of money—contracts, loans,

[20] Doty's reports begin at p. 369 of Blume's *Michigan 1814-1829*, I. For some of the early American reports, see Aumann, *Changing American Legal System*, pp. 74-77.

[21] William Wirt Blume, "Civil Procedure on the American Frontier: A Study of the Records of a Court of Common Pleas of the Northwest and Indiana Territories," 56 *Michigan Law Review* (Dec., 1957), 161-224. Hamilton, *Anglo-American Law on the Frontier*, pp. 136-137 and *passim*. Philbrick does not think there were many books in Indiana Territory (*Indiana*, pp. cxcv-cxcvi), but then he had not any early reports to go by.

[22] Blume, 56 *Michigan Law Review*, 209.

[23] Philbrick, *Indiana*, pp. clxxxlx, cxcvii-cxcviii.

[24] *Ibid.*, pp. clxxxvii-viii.

commercial paper. Whole terms of court might be given up to debt on sealed agreements and indebitatus assumpsit on promissory notes and bills of exchange. There was considerable trover, and we even find a sample or two of the ancient action of account (used before equity was introduced), which Maitland says is rare in modern times.[25] The dominance of commerce in the courts is also reflected in the extensive use of arbitration, never used except for an action arising out of a business transaction, in which the parties would put themselves upon the court rather than upon the country.

There were plenty of actions of case and the ridiculous old trespass and ejectment, complete with John Doe and Richard Roe as sureties for the plaintiff, John Denn as the lessee, and "your loving friend" Richard Fenn as the casual ejector. So assiduously did the lawyers pursue their researches that we find rare actions, such as qui tam, used against a man who had let his slave run at large,[26] and the grand old writ de homine replegiando (a sort of replevin for human beings), thrice invoked for some heartbreaking efforts to rescue persons from chattel slavery. Holdsworth tells us that this writ, which was so ancient that it appeared in Bracton, had not been used in England since the seventeenth century.[27] We might add to our antiquarian collection benefit of clergy, briefly permitted by statute in Mississippi colony for first offenses in certain crimes[28] and by no means rare or unusual in America.[29]

As in Professor Blume's Wayne County, pleading on the Southwestern frontier was of high quality. The multitude of disputed land titles, in addition to the commercial business, brought in some rather keen lawyers and promoted competition for business. "Special Pleading," wrote Rodney, "is adhered to in our Courts with as much Strictness Elegance and propriety as many of the States,

[25] F. W. Maitland, *The Forms of Action at Common Law* (Cambridge, 1941), p. 88, and *Pleader's Assistant* (Dublin, 1795), p. 36, give the words of the old writ and of the declaration based upon it, followed faithfully in *Eldergill* v. *McKoy*, 1801, Adams County Common Pleas, Judgments, Book A, Adams County Courthouse.

[26] *Green* v. *Irby*, 1808, Minutes, Adams County Court, 1804-1812, p. 252.

[27] *History of English Law*, IX, 105, 106, 120, 121.

[28] Act of Jan. 30, 1802, Sec. 34 (MS in Mississippi Archives). Abolished 1807.

[29] Arthur Lyon Cross, "Benefit of Clergy in the American Criminal Law," Massachusetts Historical Society, *Proceedings*, LXI (1928), 155-180; William K. Boyd, "Documents and Comments on Benefit of Clergy as Applied to Slaves," *Journal of Negro History*, VIII (1923), 443-447; George W. Dalzell, *Benefit of Clergy in America & Related Matters* (Winston-Salem, 1955).

so that Even the young Lawyers are obliged to read their books and be very attentive to their business or want bread."[30]

Of course the lawyers did not have to follow all the ancient rigamarole of the common law with painful exactness. In Mississippi, all the English statutes of jeofail down to the 16th of George III were made law by the assembly, and when Judge Harry Toulmin wrote a *Digest* in 1807, he wrote into it his own simple law forbidding any abatement, arresting, quashing, or reversal of any part of the proceedings for imperfections, defects, or want of form, except in demurrers.[31] Indiana had its own statutes of jeofail, one of which adopted appropriate English statutes to 1752,[32] and we may suppose the other colonies had similar statutes.

That borrowing of English statutes by statutes of colonies of the United States raises the question of how far English statutes were transported to the frontier. We shall give the question short shrift, partly because we do not know much about it, partly because English statute law as such was cut off fairly early. We have suggested already that English statutes found their way to the frontier concealed in procedural forms, and that the Northwest Territory and at least one of its offspring adopted, along with the common law, applicable statutes of England up to 1607 (having borrowed the Act from Virginia). It would take too much trouble to find out when the northwestern states all declared English statutes not in force. In 1810 Michigan Territory, in one grand sweep, outlawed the statutes of England, Great Britain, and Canada, and for good measure the coutume de Paris (more likely it was the custom of Normandy), leaving only Michigan and United States statutes and English common law and equity.[33]

Rodney held flatly that English statutes did not extend to Mississippi.[34] On the other hand, Harry Toulmin, the judge in the eastern part of the colony, took an opposite view, and his view is of sharp significance because he wrote the first digest of the terri-

[30] To C. A. Rodney, Sept. 30, 1809, *Pennsylvania Magazine of Biography and History*, XLV (1921), 183.
[31] Hamilton, *Anglo-American Law on the Frontier*, p. 121. All the above material on Mississippi comes from *ibid.*, pp. 118-121, 136-138, 141, 146-147, and notes, plus the cases that go with them. See Index.
[32] Philbrick, *Indiana*, pp. 7, 453-454.
[33] Blume, *Michigan, 1805-1814*, I, xxix ff.
[34] Rodney to T. Gammel, Oct. 2, 1805, *Pennsylvania Magazine*, XLIV (1920), 188.

torial laws.[35] The word "wrote" is used advisedly rather than "compiled," because there is a substantial foundation for the belief that Toulmin composed many passages in his digest. In addition to incorporating the public acts still in force, he wrote to the acting governor,

I have likewise, Sir, ventured a step beyond this, knowing that many of our legal provisions and mode of proceedings are founded not in the common law, but on the Statutes of England—reflecting that in the establishment of a colony in this country under the auspices of the British Government, the settlers must have brought with them the laws of the parent states—which a subsequent temporary occupation of the country by the Spaniards, occasioned by an ignorance of the acknowledged boundaries, would not be considered as abrogating. I have felt inclined to adopt [the view that] the statute as well as the common law of England, as it stood previously to the settlement of Florida, makes a part of the law of the Mississippi Territory.

Knowing full well that this opinion ran counter to prevailing view in the territory, Toulmin said he had restrained himself and limited his use of English statutes, not incorporating into the digest many that he felt would be useful.[36] From this remarkable statement we may conclude that English statutory law had an influence in the territory far beyond what might have been expected from mere far-distant inheritance, or from the utility which led America to adopt certain of the time-proved statutes. Someone capable of doing so needs to examine Toulmin's book with a view to detecting the English statutes in it.

In adopting this digest as the law of the territory, the assembly at the same time declared that all British statutes not incorporated in it should cease to have validity in the territory.[37] Among the

[35] *The Statutes of the Mississippi Territory, Revised and Digested by Authority of the General Assembly.* By the honorable Harry Toulmin, one of the United States Judges for the Mississippi Territory. Natchez, 1807.

[36] Toulmin to Cowles Mead, Washington, Jan. 19, 1807, in Mississippi Archives, M. T. A., Ser. A, Vol. 7. The courts of other and later American colonies, as far away from English colonial influence as Oregon and Hawaii, took the position that certain applicable statutes of England governed in their jurisdictions, sometime holding that the statutes formed part of the common law. See especially the second part of William Wirt Blume and Elizabeth Gaspar Brown, "Territorial Courts and Law: Unifying Factors in the Development of American Legal Institutions," 61 *Michigan Law Review* (1962-1963), 39 ff., 476 ff.

[37] Toulmin's *Digest*, p. 23. In 1849 Judge A. M. Clayton, in the high court of Mississippi, held that British statute law had been excluded from Mississippi by the Ordinance of 1787 and the Constitution of 1817 (*Boarman* v. *Catlett*, 13 Smedes and Marshall 152).

statutes of Parliament that the territorials copied either directly or at second hand were those of 13 Eliz. I, Ch. 5, and 27 Eliz. I, Ch. 4, on fraudulent conveyances, and Section 4 of the Statute of Frauds (29 Charles II, Ch. 3).[38] The statute of Henry VI on forcible entries and detainers seems to have been the basis for the Mississippi law of 1805.[39] "An Act for Limitations of Actions," 1802,[40] stems directly, as do most such American acts, from the Statute of Limitations, 21 James I, Ch. 16.

The sharp distinction ordinarily made between common and statute law does not serve truth. For example, the entire family of trespass actions without the allegation of vi et armis rests *perhaps* on a clause in the great Statute of Westminster II.[41] Where a process included the phrase "according to the statute in such case made and provided," as, for example, in the assignment by the sheriff of the defendant's bail bond to the plaintiff, the territory perforce thumbed through the statute books (or, to be honest, the form books) and copied out the appropriate passage—in this case 4 and 5 Anne, Ch. 16, Section 20.[42] The territorial statute with regard to multiple pleas is indebted to Section 4 of this same statute and to 27 Eliz. I, Ch. 5.[43] The form of the declaration under bill, used by the territory, was partly shaped by 4 and 5 William and Mary, Ch. 21, Section 3.[44] In other words, the frontiersmen borrowed a lot of English statute law, frequently without any idea they were doing so, just as a lot of common law was reduced to statute law in the west by simply enacting it in codes or laws. If anyone has carefully traced the ancestry of statutory provisions in the western colonies over a prolonged period of time, we are ignorant of the findings. One writer finds it strange that the seaboard accepted as much statute from England as it did, because, says she, the British position was that English statutes did not apply automatically, but American colonists went right on assuming or stating that they did, up to certain dates. The First Continental Congress declared in 1774 that the colonies were *entitled* to "the common

[38] Judge Edward Mayes, in Goodspeed Publishing Company, *Biographical and Historical Memoirs of Mississippi* . . . (2 vols.; Chicago, 1891), I, 101.
[39] 8 Henry VI, Ch. 9; Act of Feb. 10, 1805, Toulmin's *Digest*, pp. 263 ff.
[40] Toulmin's *Digest*, pp. 239 ff.
[41] Maitland, *Forms of Action*, p. 51.
[42] 2 Chitty on Pleading (1809) 162; Toulmin's *Digest*, p. 138.
[43] Holdsworth, *History of English Law*, IX, 266, 316.
[44] 2 Chitty on Pleading (1809) p. 2 n.i.

law of England" and "to the benefit of such English statutes as existed at the time of their colonization; and which they have, by experience, respectively found to be applicable to their several local and other circumstances."[45]

What might, by a stretch of the imagination, be called the first American court in the Mississippi Territory was a sort of crackerbarrel chancery set up by Benjamin Hawkins, that good agent to the Creeks, to deal with disputes over land claims in the Creek country:

The plaintiff enters his claim, on oath, circumstantially detailed, taken in the usual manner at the place of his residence, or before me. A copy of this I send the defendant, with an order to answer in a given time, and if it is then deemed necessary, I send this answer, with interrogations, to the plaintiff; he replies; the defendant rejoins, and I decree.[46]

Professor Philbrick feels that the omission in the Ordinance of provision for equity or chancery courts in the territories was "almost certainly" deliberate, a reflection of the strong prejudice in America against equity. But the territories felt a need for equity, and the northern ones, in spite of having erected orphans' and probate courts under the ordinance (and probably in violation of it), thought special federal legislation was needed to grant their courts equity jurisdiction. Indiana petitioned for such authority, and that Act of Congress which in 1805 granted the powers of the District Court of Kentucky to the superior courts of the territories likewise conferred upon those courts "a fairly broad but not altogether satisfactory jurisdiction in equity." The Indiana legislature straightway exceeded this authorization by creating a separate equity court; the governor and judges of Michigan Territory passed a law conferring equity jurisdiction upon the court of common law.[47] The Supreme Court of Michigan Territory, which had sat as an admiralty court from the beginning, exercised equity jurisdiction in cases that exceeded the authorization of the Act of Congress of 1805. In 1812,

[45] Elizabeth Gaspar Brown, "British Statutes in the Emergent Nations of North America, 1606-1940," *American Journal of Legal History*, VII (April, 1963), 95-135.

[46] Hawkins to John Joyce, Cusseta, Dec. 5, 1797, *Letters of Benjamin Hawkins. Collections* of the Georgia Historical Society, IX (Savannah, 1916), 264-265.

[47] Francis S. Philbrick (ed.), *The Laws of Illinois Territory, 1809-1918. Collections* of the Illinois State Historical Library, XXV (Springfield, 1950), xli, esp. nn. 100 and 101; Philbrick, *Indiana, 1801-1809*, pp. clxiii-clxiv; Act of March 3, 1805, 2 *Statutes at Large* 338.

to its law and equity jurisdiction was added divorce. Not until
March 3, 1823, did the imperial power confer chancery jurisdiction on the judges of Michigan. Congress was laboring behind
the facts.[48]

Three years before the Act of 1805, the Mississippi Territory,
without asking sanction, had already installed equity. It had done
so chiefly because of a particular set of circumstances that arose
early in the American dominion. Phoebe Calvit, a litigious and
energetic widow, had a grant from the Spanish of a lot in Natchez.
Robert Moore, a merchant, had a grant of later date to the same
property, but it was thought that Moore's grant was one of the
antedated grants given by the Spanish to their favorites after they
had determined to evacuate the district. This general question was
one of concern to many of the inhabitants. When in 1800 Moore,
in the cause of *Richard Roe* ex dem. *Robert Moore* v. *Calvit* tried
to eject Phoebe, the Adams County gentry on the bench of Common Pleas permitted the introduction of parole testimony to prove
fraud in Moore's grant. The jury brought in a verdict for Calvit,
whereupon Moore took a nonsuit, and brought the case in 1801
before the Supreme Court, which rejected parole testimony and
decided for Moore.[49] The populace was outraged.[50] Phoebe memori-
alized for a law to permit parole testimony in land cases[51] to prove
fraud, and the assembly seemed likely to pass such an act until
Governor Claiborne let it be known that this would be such a great
innovation in the laws of evidence that he could not gain his own
consent to sign such a bill. The legislature, moved by such repre-
sentations as a presentment by the grand jury of Pickering County

[48] Blume, *Michigan 1805-1814*, I, xliii ff.

[49] Adams County Common Pleas, Judgments, Book A, p. 142, in Adams
County Courthouse; W. C. C. Claiborne to Madison, Natchez, Dec. 20, 1801,
Official Letter Books of W. C. C. Claiborne, 1801-1816, ed. Dunbar Rowland
(6 vols.; Jackson, 1917), I, 28-30; Memorial to the Assembly of Phoebe Dayton,
Dec. 8, 1801, in Mississippi Archives, M. T. A., Ser. D, Vol. 36.

[50] The grand jury of Adams went so far as to indict Moore for fraud (His-
torical Records Survey, Transcription of County Archives of Mississippi, No. 2
Adams County, Vol. I, *Minutes of the Court of General Quarter Sessions of the
Peace, 1799-1801*, Jackson, 1942, p. 228).

[51] See n. 49, above. Rodney permitted parole testimony to prove Spanish land
law in *Calvit* v. *Alston*, but refused such testimony on an English grant, on
grounds that the records were available in Washington, D. C. (*Peter Nelson and
wife's lessee* v. *Thompson*). Both rulings were on the popular side. Hamilton,
Anglo-American Law on the Frontier, pp. 353-359, 239-240.

and a petition from fifty citizens,[52] turned to the expedient of authorizing equity jurisdiction, although most of the lawyers thought it would not serve the purpose.[53] Be that as it may, in the heat of a particular issue and a clash of personalities, the assembly conferred equity jurisdiction on the superior courts of the territory,[54] and such courts were, in each subsequent reorganization of the court system during the territorial period, given equity jurisdiction, with all the "powers authority and jurisdiction incident to courts of chancery," including the power to issue writs of injunction and ne exeat.[55] This account illustrates beautifully what non-deterministic historians frequently find, that rather fundamental consequences may flow from reactions to a particular event or set of occurrences, and that these consequences are not necessarily logical or inevitable. Note carefully that the frontiersmen, in the grip of strong emotions, did not invent or devise a solution western, or American, or geographical in character. They simply adopted another good old medieval English institution, and copied its forms.

Lyman Harding, who was the best lawyer in the territory, did indeed suggest, in contesting a motion by an opponent for leave to amend his bill, that chancery practice in Great Britain did not apply in America. The court took time to consider, and then made the sensible pronouncement that

We shall be guided by The practice in England So far as it is admissible here because there is no Other Safe and regular guide, for there it has been brought to perfection by long Experience and the practice of the ablest Judges, and being Contained in their books of practice They can always be resorted to—without which the practice here would be always irregular and Uncertain.[56]

[52] Nov. Term, 1801, Mississippi Archives, M. T. A., Ser. A., Vol. 3; petition dated Aug. 4, 1801, in Mississippi Archives, M. T. A., Ser. D, Vol. 36.

[53] For this tale, in addition to previous citations, see Dunbar Rowland, ed., *Mississippi Territorial Archives, 1798-1803*, Vol. I, *Executive Journals of Sargent and Claiborne* (Nashville, 1905), pp. 364-365, 367, 369-370, 376, 463, 464-467.

[54] An Act for giving Equity Jurisdiction to the Superior Courts, approved Jan. 30, 1802. MS in Mississippi Archives. Printed in *Laws of 1801-1802*, no title page, pp. 186 ff. Photo in Mississippi Archives.

[55] Toulmin's *Digest*, pp. 123-124 (Act of March 2, 1805); Edward Turner, *Statutes of the Mississippi Territory . . . Digested by authority of the General Assembly* (Natchez, 1816), p. 109 (Act of Dec. 22, 1809), p. 200 (Act of Jan. 20, 1814). Ne exeat is now unconstitutional in Mississippi.

[56] *William Conner & wife v. James Williams, Admr. of Henry Willis*, in Supreme Court, Nov. Term, 1805. Hamilton, *Anglo-American Law on the Frontier*, p. 197.

One final sample of an important subsidiary of Anglo-American law—the justice of the peace and the court of quarter sessions, made not by interaction of the frontiersman and the wilderness, but by the inventive genius of the medieval English kings and their councilors, as translated by the southern American colonies. The county court had more direct work to do in the Mississippi Territory than the quarter sessions did in England because of the absence of the vestry. Individually the justice of the peace heard small cases, kept the peace, bound over suspects, acted as coroner and notary, and so on. With three or more of his fellows, of whom one must be of the quorum (i.e., learned in the law, as in the English Act of 1362, but we suspect the justice of the peace *and* of the quorum was simply a more substantial person), he held the county court, which disposed of civil suits below a certain sum of money, heard some criminal causes, sometimes acted as a probate and orphans' court. In the immemorial fashion, they also formed the administration of the county; they were responsible for social security (apprenticing of the young, the care of the sick or aged poor—housing, nurses, doctors, and drugs); they regulated such public utilities as ferries, mills, taverns, toll bridges, and bakeries; and they saw to it that roads and bridges were built and maintained. They were the custodians of the standard weights and measures placed at certain places by the colonial government. They appointed viewers of fences to enforce the cattle and stray laws.[57]

When those worthies sat as a court, what law did they use? English, to the best of their ability. Listen to the compiler of their manual:[58]

The general guide which has been followed in selecting subjects for the assistant, is Dr. Burn's Justice of the peace and parish office: but many other books have been used in making the compilation; the principal of which are Hawkins' pleas of the Crown—Easts' Crown law—Foster's discoveries—Gilberts' law of evidence, by Loft—Blackstone's Commentaries—Haywoods duty and office of Justice of the peace. . . .

[57] Summary based on a reading of the minute books of the Adams County Court and on Toulmin's *Digest*, pp. 7, 31, 36, 85, 88, 89, 90-95, 99, 214, 216, 272, 287, 357-358, 364, 417; Turner's *Digest*, pp. 327, 345, 369. I doubt there were any public bakeries in the rural areas, but the magistrates of the city of Natchez held assizes of bread.

[58] *The Magistrates' Assistant; Being an Alphabetical Illustration of Sundry Legal Principles and Usages, Accompanied with a variety of Necessary Forms. Compiled for the Use of The Justices of the Peace, in the Mississippi Territory.* By the Honorable Harry Toulmin, Natchez, 1807. The quotation is at p. 213.

All this came straight from the frontiers of the Palace of Westminster. The Thames flowed into the muddy waters of the majestic Mississippi and transformed them, engulfed them, Anglicized them forevermore. The evidence tends to show, as a restrained judge might say, that the old, or cis-Mississippi frontier, if it fashioned anew institutions out of its contacts with the wilderness, did not do so with such a pervasive, fundamental institution as the law. It imported it from England and the Atlantic coast on which English law had been deposited. In the early days, its law was continually refreshed by recourse to the English books, for they were all the frontiersmen had.

Of course they modified or changed that law as time went on. At its source it was changing all the time; some of it was probably changed by being filtered through the East; and the frontier was adopting it just as the movement for reform of it began to stir in England. American colonies and states were notably irreverent and sometimes willing to experiment. These facts have to do with change, not with the frontier. The assembly of the Mississippi Territory and its courts wavered in exactly the same manner on heritable estates and entails as did the councils and Parliaments of Edward I. The feudal magnates wished to preserve their estates in their families intact (*de donis conditionalibus*), or at least to hang on to reversionary rights (*quia emptores*). The courts, on the other hand, used every device they could, including outrageous fictions, to dock entails and to promote free alienation of land. In 1803 the Mississippi colonial legislature forbade an old medieval dodge to break an entail when it provided that all warranties by a tenant for life were void against those in remainder or reversion,[59] but in 1812 estates were strictly limited: All estates in land or slaves are now, and henceforth shall be, estates in fee simple, "and the same shall be discharged of the conditions annexed thereto by the Common Law, restraining alienations before the Donee shall have issue." The donee, or person in whom the conditional fee is vested, shall have a pure and absolute fee, "Provided, That any person may make a conveyance, or demise of lands, to a succession of Donees then living, and the heir or heirs of the body of the re-

[59] Toulmin's *Digest*, pp. 249-250.

mainder-man and [in] default thereof, to the right heirs of the Donor in fee simple."[60]

Sometimes the statutes would return the law to an earlier common law position. On the question of a testator's power to exclude his wife from the testamentary disposition of property, the territorial courts had been following the common law as it had developed in the seventeenth century, which held that the testator could so exclude.[61] The dower Act of December 22, 1812, provided that a widow was entitled to one-third of the real, and a child's share of the personal, property, whether the husband had made a will or not. She was given a sort of simple writ of dower and summary process: if she were dissatisfied with the property that came to her, she could institute by petition proceedings in the superior or county court to get what the law allowed.[62]

There were more statutory modifications of the common law, and of course some conscious modifications by the courts. Since the latter were mostly not printed in reports until the twentieth century, we have no idea whether or not they represented ruling law and little would be served by giving examples of them,[63] except for one that probably stuck: In *Territory* v. *Ellis*,[64] the question came up of granting a new trial in a case based on a penal statute. English doctrine was that the court did not have the power to grant an application for a new trial. The remedy was a writ of error coram nobis for an error of fact, or a pardon in the case of an error of law. The judge was determined to grant a new trial, and he had only one precedent,[65] so he proclaimed that although English practice in a great degree guided the courts in America, "yet in many Cases Our practice and police [policy] here, differs widely from their's." He fell back on the differences between the American and the Brit-

---

[60] Act of Dec. 22, 1812, Sec. 10. *Acts Passed at the Second Session of the Seventh General Assembly of the Mississippi Territory* . . . (Natchez, 1812 [prob. 1813]), pp. 87-88.

[61] *Vousden* v. *Exrs. of Vousden*, Supreme Court, May 26, 1808. Hamilton, *Anglo-American Law on the Frontier*, pp. 383-385.

[62] Turner's *Digest*, p. 255.

[63] See Hamilton, *Anglo-American Law on the Frontier*, pp. 121-127.

[64] *Ibid.*, pp. 199-206.

[65] *United States* v. *Fries*, convicted of treason in the Pennsylvania U. S. Circuit Court, 3 Dallas 519. There was one more precedent he probably did not know about: *State* v. *Hopkins* (1794), 1 Bay (S. C.) 372, in which a new trial was granted to a counterfeiter because the foreman of the jury had announced that he came to court determined to hang every damned counterfeiting rascal.

ish constitutions, the latter monarchical, the former republican. In a republic the people are governed by law, not men. It was unrepublican to seek justice from the executive; it should be found in the courts. New trial granted. Rodney was, on general ground, making a decision that seems in line with what would become doctrine in America. [66] This would seem to be an American, rather than a frontier, modification.

It might be recounted, as a footnote, that even to areas annexed after long rule by countries whose law was based on Roman, the advancing American frontier carried the English law. It made the Anglo-Americans uneasy to be confronted with another type. The emigrant Scots were homogenized; the Dutch may have left some vestigial remains in New York; the frontiersmen temporized briefly with the French in certain settlements in the Northwest, and with the Spanish in the Southwest (when they permitted citations of civilians and of such Spanish law books as they had in cases that had originated before the Spanish departed), then rolled completely over the minorities. Louisiana (meaning the Orleans Territory only) offers of course the exception. The Anglo-Americans hesitated before they allowed diversity in that jurisdiction, then imposed English procedure, especially in criminal trials, and left the remainder to the law as they thought it stood before the Purchase. The inhabitants took a while to settle upon what civil law they wanted, adopting the Napoleonic Code (which had of course never governed them before) because it was certain and available, but going right on citing such Spanish law as they could adduce[67]— a strange performance all 'round. Florida embraced English law and equity. Texas firmly chose English law, merging equity with it, although the early judges sensibly said they would have none of the rigamarole associated with its practice.[68] California, which like Texas was never governed as a colony by the United States, decided almost as soon as she joined to the Union to adopt English law as the base for her own.[69]

[66] An early case was that of *Commonwealth* v. *Green* (1821), 17 Mass. Reps. 533, in which Parker, C. J., argues for the right to grant new trials, using essentially the same argument as Rodney's.

[67] Elizabeth Gaspar Brown, "Legal Systems in Conflict: Orleans Territory, 1804-1812," *American Journal of Legal History*, I, (1956), 35-75.

[68] Edwin Lee Markham, Jr., "The Reception of the Common Law of England in Texas . . . , 1840-1859," 29 *Texas Law Review* (Oct., 1951), 904 ff.

[69] Edwin W. Young, "The Adoption of the Common Law in California," *American Journal of Legal History*, IV (1960), 355-363.

As far as law is concerned, then, Turner's case falls to the ground for want of evidence. His thesis, or hypothesis, is invalid. On the positive side, however, the essence of the case is perhaps not the validity of the Turner thesis but the question of a model for the transmission of important institutions and ideas from their original home to lands and peoples far away. The data in this paper cover the simplest situation with which the historian of transfer has to deal: one in which there was continuous importation of persons, habits, ideas, and books, chiefly from the British Isles, over a period of two hundred years. The indigenous peoples were killed off or pushed back; there was little attempt to settle down with them and adapt customs and institutions to them, as the Spanish and Portuguese may have done in parts of Central and South America. There was not the problem of an ancient culture that pervaded society, as in India. Furthermore, we dealt with ideas that became popular as they became vaguely identified, in the minds of emigrants who became revolutionaries, with the seventeenth-century rebellion against the king.

Law has to operate by rules and practices and by precedents, which must be written down for any large and complex society, must be uniform within a jurisdiction, must be as well known and as certain as is possible in an institution that constantly adapts itself to society through the interpretations of judges (assisted by lawyers) and the drafts of legislators. Its practitioners therefore needed books, and the books came from England. Law was scarcely an area of thought and doctrine that could tolerate sectarians such as those that splintered religion in Britain and America. Legal heretics, even if they converted temporarily whole jurisdictions, as in New England, were in the long run brought back into the fold by the lawyers of a people desirous of public order and of solid citations of precedents for the settlement of their disputes over money and property. Society could tolerate, and even profit from, little pockets of diversity in farming—as with Richard Shryock's Germans—or in German Moravian town planning, or in social custom, speech, or dress. In law, however, on the old frontier, English institutions were enjoined on the inhabitants by the imperial government at Philadelphia and Washington, they were desired by them, they were available in a language they could read, and they were operated by lawyers trained in the traditions of those institutions. All this made for a rough unity in legal development as the Anglo-American wave swept across a great continent and on into the Pacific. Insofar as there was diversity, and there was, within a broadly uniform framework, it was produced by inherited custom, by ignorance, or by strong-willed legislators or judges, not by acquired characteristics governed by geographical determinism.

In sum, *Q.E.D.*: English law was transported to America where it was received and took root. Our thesis does not require that we adopt the theory that American democratic governmental institutions grew from a germ in the German forests of the Angles and Saxons—the fixed idea which repelled the young Turner come out of the West to the Johns Hopkins. Not so long ago the Normans won a battle among historians in which the Anglo-Saxons admired by Jefferson and Rodney were subdued. The war among another flight of crook-taloned birds, as Mr. V. Mehta called some English historians, broke out again as the nine hundredth anniversary of the Norman Conquest approached, and the adversaries are happily tearing out of each other, if not the livers, then the lights.[70]

We can stay out of the battle, because, whatever its origins, the law was English in 1607. Nor can we undertake to set up any general model for the transfer of ideas and institutions, because the law, as we have reiterated, seems a case unto itself. As far as *it* goes, however, we suggest that the generalizations we have ventured would apply in any settlement colony such as Australia, New Zealand, English Canada, Quebec, and Boer-British South Africa. They would probably carry over neatly into strongly dominated or partial-settlement areas, such as Roman Europe, Brazil, Spanish South America, and even a great part of Islam. Mixed areas, or ones in which foreign domination was short, or ones in which foreign domination met a persistent ancient culture—India, Ceylon, Southeast Asia, French and British tropical Africa—present a more complicated story. The literature is enormous and fascinating and it invites synthesis.

[70] See, for an introduction to the controversy over the extent to which Anglo-Saxon institutions survived, R. Allen Brown, "The Norman Conquest," in *Transactions* of the Royal Historical Society, Fifth Series, XVII (London, 1967), 109-130.

The Spread of the Protestant Reformation of the Sixteenth Century

A Historical Case Study in the Transfer of Ideas

Hans J. Hillerbrand

I

If it were not for the fact that for some the sixteenth century is rather distant past and contaminated by a heavy preponderance of religious ideas and concerns, one might argue that the Protestant Reformation affords a singularly interesting case study of a transfer of ideas. This is so because the Protestant Reformation was a phenomenon which by the middle of the sixteenth century had affected, with the exception of Ireland, virtually all of Europe. Major Protestant movements were found not only in Germany, but in France, Switzerland, England, Sweden, Poland, and Hungary as well. In some of these countries, such as England, Switzerland, and Germany, Protestantism actually had succeeded in accomplishing the remarkable feat of dislodging Catholicism—which had dominated the ecclesiastical scene for as long as men could remember—thereby establishing itself as the official religion. A cluster of factors brought about this official recognition, and it would be hopelessly naïve to suggest that only religious or ideational considerations were operative in the swiftly moving course of events. Still, it can hardly be argued that they were completely absent. This assumption, accordingly, that novel religious notions made their impact throughout Europe, forms the underlying rationale for this essay.

To speak of the European dimension of the Protestant Refor-

MR. HILLERBRAND *is a professor at Duke University with appointments in the Department of History and the Divinity School. Among his publications is a volume in the Harper Documentary History of Western Civilization entitled* The Protestant Reformation.

mation as a case study for a transfer of ideas raises the question of how this simultaneous manifestation of Protestant thought throughout Europe should be understood. Two basic answers offer themselves and have been put forth by Reformation scholars. One is to see the European dimension of the Protestant Reformation as the result of an autochthonous emergence of similar or possibly identical movements for ecclesiastical reform. If a common temper characterized the rise of Protestantism, this temper was not attributable to a common source. According to this perspective, which might be called the "parallel-source" theory of Reformation origins, the spread of the Reformation cannot be seen as the result of a single event or man. On the other hand, one can see the European expansion of the Reformation in terms of a transfer of certain ideas from a single source, or a cluster of sources, across Europe. The designation "single-source theory" seems appropriate here. In this case the crucial question becomes the identity of this source. The chronological priority of the German Reformation and of Martin Luther suggests the clue for the subsequent reformatory development.

These two approaches determine the method of scholarly investigation. One can examine European society on the eve of the Reformation with a view to capturing the *zeitgeist* and the general conditions that precipitated the parallel emergence of what we might call revolutionary ecclesiastical movements. Thereby the intellectual and religious climates of the early sixteenth century become important focuses of investigation. Accordingly the general temper of the time is more important for an understanding of the European dimension of the Reformation than is any man or event.

The postulate of a priority of Luther or the German Reformation, on the other hand, calls for a careful examination of both the transmission and reception of Luther's ideas throughout Europe. The question of the condition of European society at the time is relegated here to a secondary place.

A survey of Reformation historiography shows that both approaches have been taken, without a definitive consensus of scholarly opinion being discernible. The two most recent surveys of Reformation history, G. R. Elton's *Reformation Europe* and A. G. Dickens' *Reformation and Society in Sixteenth-Century Europe*, speak briefly, though distinctly, about the "expansion" of Lutheranism or about "a very rapid radiation in all directions"[1] and thus seem to come down on the side of the "single-source" theory of Reformation origins. On the other hand, Leonard Trinterud, in his "Reappraisal of William Tyndale's Debt to Martin Luther," has rejected the writing of Reformation history in such a way as to make the Reformation begin in a given country with the first incidence of Lutheran ideas there.[2] This same position was taken by the French historian Lucien Febvre, whose essay "Une question mal posée: Les origines de la Réforme française et le problème des causes de la Réforme" argued that a study of the origins of the Reformation must not be undertaken in terms of "specificité, priorité, nationalité."[3] As a more specific illustration it might be noted that Oskar Farner, the biographer of Huldrych Zwingli and thereby of the early Swiss Reformation, has gone to considerable lengths to reject any influence of Luther on Zwingli.[4]

II

No study of the spread of the Reformation is available, and this lacuna makes a tentative investigation of the problem both possible and necessary. Our investigation will argue the "single-source" theory and it hopes to show that the European dimension of the Reformation receives its clue from a transfer of "Lutheran ideas" from Germany abroad. Moreover, it will be argued not only that these ideas made their way from Germany to Europe at large, but that such transfer entailed at once their reception abroad and a significant impact upon their respective societies. This latter point seems particularly important inasmuch as the "transfer," "reception," or "impact" of ideas denote different facets of a general phenomenon which must be properly distinguished if the actual situation is to be understood. A "transfer of ideas" is impossible without a concomitant "reception" of those ideas. To be specific, the assertion of a transfer of Luther's ideas throughout Europe does

[1] G. R. Elton, *Reformation Europe* (Cleveland, 1964), p. 104; A. G. Dickens, *Reformation and Society in Sixteenth-Century Europe* (New York, 1966), p. 87.
[2] L. J. Trinterud, "A Reappraisal of William Tyndale's Debt to Martin Luther," *Church History*, XXXI (1962), 244.
[3] Febvre, *Au Coeur Religieux du XVIᵉ Siècle* (Paris, 1957), p. 70.
[4] O. Farner, *Huldrych Zwingli. Seine Entwicklung zum Reformator* (Zürich, 1946), pp. 310 ff.

not in itself prove that these ideas played a significant role in their new environments. The notion of a "transfer of ideas" is obviously a shorthand expression that encompasses three distinct aspects: the existence of the idea, its transmission, and its reception.

If we speak of a transfer of "Lutheran ideas" we must define what is meant by "Lutheran." This is difficult for two reasons. For one, even an intensive scholarly preoccupation with Luther during the past decades has not succeeded in establishing a consensus about the main thrust of his theology. Particularly, the question of the nature of the "Protestant" reorientation of his thought between 1513 and 1518 is not easily answered, and, similarly, the relationship of Luther's assertions concerning justification, Scripture, or the vernacular Scriptures vis-à-vis authentic Catholic theology in the early sixteenth century is difficult to establish.[5] Second, we are concerned only with a chronologically restricted period of Luther's literary activity, namely, that of the time from the outbreak of the indulgences controversy to the establishment of his European fame. For the latter date, the year 1523 is suggested somewhat arbitrarily. Even at that date Luther's "complete" theology could not be disseminated abroad, but only his published writings. The picture of Luther's theology that can be drawn from the writings of these early years is fragmentary. Thus Luther's particular understanding of the Lord's Supper, as subsequently expressed in the communion controversy with Zwingli; the details of his anthropology, as delineated in his encounter with Erasmus; or the concept of justification, as propounded by his second commentary on Galatians—all remain enigmatic on the basis of the published writings between 1518 and 1523. Moreover, since some of his significant reflections were not published at all—the first Psalms lectures, for instance, or the lectures on Romans—the generally available work did not convey the full scope of his theology even as of that time.

An analysis of the writings commonly available shows that Luther conveyed a relatively vague program of ecclesiastical and theological reform—more a mood or temperament than a detailed theological exposition, more a broad assertion than a carefully delineated position. This is confirmed by the fact that Luther's most

[5] The scholarly discussion about Ernst Bizer, *Fides ex Auditu* (Neukirchen, 1958), which ventured a reinterpretation of Luther's theological beginnings, is here a good case in point.

popular work prior to the publication of his *The Babylonian Captivity of the Church*, in 1520, was his exposition of the Lord's Prayer, a tract containing little specifically theological reflection.[6] The *Babylonian Captivity*, however, indicates that Luther's theological dissent from Catholicism also found a very specific expression, so that we must not overstate the general character of his writings.

Our use of the term "Lutheran"—or its broader though anachronistic parallel, "Protestant"—will be influenced by these considerations. In other words, the question is not so much what we today would consider a valid statement of Luther's theology for the years between 1518 and 1523, but rather what the people of the time were able to conclude concerning the Wittenberg professor. The popular conception of Luther is thus more important than the accuracy of this conception. Not what Luther meant to convey in his writings—or indeed what he himself stood for—is important, but what people took him to say and what they associated him with in the early years of the Reformation.

This means, of course, that the contemporary use of the label "Lutheran" or "Martinian" will be accepted as legitimate and useful for our purposes. If, for example, the demand for the vernacular Scriptures was seen as peculiarly "Lutheran," and thus heretical, then it must be accepted as such, even though theological examination might show that the vernacular Scriptures were in principle not alien to Catholicism.

Finally, it is to be observed that the general notion of a transfer of Lutheran ideas itself says nothing about the geographic dimension of this transfer which may have taken place either on a larger or a smaller scale, affecting Europe at large or only specific countries. In other words, even if, for example, no Lutheran influence were discernible in Switzerland, the situation in France or England might be different.

These considerations, then, suggest a threefold development of the argument of this essay: to establish, first of all, the extent to which Luther's ideas were actually transferred throughout Europe; to investigate, second, the means as well as the characteristics by which this transfer took place; and to assess, finally, the general

[6] *D. Martin Luthers Werke* (Weimar, 1883-), II, 74 ff. Hereinafter cited as *WA*.

influence of Luther's ideas so disseminated upon the Reformation in Europe.

III

Before we can address ourselves to the first point—the transmission of Luther's ideas—a few general comments must be made about the conditions of European society on the eve of the Reformation. Our concern is primarily with the ecclesiastical situation, even though the political and economic also are relevant. The basic question can be formulated as follows: Were the ecclesiastical conditions of the early sixteenth century such as to denote a precarious equilibrium that necessitated some kind of revolutionary or reformatory upheaval? Was Europe in the early sixteenth century "crying for Reformation"?[7]

The answer is that we know far too little about the time to offer more than tentative statements. Detailed research about the conditions in specific places is only beginning.[8] Still, the general conclusion at this point appears to be that European society was far more stable than has traditionally been assumed. In other words, if Luther and the other early reformers had died in their cradles, the Catholic Church might well have survived the sixteenth century without a major upheaval.

This is not to say, however, that there were not a number of problems beneath the surface. The sources reveal a considerable dissatisfaction with the ecclesiastical establishment. Denunciations of the Catholic Church are discernible, and every humanist worth his salt condemned the church. Colet's convocation sermon of 1512, Sebastian Brant's *Ship of Fools*, and *The Letters of Obscure Men* serve here as random illustrations. There are others, above all the official *gravamina* that were repeatedly compiled in Germany to express the grievances against the church.[9] Two themes occur again and again: charges of clerical immorality and resentment against the church's financial demands.[10]

[7] O. Chadwick, *The Reformation* (London, 1965), p. 1.

[8] See here the divergent conclusions of E. W. Zeeden, *Die Entstehung der Konfessionen* (Munich, 1965), p. 7, and B. Moeller, "Frömmigkeit in Deutschland um 1500," *Archiv f. Reformationsgeschichte*, LVI (1965), 30.

[9] B. Gebhardt, *Die gravamina der Deutschen Nation gegen den römischen Hof* (Breslau, 1895).

[10] See here the comments in H. A. Oberman, *Forerunners of the Reformation*

One must speak, then, of a latent dissatisfaction with the Catholic Church. While neither the available sources nor the present state of research allows a definitive statement about the intensity of this dissatisfaction, about its existence there can be no doubt. It was European-wide, discernible in England no less than in Germany, in France no less than in Switzerland. A common temper thus characterized the European scene, more intense at some places than at others, but present everywhere. Its exponents must naturally be sought among the literate segment of the populace—the burghers of the towns and the humanists. Though numerically insignificant, there were men throughout Europe who were basically cool toward the church. To these should be added the presence of a new theological temper. Though this temper took several forms, all of those men who displayed it shared in the reaction against late medieval scholastic theology. The most significant expression of this new theological approach was the Christian humanism of Erasmus and his program of the *philosophia Christi*. Erasmus' goal was to return to the simplicity of Jesus' teachings as well as to the authenticity of the writings of the church fathers. The tenor of his writings was in keeping with the theological consensus of the time. Where it was not, a nebulous vocabulary obscured the sentiment. The essential theological agreement with the medieval tradition must not obscure the fact, however, that some of the humanist formulations spoke a new theological language. Jacques Lefèvre, for example, propounded a theology characterized by the primacy of the grace of God, which stood in contrast, therefore, to the widely held stress on the works of man and has led to the suggestion that Lefèvre's theological orientation antedated Luther's reformatory insight.[11] Above all else, the way Erasmus and his fellow humanists went about stating their case revealed their distinct divergence from theological tradition. If nothing else, the form of their work was different. It was characterized by a fresh Latinity, and the authorities cited were not the scholastics but the early church fathers.

(New York, 1966), pp. 4 ff., which stress four recurrent criticisms: the amorality of the laity and higher and lower clergy; absenteeism; the poor training of the clergy; a laicizing religiosity.

[11] W. F. Dankbaar, "Op de grens der Reformatie: De rechtvaardingsleer von Jacques Lefèvre d'Etaples," *Nederlands Theologische Tijdschrift*, VIII (1954). For an opposite view, note H. Dörries, "Calvin and Lefèvre," *Zeitschrift für Kirchengeschichte*, XLIV (1925).

A word must be said concerning the flow of communication among European countries. Such communication was accomplished in a variety of ways which actually had been intensified by the early sixteenth century. The invention of movable type increased the dissemination of ideas during the final decades of the fifteenth century in dramatic fashion. A book could be—and indeed was—far more easily and more cheaply produced than before. The size of editions swelled considerably, and, since books could easily be shipped from one location to another, Europe became increasingly a single market. The significance, both economic and ideological, of the book printers and the booksellers was substantial, for books must not only be written but also published and sold. And this they were, in a manner comparable to the revolution in the paperback market in our own day. The book publishers slowly found their way into the guild system of the cities, and they did so with increasing economic prosperity and social success.

Of equal importance was the existence of a common language of intellectual intercourse, for this enabled the academic and theological community throughout Europe to engage in scholarly dialogue unhindered by linguistic obstacles. The extensive correspondence between academicians and humanists across the boundaries of Europe—the letters of Erasmus take up eleven volumes in their modern scholarly edition, those of his fellow humanist Vadian, seven—shows not only the significance of Latin as the common language but also serves as a gauge for the intensity of the scholarly dialogue.[12] These letters reflected a wide range of concerns; they dealt with matters of current interest no less than with questions of scholarship.

The manifold traits of European society in the early years of the sixteenth century, as they have been sketched in the preceding paragraphs, allow two generalizations. For one, Europe was characterized by a general ecclesiastical uneasiness which expressed itself in many ways and with varying degrees of intensity. Second, European society possessed numerous possibilities of intellectual interaction and, what is more, actually utilized them in increasing fashion. The notion of the *corpus Christianum*, the one Christian body, was real indeed.

[12] A comprehensive study of the correspondence of the leading figures in the sixteenth century remains very much a scholarly desideratum.

IV

This, then, was the situation in which occurred Luther's publication of his Ninety-five Theses in 1517. The course of events between the publication of these Theses and the excommunication of their author in 1521 is well known and need not be reiterated here. Important for our consideration is the dramatically increasing popularity of Luther during those years. Virtually unknown in 1517, Luther was assuredly one of the most famous of Germans by 1521, the year the papal nuncio Aleander exasperatedly noted that nine-tenths of Germany shouted "Luther."[13]

Another way of describing this popularity of Luther is to say that a transfer of ideas—those of Luther—occurred in Germany itself and turned the theological reflection of one individual into a widespread movement for ecclesiastical reform. Whatever one may conclude about Europe, the rise of the Reformation in Germany must be attributed to Luther. This can be shown in any number of ways—Luther's central importance in the actual course of events, the label "Martinians" given to his followers—but perhaps above all by the fact that all of the subsequent German reformers, such as Oecolampadius, Melanchthon, Jonas, or Bucer, explicitly acknowledged that they owed their theological quickening to Luther.

While the examination of the German scene would be interesting, our concern here is with the European dimension of Luther's message. This means that, first of all, the extent of the spread of Luther's ideas throughout Europe must be considered. Significant evidence for this spread comes from the correspondence of several important figures of the time. The humanist Christoph Scheurl sent copies of Luther's Theses to friends in November, 1517, and January, 1518.[14] Similarly, in April, 1519, Erasmus wrote to Bishop John Fisher in England about the Wittenberg professor. In October he remarked, "I hear that Luther is approved by eminent men,"[15] and he told Elector Frederick of Saxony at about the same time, "Certe hic video libros illius ab optimis" "Indeed, I see how his books are read most eagerly by eminent men."[16] In May, 1519,

[13] P. Kalkoff, *Die Depeschen des Nuntius Aleander* (Halle, 1897), pp. 192-193.

[14] F. von Soden and J. Knaake, eds., *Christoph Scheurls Briefbuch* (Potsdam, 1867), pp. 153, 160.

[15] *Opus Epistolarum Des. Erasmi*, III, 239, 409.

[16] *Ibid.*, III, 522-523, 531.

Erasmus commented in some detail on Luther's writings.[17] These quotations, while few in number, illustrate that Luther's theological pronouncements were widely noted. Luther's own correspondence confirms this evidence for the spread of his ideas. In 1519 Luther received several expressions of approval from as far away as Italy,[18] and he was told by Erasmus, "I cannot find words to describe the storm which your books have excited here."[19] Luther had evoked excitement, and Erasmus, still somewhat uncertain about his own position in the matter, did not hesitate to voice his amazement.

The extant and cited correspondence reveals only a small portion of what must have been communicated, but even what is available for our scrutiny indicates that personal contact played an important role in the transfer of Luther's ideas.[20] The letters not only show that acquaintances and colleagues informed one another of Luther's activities and commented on the spread of his writings; they also indicate that Luther's writings were circulated at the same time—somewhat like sending reprints of scholarly articles today. "I send you the theses," wrote Christoph Scheurl, and Zwingli spoke of "having received the books of a certain author."[21] Several entries in Zwingli's correspondence of June and July, 1519, show how Zwingli organized the colportage of Luther's books,[22] an activity especially stressed by Zwingli's first biographer, Oswald Myconius.[23]

Obviously the circulation of Luther's books would have been impossible if they had not been available in the first place. And this brings us to the men who produced them, the printers, who occupy a central place in the spread of the Reformation. Books make money and communicate ideas: this dual characteristic makes it impossible to say what motivated the men who published Luther's tracts during the third decade of the sixteenth century—

[17] *Ibid.*, III, 590.
[18] *WA Briefe* (Letters), I, 199, 205-206, 331 ff.
[19] *Opus Epistolarum Des. Erasmi*, III, 604.
[20] Note, for example, the comments about the spread of Luther's ideas in Nuremburg, *WA Br.*, I, 152; also note *Konrad Peutingers Briefwechsel* (Munich, 1923), p. 299.
[21] *Huldreich Zwinglis Sämtliche Werke*, I, 285.
[22] *Ibid.*, I, 7, 193, and 195.
[23] Oswald Myconius, *De Huldrichi Zwinglii fortissimi herois ac theologie vita et obitu. 1532.* A German translation is found in *Ulrich Zwingli. Eine Auswahl aus seinen Schriften* (Zurich, 1918), p. 6.

whether it was the desire to propagate new religious ideas or the hope of making a good profit. The fact is that by seeking to do the latter they also did the former. No copyright laws thwarted their entrepreneurial enthusiasm or prevented them from reprinting anything in sight. Accordingly, they printed prolifically.[24] If a contemporary sentiment is needed, it comes from the pen of John Foxe, the English martyrologist, who devoted a separate chapter to the "arte of printing" and observed that "the Pope, that great Antichrist of Rome, could never have been suppressed . . . except this most excellent science of printing had been maintained."[25] One need only check the places of the reprints of Luther's tracts between 1518 and 1522 to note the geographic dimension of a printing enterprise that nowadays would be severely handicapped by the laws of copyright. The printers of Wittenberg at times even published material that Luther did not want to have published. This aspect of the matter annoyed him no end, but on the other hand he was glad to have their services and had no serious objection to these sometimes overly enthusiastic colporteurs of his message.

By the end of 1520 eight collections of Luther's writings had been published, including two in Dutch. Luther's *Sermon on Indulgence and Grace*, of 1518, was reprinted thirteen times in 1518, five times in 1519, and four times in 1520. His exposition of the Lord's Prayer, of 1519, saw eighteen reprints, five of which were translations; his *Instruction Concerning Several Propositions* also had eighteen reprints, his *Sermon on the Preparation for Dying*, of 1519, twenty-two, and the account of his appearance before the German diet at Worms, no less than twenty-nine.[26] All in all, there were some 1,350 reprints of Luther's tracts between 1518 and 1519, twenty-two, and the account of his appearance before the instance, we reach a total of over one million copies of Luther's writings in circulation by 1524.[28]

[24] P. Leeman-van Elck, "Der Nachdruck in zürcher Sicht," *Zürcher Taschenbuch* (1943), pp. 106 ff.

[25] S. R. Cattley and George Townsend, eds., *The Acts and Monuments of John Foxe* (8 vols.; London, 1843-1849), III, 721.

[26] The works cited are found in Vol. II of *WA*.

[27] See here the bibliographical information in J. Benzing, *Lutherbibliographie* (Baden-Baden, 1965).

[28] The figure of one thousand copies is proposed, with documentation, by L. W. Holborn, "Printing and the Growth of a Protestant Movement in German," *Church History*, XI (1942).

In February, 1519, the Basel printer Johann Froben advised Luther of his activities on behalf of the colportage of Luther's writings.[29] Froben's letter indicated the geographic distribution of his efforts—France, Spain, Italy, England, Brabant.[30] The future reformer Wolfgang Capito wrote Luther at the same time, "Your writings have been made public throughout Italy, France, Spain, and England."[31] For Switzerland, Froben and Zwingli offered conclusive evidence of the spread of Luther's writings.[32] For other countries similar statements may be made. In Hungary, the bull of excommunication against Luther was read in the important churches in 1521, which is an indication that his writings had found their way into the country.[33] In Scotland a bill was passed in 1525 prohibiting the importation of Luther's "dampnable opunyeounis."[34] In Sweden, Bishop Hans Brask prohibited, in 1522, the sale, purchase, and reading of the books of Luther under pain of excommunication.[35] In England, Luther's books were read in 1519 and publicly burned in 1521.[36] Again Froben was an important agent.[37] Zwingli was told by an English humanist, William Nesenus, that Luther's books were bought everywhere.[38] An English canonist, Christopher Urswyke, who died in 1522, had two of Luther's published sermons copied.[39] The receptacle for Luther's message in England seems to have been Cambridge. There, the White Horse Tavern (where, according to John Foxe, Luther's doctrines were first discussed by a group of university dons) was dubbed "Little

[29] *WA Br.*, I, 331.

[30] *Ibid.*, I, 332.

[31] *Ibid.*, I, 336.

[32] There is no recent study of book publishing at Basel which could throw considerable light on the contribution of printers like Froben to the spread of Luther's ideas. A useful older work is I. Stockmeyer and B. Reber, *Beiträge zur Basler Buchdruckergeschichte* (Basel, 1840), and also C. W. Heckethorn, *The Printers of Basel in the XVth and XVIth Centuries* (London, 1897).

[33] M. Bucsay, *Geschichte des Protestantismus in Ungarn* (Stuttgart, 1959), p. 20.

[34] Acts of the Parliament of Scotland II, 295, as cited in J. H. Burleigh, *A Church History of Scotland* (London, 1960), p. 121. Also cited there is a royal warrant against "sundry strangers and others" who are "possessed of Luther's books and favoured his errors."

[35] *Handlinger rörande Skandinaviens historia*, XVII, 220, as cited in J. G. Hoffman, *La Réforme en Suede 1523-1572* (Paris, 1945), p. 93.

[36] A. G. Dickens, *The English Reformation* (New York, 1964), p. 69.

[37] *WA Br.*, I, 332.

[38] *Huldreich Zwinglis Sämtliche Werke*, VII, 384 ff.

[39] J. K. McConica, *English Humanists and Reformation Politics* (Oxford, 1965), p. 71.

Germany."[40] Erasmus had told Luther as early as May, 1519, that "You have friends in England who think very highly of your books."[41]

For France the evidence is also abundant. Thus, one eminent contemporary source noted that Luther "wrote several books which were printed and distributed throughout Germany and France."[42] In April, 1519, Lefèvre asked Beatus Rhenanus to convey greetings to several men "whom I cherish in Christ," and he included Luther in the list.[43] One month later a letter from Paris noted that "the works of Martin Luther are read by all learned men."[44] Martin Dorp wrote from The Hague in November, 1519, "Luther, about whom I wrote you recently, stands in high favor here."[45]

Obviously, we have only sampled the evidence. But there can be little doubt that by 1522, the year of Luther's excommunication by the Catholic Church, Luther's thought had reached every corner of Europe. This was primarily the result of the export of Luther's books, of course, but in addition to the place of books in this transfer of ideas, the role of people must not be overlooked. Not only the printed page but men carried the Lutheran ideas abroad. The carriers were those who traveled professionally and constantly between Germany and other places; mostly they were merchants and academicians who brought the news of the theological development in Germany, sometimes as uninvolved reporters, sometimes as enthusiastic partisans. Again, the evidence is rich and allows only a sampling. With respect to England, the role of the merchants in spreading the Lutheran message across the channel has been established.[46] A similar observation may be made about Sweden, where the Lübeck merchants became evangelists for the Lutheran cause, quite effective ones, as it turned out, in light of their constant communication with Sweden.[47]

[40] Dickens, *The English Reformation*, p. 68; the reference from Foxe is from *The Acts and Monuments of John Foxe*, V, 415-416.

[41] *Opus Epistolarum Des. Erasmi*, III, 606.

[42] V. L. Bourilly, ed., *Journal d'un Bourgeois* (Paris, 1910), p. 80.

[43] A.-J. Herminjard, *Correspondance des Réformateurs* (Geneva, 1878), I, 45.

[44] Note also the letter, dated April 7, 1521, from Glareanus to Myconius. Herminard, *Correspondance*, I, 62.

[45] *Opus Epistolarum Des. Erasmi*, IV, 128.

[46] Dickens, *The English Reformation*, p. 69.

[47] This is supported by a contemporary chronicle reprinted in *Historiska Handlinger* (Stockholm, 1661—), XII, Pt. 2, 1, as cited in Hoffman, *La Réforme en Suede*, p. 93.

Then there were the students who attended German universities and returned to their native lands with news of the Lutheran message. Naturally, not all of them savored the Lutheran teaching firsthand, but since Luther was the foremost topic of theological provenance, all of them did hear enough to form an opinion. For Luther's own university, Wittenberg, the statistics show an interesting confirmation of the student appeal of the "new theology": the number of students increased enormously from 1516 (162 students) to 1518 (273 students) and 1520 (579 students). At the same time, enrollment at the universities of Leipzig and Erfurt remained constant, and that of the university of Cologne dropped from 364 in 1516 to 235 in 1520.[48] Needless to say, not all of the additional students at Wittenberg came from abroad; those who did aided in the advance of Lutheranism upon their return home. The records show twenty-one *new* students from abroad enrolled in the fall of 1519, a small but significant number.[49] The increased enrollment at Wittenberg was conspicuous enough to cause several territorial rulers to demand that students from their lands leave the university.[50]

V

The fact that Luther's ideas were transferred from Germany abroad would seem, therefore, firmly established. What was the nature of this transfer? To begin with, it was bound to take place in circumscribed fashion. As we noted earlier, only the published work of Luther from the first few years of the Reformation, perhaps that of the time between 1518 and 1522, can have constituted the reservoir from which Luther's ideas could be transferred abroad. Theologically, it conveys only a fragmentary segment of his thought. Moreover, Luther's thought was in a state of flux during this time. For example, his *Resolutions* of 1518, an otherwise elaborate ex-

[48] K. Aland, "Die Theologische Fakultät [in Wittenberg] und ihre Stellung im Gesamtzusammenhang usw," in K. Aland, *Kirchengeschichtliche Entwürfe* (Gütersloh, 1960), pp. 283-284.

[49] C. E. Förstemann, *Album Academicae Vitebergensis* (Leipzig, 1841), I, 99 ff., as cited in E. G. Schwiebert, "The Reformation from a New Perspective," *Church History*, XVII (1948), 21. Schwiebert notes (*ibid.*, p. 11): "A study of the *Album* shows a rather striking correlation between the spread of the German Reformation in different regions as reflected in the enrollments in the university."

[50] W. Friedensburg, *Geschichte der Universität Wittenberg* (Halle, 1917), p. 147.

planation of the Ninety-five Theses, shows him quite indefinite about such crucial issues at religious authority or the papacy. Accordingly, a fragmentary Luther vied for acceptance, one that was possibly not even distinctly "Lutheran" in the sense of the subsequent ecclesiastical tradition or even as modern research has pictured Luther's theology. The writings available conveyed certain basic religious notions—an emphatically christological orientation, the repudiation of so-called human traditions, the affirmation of the primacy of Scripture in the formulation of religious truth, the open rejection of the Catholic Church and the pope wherever the new religious insights clashed with ecclesiastical tradition. To these notions must be added an intense stress on personal religion and a disregard of external rites and observances. If such is a correct description of the character of Luther's writings during the early phase of his reformatory career, it will be immediately obvious that these were themes that also were part and parcel of the larger reformatory concerns of the early sixteenth century.

Whether Luther's description of the Catholic teaching was always accurate, or whether his own thought was as novel as many of his contemporaries took it to be, must not be considered important. The important thing is that Luther called in bold and dramatic fashion for an examination of the faith of the Christian Church, stating categorically that, if need be, the ecclesiastical tradition of centuries had to be rejected.

As a further delimitation of Luther's influence we should note that his tracts which lent themselves to dissemination had to be in Latin in order to break the linguistic barrier between Germany and the rest of Europe. This limitation did not, of course, apply to Switzerland, but elsewhere Luther's German writings were of little use in propagating the new message. Only his Latin tracts could be communicated effectively to those whose mother tongue was French, Polish, or English. The number of his Latin writings was relatively small—ten in 1518, thirteen each in 1519 and 1520, and nine in 1521. This meant that Luther's message underwent an important modification as it was transferred abroad. In Germany, Luther had been able to address himself directly to the people and had made an explicit effort to do so. Indeed, his Catholic opponents chided him on this point, but what to them was vice was to him assuredly virtue. The extensive number of reprints of Luther's ver-

nacular tracts offers conclusive evidence for his success in speaking
to the common man.

Such immediate communication was impossible elsewhere in
Europe, where the "Latin" Luther could not speak to the people
but only to those in academic circles. Accordingly, the immediate
popular response to the reformatory proclamation found in Germany did not occur elsewhere in Europe and, for linguistic reasons,
could not. An intermediary was necessary; moreover, the transmission of Luther's ideas had to focus on essentials. Not the details of the new thought but catchy slogans—such as "Scripture"
versus "man-made traditions," salvation by "faith" and not "works"
—were important. Above all, Luther was taken as a symbol for a
basic hostility against the Catholic Church.

The effectual transmission of Luther's ideas, then, required the
support of followers on foreign soil. As matters turned out, these
followers did appear and the spread of the new ideas was not dependent upon outside literary influence but could utilize the efforts of indigenous colporteurs: Olavus Petri in Sweden, William
Tyndale in England, Huldrych Zwingli in Switzerland, Patrick
Hamilton in Scotland, Francis Lambert and Guillaume Farel in
France. These men labored in countries where Protestantism eventually rose to be a movement of major proportions, while by decided contrast countries like Italy or Spain, where there was no
Protestant success, did not produce a similar reformatory figure.
This fact suggests the significance of indigenous reformers, without
whom the ecclesiastical transformation in the various countries
would not have been possible. In a way, therefore, these men were
more important for the ecclesiastical transformations in their countries than was Luther.

Were there common characteristics among these reformers?
The answer must be "yes." Several of them actually had been to
Germany, had savored the new theology firsthand, and then had
returned to their native lands. Youthfulness is another outstanding
characteristic of the reformatory figures. They were little known
and not part of what might be called the academic or ecclesiastical
"establishment." As a matter of fact, the established academicians
remained conspicuously aloof from the new theology. The formation of Protestantism throughout Europe—as well as in Germany
itself—was attributable to men along the fringe of the "establish-

ment." The names of the reformers, from Luther on to Zwingli, Tyndale, Bilney, Frith, Cranmer, Petri, Oecolampadius, Lambert, Barnes, and the rest, are the names of men who, no matter how brilliant, in 1520 occupied neither positions of hierarchical responsibility nor academic dignity. Since all of them were young men when the storm broke, one may conjecture that some might have attained such stature in later years; when the momentous decisions were made, however, they were unknown.

An additional characteristic was their "humanist" orientation. Again, this corresponds to the situation in Germany, where all the reformers had been—and in large measure remained—humanists. Zwingli in Switzerland, Farel in France, Tyndale or Barnes in England—they all had been indebted to Erasmus before they became indebted to Luther. That Erasmus had spent a period of time at Cambridge, where subsequently the first rumblings of reformatory concern in England manifested themselves, is surely more than coincidental.

The actual propagation of Protestantism by these men took the form of an amalgamation of basic notions of Luther and elements of their own theologies. Neither was all of Luther's theology communicated abroad nor were the men who embraced the new theology devoid of theological background of their own. An encounter took place and the result was not a rigid replication of Luther's thought, but the formulation of a theology that was both anti-Catholic and vaguely Lutheran. This synthesis explains the immense variety of theological emphases that characterized the European scene, making, for example, the Reformation in Hungary quite different from that in England, and that in Sweden different from that in Poland.

One would hardly expect the various reformers to have incorporated all of Luther's thoughts—especially since the notions reaching them were, as we already have noted, so general as to require further implementation. Obviously, the theologians who subsequently carried the Protestant message forward in their countries had pondered theological issues before they heard the name of Luther. And this intellectual speculation surely had left its influence, making Luther only one of several factors in their theological development.

The transfer of Luther's ideas abroad was thus twofold, direct and indirect—the former through his writings as they were read in European countries other than Germany, the latter through indigenous reformers who became exposed, in one way or another, to Luther's thought. The former influence was limited (for reasons already shown), the latter broad and far-reaching.

This relationship between Luther's influence and that of native reformers explains at once the curious fact that so very few of Luther's writings were translated into non-German vernaculars—a few into Dutch, and two or three into English and French. On the other hand, many of Luther's early German writings were translated into Latin and, as the case of William Tyndale so tellingly shows, he was extensively plagiarized.[51] A second comment to be made about the relationship between Luther and the European reformers has to do with the full impact of Protestantism in the various countries. As we have noted, Luther's writings quickly became known abroad. The response, however, was a different matter and was long in coming. While there are exceptions, such as England and Sweden, widespread agitation for an ecclesiastical transformation generally did not come until the late 1530's, a full decade after the new theology had first swept through Europe. Explanations for this delay are difficult; the slowness in the formulation of an indigenous theology with direct popular appeal surely was a major factor.

VI

Several remarks are now in order. They pertain both to the way Protestant thought spread and to the significance of this spread for an understanding of the Reformation. Even if one assumes, as I do, that the European dimension of the Reformation is largely attributable to the impact of Luther, the question remains whether this impact was furthered by extraneous factors which themselves had little if anything to do with the Wittenberg reformer. The existence of such factors must be acknowledged, but at the same time

[51] Trinterud, *A Reappraisal*, p. 28. Since the concern of our study is to reflect on the possible immediate impact of Luther's ideas abroad, such wider questions as the Lutheran character of Tyndale's theology are not considered here. For the general problem of the long-range "Lutheran" influence in England, see, aside from the studies of Trinterud and the older work of H. E. Jacobs, the recent monograph by N. S. Tjernagel, *Henry VIII and the Lutherans: A Study in Anglo-Lutheran Relations from 1521-1547* (St. Louis, 1965).

the significance of Luther's writings must be underscored, for no explanation of the expansion of the Reformation will be adequate unless it notes that these writings struck a responsive chord among his contemporaries.

But it would hardly have done so had there not been other factors involved. The practical ease of the communication of ideas is important here—even, incidentally, in John Foxe's narrative of the Reformation, for he introduced his chapter on the Reformation with the remark "the science of printing being found, immediately followed the grace of God; which stirred up good wits aptly to conceive the light of knowledge and judgment."[52] The latent anti-ecclesiastical sentiment throughout Europe also must be cited. Not that it offers the primary clue, for one cannot find any parallel between the intensity of this sentiment and the subsequent success of the Reformation, but its presence undoubtedly influenced the course of events. The discontent of the humanists must be mentioned next. In many ways the humanists were the most vocal critics of the church and of the prevailing theological temper, and the spread of Luther's ideas was furthered by their identity with humanist reform concerns. But it was only a seeming identity, as the subsequent parting of the ways of many humanists and the Protestant cause was to show.[53] In a sense, therefore, the humanists who carried Luther's banner supported a cause which was really not their own. If the initial transfer of Luther's ideas was largely due to the humanists, then the success of the Reformation is in some measure to be attributed to a misunderstanding on their part.

There also can be little doubt that the spectacular notoriety of Luther had something to do with the impact of his writings. The point here is simple: Luther propagated not only ideas, but he lived a spectacular life—from his first reaction to the sale of indulgences by Archbishop Albert of Hohenzollern in 1517 to his defiant refusal to recant before the German diet at Worms in 1521. Luther was not merely a theologian or an academician but a man of action, a public figure. He was a notorious figure, but at the same time an underdog, a somewhat uncomfortable position that always arouses sympathy. Moreover, it was not only his ideas, which many

[52] *The Acts and Monuments of John Foxe*, IV, 253.
[53] B. Moeller, "Die deutschen Humanisten und die Anfänge der Reformation," *Zeitschrift f. Kirchengeschichte*, LXX (1959).

people must have found far too complicated, but his personal courage that won support.

An additional point is relevant here. From 1521 onward, contemporaries encountered not only Luther's striking notoriety, but also a large number of his supporters. Such support took many forms. Above all, there was the literary assistance, which from 1520 onward began to flood the market with numerous pamphlets echoing Luther's ideas. In addition, there was political support which was afforded Luther by his territorial ruler and other rulers of the German Empire. In other words, by the time Luther's ideas found their way abroad, their author was no longer a solitary figure standing *contra mundum*, but was the spokesman for a large body of followers. This made the aceptance of his ideas immeasurably easier.

Luther was a catalyst whose bold proclamation laid bare elsewhere in Europe the spiritual aspirations already present among men of religious concerns. Yet if he was only that, no real "transfer" of ideas would have taken place, only a "republication" of ideas, to use a phrase so popular among the English Deists when they spoke about natural and revealed religion in the eighteenth century. But it was more than that. Ideas were transferred. While contemporary scholarship may deny the newness of Luther's ideas and insist that what he said can be found among certain "pre-reformers," the fact is that Luther's slogans were, for all practical purposes, new. They had not been widely heard before.

Thus a transfer did indeed occur, a transfer of several key theological issues that were to be the main pronouncements of the Christian tradition which came to be known as Protestantism. Indeed, Luther gave European coinage to one additional idea—the notion that, if necessary, true biblical religion must be restored even against the Catholic Church and the pope.

VII

What about the significance of this transfer of ideas for the European dimension of the Reformation? Is Luther the crucial figure for the European Reformation? Before this question can be answered a careful definition of the term "Reformation" is necessary, for only then can Luther's influence and significance be placed in their proper setting.

The term "Reformation" can be applied in its broader sense to any effort to reform the life and thought of the Catholic Church.[54] In this general and comprehensive sense, efforts at "reformation" were variously undertaken in the early sixteenth century. Its most eminent representative may well have been Jacques Lefèvre, John Colet, or Erasmus, though there were others. It was not only an effort to correct ecclesiastical abuse, but it was at the same time a reinterpretation of traditional theological emphases with affirmations that at times sounded quite Protestant.

"Reformation" also can be used in a restricted sense, however, with a definition that pertains to a theological reinterpretation that not only departed from the tradition of scholasticism but also was willing to break with the Catholic Church. The real issue was explicit dissent from the church.

According to the broader definition, Luther contributed nothing new, and several reformatory efforts, such as those of Bishop Briçonnet at Meaux, clearly antedate him and his ideas. On the other hand, the formalization of an ecclesiastical reconstruction *against* Rome does depend on the contribution of Martin Luther. Prior to his arrival on the scene no such "radical" efforts at ecclesiastical renewal are discernible.

Lucien Febvre, who in his essay "Les origines de la Réforme française et le problème des causes de la Réforme," of 1929, was willing to use the broader definition of the term and thus see Lefèvre as the signal figure of the French "Reformation," proposed in an essay of 1945 the labels "rénovations, révolutions, révisions" for what customarily is referred to as Pre-Reformation, Reformation, and Counter-Reformation. This suggestion never received widespread attention, but his distinction between "rénovation" and "révolution" underscores our own distinction between a general reformatory concern and a reformatory concern propounded in opposition to the Catholic Church.[55]

The transfer of Luther's ideas, no matter how circumscribed, constituted in every single instance the crucial factor precipitating the rebellion against the Catholic Church—in other words, the Reformation. Zwingli's recollection and admission that Luther

[54] G. B. Ladner, *The Idea of Reform: Its Impact on Christian Thought and Action in the Age of the Fathers* (Cambridge, 1959), pp. 402 ff.
[55] Febvre, *Au Coeur Religieux*, p. 161.

"prompted him to be bold" throws the best light on the situation, and the printer Froben's quotation from the Parisian faculty that "some of the scholars already have said that they had wished for a long time that those who expound Scripture would do it so freely" exhibits real insight.[56] There may have been deviation from the late medieval scholastic consensus (Lefèvre), reflection about a Pauline theology (Zwingli), exposure to humanism and the Lollard tradition (Tyndale)—all quite independent of Luther. But there was no conscious rebellion against Rome, neither in England, France, Switzerland, nor anywhere else. One can hardly imagine, therefore, how there could have been a "Reformation," defined as "révolution," without that youthful professor at a second-rate academic institution: Martin Luther.

[56] *Huldreich Zwinglis Sämtliche Werke*, V, 722; *WA Br.*, I, 332.

German Socialists and Russian Soviets

The Transfer of Workers' Councils from Russia to Germany in 1918

John Raphael Staude

As an example of the transfer of ideas from one cultural setting to another, this essay deals with the attempt of German socialists to transfer an idealized institution, the Russian soviet (council of workers' and soldiers' deputies), from Russia to Germany in 1917-1918. By 1917 the German socialists were split into three groups: Majority Socialists (SPD), Independent Socialists (USPD), and several leftist splinter groups, notably the Spartacists and Left Radicals who formed the nucleus of the German Communist party (KPD) established at the end of 1918. The following pages undertake to describe the attitudes of each of these groups to the Bolshevik Revolution, and to show how their attitudes conditioned their conceptions of the role of workers' councils in Germany.

I

Although workers' councils had been created in Russia in 1905, it was not until they reappeared in that country during March, 1917, that they attracted the attention of the German working class.[1] The peace resolution of the Petrograd Soviet, which urged the proletariat in every country to unite and "take into their own hands the questions of war and peace," was welcomed by all Ger-

MR. STAUDE *is assistant professor of history in the University of California at Riverside. He is the author of* Max Scheler: An Intellectual Portrait (*New York, 1967*).

[1] Walter Tormin, *Zwischen Rätediktatur und sozialer Demokratie. Die Geschichte der Rätebewegung in der deutschen Revolution 1918/1919* (Düsseldorf, 1954), p. 26; Eberhard Kolb, *Die Arbeiterräte in der deutschen Innenpolitik 1918/1919* (Düsseldorf, 1962), p. 56; and Albert Schreiner, ed., *Revolutionäre Ereignisse und Probleme in Deutschland während der Periode der grossen sozialistischen Oktoberrevolution 1917/1918* (East Berlin, 1957), p. 5.

man socialists.[2] *Vorwärts*, the leading Majority Socialist newspaper, indicated a sense of pride and solidarity with the Russian proletariat and peasantry who had thrown off the yoke of tsarism that had oppressed them for centuries.[3] The Independent Socialist organ, the *Leipziger Volkszeitung*, acclaimed the Petersburg Soviet as the first institution established to represent the Russian proletariat.[4] Even the radical Spartacists welcomed the March Revolution, seeing the revival of the Petersburg Soviet as a continuation of the revolution begun in 1905, though they considered the new government in Russia to be "not an end, but only a weak beginning."[5] Recognizing that this new revolution could serve as a means for the "political education" (i.e., radicalization) of the German working class, the Spartacists publicized events in Russia in their clandestine publications and by word of mouth, publishing proclamations and documents of the All-Russian Congress of Soviets, and insisting that it was the duty of the German proletariat to strive for peace along with their Russian brethren.[6]

The first workers' councils (*Arbeiterräte*) established in Germany were inspired by the March Revolution in Russia, although some shop councils (*Betriebsräte*) were in existence before the war.[7] The appalling state of the food rations, as a result of the Allied blockade and the extremely poor turnip harvest, provoked thousands of workmen to go on strike in Leipzig on April 16, 1917. Two days later 200,000 workers in Berlin also went on strike. In both cases the striking workers created workers' councils modeled on the Petersburg Soviet to present their grievances to the German government.[8] Strikes soon occurred in many other German cities. These, too, were probably inspired by the successful overthrow of

[2] John L. Snell, "The Russian Revolution and the German Social Democratic Party in 1917," *American Slavic and East European Review*, XV, (1956), 339, and Arno Mayer, *Political Origins of the New Diplomacy, 1917-1918*, (New Haven, 1959), pp. 293 ff.

[3] *Vorwärts*, March 5, 1917.

[4] *Leipziger Volkszeitung*, March 8, 1917.

[5] Snell, p. 339.

[6] *Ibid.*

[7] Tormin, p. 26; Schreiner, p. 13; and Klaus Mammach, *Der Einfluss der russischen Februarrevolution und der grossen sozialistischen Oktoberrevolution auf die deutsche Arbeiterklasse. Februar, 1917–Oktober, 1918* (East Berlin, 1955), p. 32. On the development of shop councils in Germany, see Peter von Oertzen, *Betriebsräte in der Novemberrevolution* (Düsseldorf, 1963).

[8] Arthur Rosenberg, *The Birth of the German Republic, 1871-1918*, trans. Ian F. D. Morrow (2nd ed; New York, 1962), p. 208.

tsarism in Russia, but only in Berlin and Leipzig, both strongholds of the left-wing Independent Socialists, were workers' councils actually established.

These first councils in Germany were not conceived of as permanent political institutions. They had specific limited responsibilities, and they voluntarily dissolved themselves after they had presented the strikers' demands to the government. The demands of the Leipzig Workers' Council are worth mentioning because they were later adopted by many of the other councils established in Germany after the Bolshevik Revolution: (1) issuance of sufficient supplies and cheap provisions for the populace; (2) a government declaration of willingness to conclude peace immediately, renouncing all plans for annexations; (3) abolition of martial law and of censorship; (4) immediate repeal of the hated compulsory labor laws, instituted at the outset of the war; (5) freedom of assembly; (6) immediate liberation of all political prisoners and abandonment of all political trials; (7) complete civil liberty; and (8) introduction of universal, equal, direct suffrage in elections to all offices in the federal, state, and municipal governments.[9] This program, which by the end of the year, expressed the hopes of most German socialists, was really little more than a modest middle-class program of reform, and it was bitterly criticized as such by the Spartacists and Left Radicals, who called it "bourgeois" and "a stab in the back of the proletariat."

The strikes in April were followed by the Reichstag peace resolution in July. In the fall, the Michaelis government was overthrown and replaced by the semi-parliamentary government under the Bavarian Catholic, Count Georg von Hertling. Meanwhile, there was much talk of election reform in Prussia, which finally resulted, in December, in the introduction of a proposal for reform of the suffrage in the Prussian *Landtag*. These events aroused the hopes of the working class. Peace and democracy appeared to be within easy reach.

In this climate of rising expectations the news of the overthrow of the provisional government and the establishment of a socialist government by the Bolsheviks in Russia was especially welcome. Whereas Kerenski had carried on the war, Lenin and Trotski ac-

[9] *Ibid.*, p. 209.

tually had begun to initiate armistice negotiations immediately after the Bolsheviks came to power. The intense longing for peace in Germany and Austria-Hungary was soon transformed into a warm sympathy for the Bolsheviks. One historian, Arthur Rosenberg, goes so far as to say that the German working class now "came to look upon it as their duty to support the Russians as against General Hoffmann," the German commander on the Eastern Front.[10]

From November, 1917, to January, 1918, *Vorwärts* reported events in Russia favorably, insisting, however, that although the German Socialists shared the same goal as the Bolsheviks—the liberation of humanity through socialism—German Socialists rejected the violent methods of the Bolsheviks. For Germany the only way to socialism would be the peaceful way: through parliamentary legislation. Thus, although the Majority Socialists welcomed the Bolshevik Decree of Peace as a "truly socialist" measure, they firmly rejected the slogan, "Without revolution, no peace."[11]

As might be expected, the more radical *Leipziger Volkszeitung* expressed warm sympathy for their victorious Russian comrades. The Bolsheviks were "the vanguard of humanity, the vanguard of peace." Clara Zetkin, writing in the same newspaper two weeks later, announced that the Bolshevik revolution had ended the period of bourgeois revolutions and inaugurated a new epoch in world history. The "dictatorship of the proletariat" had been realized in Russia and would soon spread to other parts of the world.[12] Whereas Friedrich Stampfer, the editor of *Vorwärts*, considered the Bolshevik revolution a unique response to Russian conditions, something that could never occur in Germany,[13] Clara Zetkin urged the German proletariat to imitate the Bolshevik example.

The Spartacists acclaimed the Bolshevik victory in glowing terms, as well:

For the first time in world history the proletarian masses have actually succeeded in seizing the reigns of government. With heroic courage beyond compare, prepared to sacrifice their own life's blood, the Russian proletariat is now struggling, valiantly supported by the peasantry,

[10] *Ibid.*, p. 210.
[11] *Vorwärts*, Nov. 10, 1917.
[12] *Leipziger Volkszeitung* (Frauenbeilage), Nov. 30, 1917.
[13] *Vorwärts*, Nov. 16, 1917.

to consolidate its newly acquired power. The goal is twofold: to put an end to the useless slaughter of the war and to inaugurate the realization of socialism.[14]

The Spartacist leader, Rosa Luxemburg, was not so sanguine. Learning of the Bolshevik takeover while in prison in Leipzig, Rosa criticized the Bolsheviks for dispersing the Constituent Assembly (which they, themselves, had convoked) and for restricting the suffrage.[15] Her apprehensions were not shared by her party, however, and her reflections on the Russian Revolution were not published until after her death.[16]

In considering German socialist responses to the Russian revolution, the tiny but influential group of Left Radicals must also be mentioned because of their great sympathy for Russian Bolshevism. Led by Johann Knief and Paul Frölich, the Left Radicals' headquarters were in Bremen. At the time of the Bolshevik revolution they could claim hardly more than a hundred members in all of Germany, and most of these were former Majority Socialists who had become dissatisfied with the Social Democrats' close collaboration with the army and heavy industry in the war effort. Unlike the Spartacists, who sought to influence the SPD from within, the Left Radicals advocated splitting away from both the SPD and the USPD to form a separate revolutionary party. In this respect they were the true forerunners of the German Communist party established at the end of 1918. Strongly influenced by Karl Radek, who contributed regularly to their weekly, *Arbeiterpolitik*, the Left Radicals maintained close ties with Lenin, Zinoviev, and other members of the Bolshevik Central Committee in Russia. During the summer of 1917 *Arbeiterpolitik* published translations of speeches and articles by leaders of the Petersburg Soviet and by members of the Bolshevik Central Committee, thereby introducing German socialists for the first time to the actual modes of operation of the Russian soviets. As might be expected, the Left Radicals greeted the Bolshevik revolution ecstatically. In early 1918 they began disseminating illegal pamphlets describing how the Russian

[14] *Spartakusbriefe*, Nov. 7, 1917, quoted in Schreiner, p. 147.
[15] Peter Nettl, *Rosa Luxemburg* (London, 1966), II, 702.
[16] First published in 1922, Rosa Luxemburg's pamphlet, *The Russian Revolution*, is available in an English translation published by Ann Arbor Paperbacks, 1961.

workers and peasants had overthrown the capitalistic provisional government and established a true dictatorship of the proletariat.[17]

Thus, although some German socialists acknowledged the Bolshevik revolution with more reserve than others, they all welcomed the advent of socialism in Russia, and many felt that the German proletariat could learn from the Bolshevik example. Above all, the German socialists welcomed the Bolsheviks as harbingers of peace.

II

Leon Trotski was fully aware of the longing for peace in the hearts of the soldiers and workers of the Central Powers, and he carefully played upon these feelings in his speeches at Brest-Litovsk. There, appealing to world opinion, he tried to show that Russia's desire for a peace without annexations or indemnities was being thwarted by German lust for conquest. The intervention of General Hoffmann into the negotiations on January 12, when he warned the Russians that Germany was the victor and that they had better take this fact into account in making their proposals, shattered the illusions, of German socialists as to the government's war aims.[18]

The events in Brest-Litovsk in January resulted in an outbreak of strikes that began in the Manfred Weiss munitions factory near Budapest (January 14), spread to Vienna, and soon swept across Germany, reaching Berlin on January 28 when 400,000 workers in Berlin went on strike and formed a 414-man workers' council with one delegate representing approximately a thousand workers. This Berlin Workers' Council elected an eleven-man Executive Committee (*Vollzugsrat*) from among the Revolutionary Shop Stewards, headed by the Independent Socialist, Richard Müller, to lead the strike and to present their demands, which were similar to those of the earlier Leipzig Workers' Council described above. This new workers' council differed from the earlier ones in Germany in that it was formed *before* the strike and decided on the timing and tactics of the strike. Nevertheless, it was still closer to the Petersburg Soviet of 1905, which directed revolutionary actions, than to the Petrograd Soviet of 1917, which became an organ of

[17] Tormin, pp. 40-41. Karl Radek's articles for *Arbeiterpolitik* are reprinted in his collected essays, *In den reihen der deutschen Revolution 1910-1919* (Munich, 1921).

[18] Rosenberg, p. 206, and Gerald D. Feldman, *Army, Industry, and Labor in Germany, 1914-1918* (Princeton, 1966), p. 447.

state under the control of the Bolshevik party. As Rosenberg says, the Berlin Workers' Council was "no more than a mouthpiece of the striking workmen. It took the place of the trade unions, not of the Reichstag."[19]

The absence of any socialist demands from the Berlin Workers' Council is significant. The council, which was made up of both Majority Socialists[20] and Independents—but not of Spartacists—had no intention of raising the question of socialization of industry or even the limitation of war profits. (After all, the Berlin strikers were among the best-paid workers in Germany.) They demanded nothing more radical than immediate peace, better food supplies, and suffrage reform, as well as the replacement of the military dictatorship with a middle-class democratic government. This program indicates that the strikers were closer ideologically to their representatives in the Reichstag than to the militant Revolutionary Shop Stewards and Spartacists. Arthur Rosenberg admitted this when he commented later that only if the strike had been directed by the Spartacists and the Independents alone, with the Majority Socialists deliberately excluded, might the January strike have been a truly "proletarian class action" instead of a "pacifist demonstration with middle class democratic aims." He concluded that in January, 1918, the formation of a republic—not to mention the bolshevization of Germany—was beyond practical possibility.[21]

The strike in Berlin, and similar strikes in other industrial centers in Germany, were dealt with ruthlessly by the authorities. In Berlin a state of seige was proclaimed, the socialist press was outlawed, and meetings of the strikers were forcefully disbanded by the police. The big munitions factories were militarized, and the strikers were ordered to return to work the next day on penalty of facing a court martial if they refused. By February 4 the strike was broken.[22] Large numbers of exempted workers who had participated in the strike were now drafted into the army and a "B-18" (Ber-

---

[19] Rosenberg, p. 213.

[20] The Majority Socialist leaders in Berlin did not want the strike in the first place, but once it broke out they joined the workers' council in order to keep control over the Berlin workers.

[21] Rosenberg, pp. 212-214.

[22] Franz Borkenau, *World Communism: A History of the Communist International* (2nd ed.; Ann Arbor, 1962), p. 91; John Wheeler-Bennett, *Brest-Litovsk, the Forgotten Peace, March 1918* (2nd ed.; London, 1963), p. 192; and Feldman, p. 451.

lin—1918) was stamped in their files to make sure that they would
not be exempted again. However, in sending these untrained, dis-
affected workmen to the front the government created new problems for itself, for these "B-18ers" proved to be excellent agitators.
They spread pacifist propaganda, fraternized with Russian troops
on the Eastern Front, and did much to demoralize the German
army wherever they went.[23]

As a result of the January strikes, workers throughout Germany were introduced to the idea of the workers' council. Their interest in this new instrument of political class struggle was often
further intensified by Bolshevik propaganda, which began to be
distributed in Germany in early 1918 through the Russian Embassy in Berlin and through the Spartacist and Left Radical press
and clandestine publications. Nevertheless, specific information
was rather scarce about the actual workings of the soviets in Russia.
The government encouraged the news media to disseminate stories
of anarchy and hardship in Russia, while accounts of the positive
achievements of the new government were suppressed. To most
Germans the meaning of the term "workers' and soldiers' council"
remained rather vague. It seldom implied a concrete program, yet
its very mention invoked radical hopes, and it soon became closely
associated with the idea of a revolutionary overthrow of the monarchy. Spartacist, Left Radical, and Bolshevik propaganda did
much to promote this association of the concept "workers' council"
with "revolution," although few of the workers' councils established in Germany before November, 1918, actually advocated the
violent overthrow of the government.[24]

It is difficult to determine the extent to which the growth of the
workers' council concept in Germany in the summer and fall of
1918 resulted from the spread of Bolshevik propaganda. The Soviet Embassy in Berlin actively supplied the Independents with considerable sums of money, with weapons, and with confidential information purchased from officials of the German government. Furthermore, through its control of at least ten Social Democratic
newspapers, the Soviet Embassy was able to spread pro-Soviet propaganda throughout the country. By October a good deal more in-

[23] Ralph H. Lutz, *The Causes of the German Collapse in 1918* (Stanford,
1934), p. 110.
[24] Tormin, p. 48.

formation about the Russian soviets was filtering into Germany and Lenin's *State and Revolution* was being serialized in the radical press.[25]

During the summer of 1918 the ranks of the Independent Socialist party swelled, and the left wing of the party became increasingly radicalized as a result of growing discontent with the military dictatorship, food shortages, and general war-weariness. More particularly, many of the rank and file in the German labor movement had become disgusted with their leaders in the SPD and the trade unions, whose close collaboration with the government appeared to be prolonging the war.[26] At a party congress in July, Ernst Däumig, who was then the leader of the Revolutionary Shop Stewards and a member of the Executive Committee of the Berlin Workers' Council, demanded that the party adopt the Bolshevik slogan, "All Power to the Workers' and Soldiers' Councils." At the time his proposal was rejected, but a month later at another party meeting in Berlin where the Revolutionary Shop Stewards wielded a stronger influence, the members passed a resolution commending the Russian proletariat for their achievements in holding off the counter-revolution and creating the first truly socialist state. In a separate meeting of the Revolutionary Shop Stewards, Däumig was able to ram through a much stronger motion which denounced the military dictatorship and demanded its immediate overthrow and its replacement by a council government based on the Russian model (*ein Räterepublik nach russischem Muster*).[27]

On October 7 the Left Radicals joined the Spartacists in a combat partnership (*Kampfgemeinschaft*) to prepare for revolution. They called on the people of Germany to form workers' and soldiers' councils immediately, which would be prepared to take over industry, agriculture, and the army as well as the national government. Demanding the immediate forceful overthrow of the government and the establishment of a *Räterepublik*, the radicals con-

---

[25] Ernst Drahn and S. Leonhard, *Unterirdische Literatur im revolutionaren Deutschland wahrend des Weltkrieges* (Berlin, 1920), p. 114; Charles Burdick and Ralph H. Lutz, eds., *The Political Institutions of the German Revolution, 1918-1919* (New York, 1966), p. 90; and Louis Fischer, *The Soviets in World Affairs* (Princeton, 1951), I, 75.

[26] Feldman, pp. 459 ff., and Richard Comfort, "Free Trade Unions and Council Government in Hamburg, November 1918 to March 1919," *International Review of Social History*, IX (1964), 55-56.

[27] Schreiner, p. 305.

demned the leaders of the SPD and the Free Trade Unions as "traitors to the working class" for their collaboration with the government in the war.[28] Thus by the fall of 1918 the radical left wing of German socialism had come to the point of abandoning social democracy altogether and demanding nothing less than a "dictatorship of the proletariat through workers' and soldiers' councils."[29]

This extreme point of view was not generally shared among the rank and file of the German labor movement. As a result, the radicals were seldom able to gain much influence in these very workers' and soldiers' councils that they so vociferously acclaimed. When they saw that they could not win control over the existing councils, the radicals denounced them as "bourgeois" and urged the proletariat to establish truly revolutionary proletarian councils instead.[30] On the other hand, even the moderate Independents and Majority Socialists recognized that the concept of the workers' and soldiers' council had acquired a symbolic significance to the German proletariat since the January strikes. Therefore, although they repudiated the idea of a Soviet-type dictatorship, by November, 1918, most socialists agreed that workers' and soldiers' councils were an essential part of any contemporary revolution.[31]

III

It is generally agreed among historians of the German revolution that neither the preparations of the Revolutionary Shop Stewards nor the revolutionary propaganda conducted by the Spartacists and Left Radicals significantly influenced the developments leading to the revolt of the sailors in Kiel and the subsequent spread of the revolution across Germany in November, 1918. If the radical movement had really been the decisive element, the revolution would have started in Berlin where preparations for it were being made. However the capital fell only after the revolution already had triumphed in the rest of Germany. Although the radicals were planning a revolution, the one that occurred was neither planned nor expected. In almost every case (Munich being the main ex-

[28] *Ibid.*, p. 244; Drahn and Leonhard, p. 114; and Tormin, pp. 48-52.
[29] Borkenau, p. 145.
[30] Tormin, p. 54.
[31] *Ibid.*, p. 48.

ception) the revolt originated spontaneously among the troops who recognized that the war was lost and refused to continue obeying their superiors. These mutineers then set up soldiers' councils, as the Russians had done in 1917, to distribute supplies and organize troop transports home.[32] The revolt quickly spread to the civilian working class and shifted its focus to wider political questions, particularly regarding the co-operation of the trade unions with the army and industrialists in the organization of labor during the war. Thus, the "revolution," and with it the council movement, was initially more a spontaneous protest against the conduct of the war both at home and at the front than a planned transformation of the German political system.[33]

When the revolution broke out in November, the workers and soldiers set up councils all over the land. They had been prepared to think in terms of councils by the example of the Russian revolutions and by Bolshevik propaganda over the preceding months. However—and this point cannot be emphasized strongly enough— in Germany the councils did not organize and direct the revolution; they were, in most cases, more a *result* than a *cause* of the revolt. They were generally established *after* the revolution already had broken out—more symbols of the revolution triumphant than executive organs of the revolutionary masses, as they had been in Russia.

Very often the workers' and soldiers' councils that sprang up in November claimed to be the highest political organs in the towns.[34] Some even announced that they represented the advent of the dictatorship of the proletariat.[35] Such utterances indicate the wide influence of radical propaganda at the time, despite the fact

[32] See, for example, the description of the activities of the Kassel Workers' and Soldiers' Council by its former chairman, Albert C. Grezsinski, *Inside Germany* (New York, 1939), p. 51.

[33] I am particularly indebted to the work of Richard Comfort for this interpretation of the German Revolution. See his *Revolutionary Hamburg* (Stanford, 1966), and his unpublished paper, "Revolution by Consensus and by Force: Berlin, 1918-1919," presented before the American Historical Association, Dec., 1966.

[34] The most radical councils were those established in the seaports of northern Germany where the revolution began. In Hamburg, for example, the left-wing Independents, by uniting with the Spartacists, were able to create a revolutionary council modeled on the Petersburg Soviet.

[35] Eric Waldman, *The Spartacist Uprising of 1919 and the Crisis of the German Socialist Movement: A Study of the Relation of Political Theory and Party Practice* (Milwaukee, 1958), p. 86.

that the radicals were a small minority. Undoubtedly, however, most of the workers' councils were dominated by Majority Socialists, and unfortunately for them the SPD lacked a clear program. The German Social Democrats had for so long envisioned socialism in apocalyptic terms that when they were faced with the possibility of actually instituting socialism through nationalization of key industries and democratization of the army and the bureaucracy, they faltered and decided to leave the question of social and economic reorganization for the forthcoming National Assembly. In short, the Majority Socialists considered the councils at best as nothing more than a provisional government, responsible for maintaining order until a new parliamentary government could be elected.[36] In most places the old bureaucracy remained in office and the councils acted less as permanent administrative agencies than as temporary supervising authorities. Therefore, despite all the radical propaganda, the practice of most of the councils was very moderate.

Neither the Majority Socialists nor the Independents had any intention of establishing anything even remotely resembling a dictatorship on the Bolshevik model. Both parties agreed that the entire nation should be called on to decide by majority vote the future fate of the revolution. The SPD had opposed the revolution before it broke out, and once it began, its leaders did everything they could to restore law and order as quickly as possible. Under pressure of circumstances, the leaders of the SPD decided for a middle-class republic. For them the goal of the revolution lay in the elimination of the monarchy, replacing it with a parliamentary constitution based on equal suffrage. Threatened by radical demands of "All Power to the Workers' and Soldiers' Councils," the leaders of the SPD became increasingly suspicious of the councils and their opposition to them hardened. Many of the SPD leaders felt that as soon as the National Assembly was called, the councils should be dissolved for good. They felt that the political revolution could only change the state from a monarchy into a republic. Socialism could only be realized gradually through parliamentary legislation, not through the councils.[37]

[36] Tormin, p. 68.
[37] Rosenberg, p. 272; Waldman, p. 84; Comfort, *Revolutionary Hamburg*, pp. 96-99.

The Independents, always more radical than the Majority Socialists, believed that the *political* revolution should be a *social* revolution at the same time. They recognized that thus far only the political power of the old order had been broken; they urged that the means of production should be socialized and the power of the old bureaucracy and officer corps should be broken. They agreed with the radicals that the elimination of bourgeois class rule would necessitate a transition period of the dictatorship of the proletariat, which was to be exercised through the workers' and soldiers' councils, and they were willing, temporarily, to restrict the suffrage during this period. They were, however, convinced that *after* the economy was socialized, the nation should be governed by a democratic parliament elected by all the people, not by a proletarian dictatorship.[38]

In the popular mind, council government and parliamentary government were considered to be contradictory. The majority of the middle class identified council government with the Soviet dictatorship in Russia and bitterly opposed a council system, although, in fact, the councils in Germany had not produced a dictatorship.[39] On the other hand, the radicals thought of parliamentary government as being nothing but a front for bourgeois class rule, a way of legalizing the exploitation of the proletariat by the capitalists. The polarity between the two conceptions hardened rapidly, and all attempts at compromise between the two systems were rejected by radicals and conservatives alike.

Radical propaganda spread among the workers, many of whom were becoming rapidly disillusioned with the new democracy which showed so little progress in terms of democratization of the bureaucracy, the army, and the trade unions. Although the radicals were never more than a small minority, in the days before the convocation of the first all-German Congress of Workers' and Soldiers' Councils, their ideas were widely publicized and discussed, and at the time it appeared that they had a much larger following than they had in fact. Their position, then, deserves some attention.

[38] Richard Müller, *Vom Kaiserreich zur Republik* (Vienna, 1924), p. 131. Müller, an Independent, was chairman of the Berlin Workers' and Soldiers' Council during the November revolution.

[39] Waldman, pp. 104-105.

In a front-page article in the *Rote Fahne* of November 18, 1918, Rosa Luxemburg spelled out the Spartacist program for transforming the "limited revolution" into a genuine proletarian revolution in which all power would be vested in the hands of the workers' and soldiers' councils: (1) completion and re-election of local workers' and soldiers' councils, (2) transfer of the executive power of the new government from the *Vollzugsrat* (the Executive Committee of the Berlin Workers' and Soldiers' Council) to the whole workers' and soldiers' council, (3) convocation of a national congress of councils as soon as possible, (4) organization of the rural proletariat and small farmers, who as a class were still untouched by the revolution, (5) formation of a Red Guard to protect the revolution, (6) removal of the agencies taken over from the Empire—the administration, the judiciary, and the army, (7) immediate confiscation of dynastic property and estates to supply food for the starving masses, and (8) convocation of a Workers' World Congress in Germany to emphasize the international character of the German Revolution.[40] Rosa was particularly distressed by the Ebert government's call for a constituent national assembly, for she recognized that any parliament would act as "a bourgeois counterweight" to the councils, thereby shifting the revolution onto the track of a bourgeois revolution and thwarting its socialist aims.

The Spartacists strongly advocated the council system in preference to "bourgeois democracy," not because they believed the former could produce a better representation of public opinion, but because they recognized that it could be used with great advantage to weight the balance in favor of the more radical elements in society since the franchise was limited to the workers and soldiers. As Eric Waldman writes in his history of the Spartacists:

The council system could actually facilitate the perpetuation of a minority rule and still make it appear to be backed by a sizeable majority. The Russian manipulation of the Soviets had clearly demonstrated their utility to the Spartacists. This could only be achieved when the workers' and soldiers' councils were the sole organs of state power and were not subordinate to any other type of governmental agency such as the Provisional government.[41]

[40] *Ibid.*, pp. 106-107.
[41] *Ibid.*

On November 20, 1918, Rosa stated her position on the proposed National Assembly in the *Rote Fahne*. Denouncing the Independents for approving of the National Assembly, she warned that "The civil war they seek to banish from the revolution cannot be banished." The idea that socialism could be introduced without a class struggle through parliamentary majority decisions was utterly ridiculous, "a petit bourgeois illusion." The National Assembly was simply a superannuated inheritance from the bourgeois revolutions of the past. Whereas the present fight over the national assembly was being carried on under the battle cry "democracy or dictatorship," she insisted that the real question of the day was rather "bourgeois democracy or social democracy?" As opposed to the convocation of a bourgeois national assembly, she urged the creation of a truly proletarian legislature based on workers' councils.[42]

The greatest weakness in Rosa's ideology was her naïve belief that the masses, if left to themselves, would spontaneously produce social democracy. Her fear of Leninism, coupled with her strong commitment to "revolutionary democratic" procedures, prevented her from recognizing the political neutrality of a council system. Looking back we can see that in both Russia and Germany the councils were only as strong as the parties that controlled them. The establishment of workers' councils nowhere led to the "social democracy" Rosa anticipated. Furthermore, Rosa and the Spartacists failed to realize that the majority of the German people in 1918 were convinced that the revolution already had established a new order of society, and that after four years of war which had ended in defeat, the people were tired of strikes and chaos. The Spartacists were mistaken to put their hopes in the council movement. Hardly any of the councils were controlled by radicals who wanted to emulate the Russian example by demanding that all political power be vested in the council system. The overwhelming majority of councils considered their existence temporary, pending an eventual return to legally established political authority.

IV

All hopes that the radical viewpoint might prevail were dashed shortly after Rosa Luxemburg's editorial was published when, on

[42] *Ibid.*, pp. 110-112.

December 16, the first Reich Congress of Workers' and Soldiers' Councils convened in Berlin. The Russians sent a delegation to the congress, hoping to gain influence over the German councils, but the provisional government refused to allow the delegation to enter Germany, and only Karl Radek, in disguise, reached Berlin. Shortly after the congress began it was interrupted by a delegation claiming to represent the "revolutionary working class of greater Berlin." The delegation, speaking for a large body of workers demonstrating outside the meeting hall, demanded that: (1) Germany be declared a unified socialist republic, (2) complete power be placed in the hands of the workers' and soldiers' councils, (3) the Executive Committee be the supreme executive power in the land, (4) Ebert's Council of People's Commissars be abolished, (5) measures be taken to protect the revolution by such means as the formation of a Red Guard and disarmament of the counter-revolution, and (6) the Central Council declare its solidarity with the world revolution. These demands provoked an uproar and cries of "Berlin is not Germany," but the congress chairman assured the demonstrators that the congress would decide on the petition in the course of its discussions, and the demonstrators withdrew peaceably.[43]

On December 17 the members of the Executive Committee of the Berlin Workers' and Soldiers' Council debated among themselves whether or not to support a parliamentary system. Ernst Däumig, leader of the Revolutionary Shop Stewards, upheld the radical viewpoint, but his motion that Germany adopt a council rather than a parliamentary system met defeat. On December 19 the congress voted on the future of the council system. Max Cohen, a member of the Executive Council, spoke first, urging the delegates to choose parliamentary over council government. Speaking of the heavy burdens on the new republic, he warned that "there cannot be a central power with strong authority . . . unless it be supported by the overwhelming majority of the German people."[44] The only organ that could ascertain this will of the people, he maintained, was a National Assembly elected by universal suffrage. His speech received tremendous applause. Däumig spoke for the opposition. He saw at once that the parliamentarians had won the

[43] Burdick and Lutz, pp. 216-218.
[44] *Ibid.*, p. 222.

day. Disheartened, he warned that the councils had signed their own death warrant. Once the National Assembly met, the council system was bound to disappear, he said. However, comparing the German November revolution with the Russian revolution of 1905, he predicted that the councils would be reborn when the time was ripe.

The delegates voted overwhelmingly, four hundred to fifty, in favor of holding elections for the National Assembly the next month. Though Däumig decried this decision as the "suicide of the council system," the vote simply reflected the attitude of the majority of the German workers, who shared the middle class view that Germany should be a parliamentary democratic republic. Only a handful of radicals ever wanted a Soviet-type dictatorship in Germany.

As the Congress of Workers' and Soldiers' Councils drew to a close, the delegates authorized the formation of a Central Committee (*Zentralrat*), which was empowered to review and control the Council of Peoples' Commissars and the Prussian Cabinet. The Central Committee replaced the Berlin Executive Committee in matters concerning national affairs, although the Executive Committee continued to function in its activities regarding the city of Berlin. The Independents then decided, after a heated discussion of the authority of the new Central Committee, not to participate in it. As a result the Majority Socialists elected all twenty-seven members of the Central Committee. Although the three Independents in the cabinet remained in office until mid-January, their decision not to participate in the Central Committee weakened their position in the cabinet.

In effect, the election of the Central Committee marked the turning point of the revolutionary movement, for now the Majority Socialists were in complete control, and their radical opponents went onto the defensive without any national political apparatus to articulate their political goals. The advocates of a dictatorship of the proletariat exercised through workers' and soldiers' councils were defeated by the councils themselves. The national congress of councils simply confirmed what should have been evident from the start, that the council movement was a spontaneous expression of dissatisfaction with the conduct of the war and with the organization of the trade unions. Council members wanted to *reform* the existing military, industrial, and administrative structures, not to *replace* them.

Conclusion

In reviewing the history of workers' and soldiers' councils in Germany and Russia, one is immediately struck by the great differences between them. In Russia the councils developed from revolutionary organs of class struggle into agencies of government controlled by the Bolshevik party. In Germany the radicals were never able to wrest control of the councils from the moderate Majority Socialists, who were committed to the democratic traditions of Western socialism and who had no desire to substitute a council system for parliamentary democracy as the Bolsheviks had done. The Independent Socialists, who wanted to establish social democracy through a council system, avoiding the pitfalls of both bourgeois democracy and a proletarian dictatorship, were hampered by internal divisions in their own party and by Bolshevik and Left Radical propaganda for a council dictatorship. When German socialists were called upon to choose between a bourgeois parliamentary democracy and a council system that might be subverted into a proletarian dictatorship, they came down overwhelmingly on the side of parliamentary democracy.

One must not overlook the similar fates of the councils in Germany and Russia, however. In both countries the councils, which were the spontaneous creation of protesting workers, came to serve the objectives of the parties that controlled them. Once they had attained power in Russia the Bolsheviks found that the councils which had been useful in helping them to power could be retained in the new order as organs for controlling the proletariat. The German Majority Socialists, on the other hand, having attained power in the November revolution, found the councils to be a liability rather than an asset. The councils were difficult for the party leaders to work with for several reasons: (1) Council leaders were generally politically and administratively inexperienced. The judgment of *Vorwärts* on the Berlin *Vollzugsrat* is typical of the attitude of the SPD to the councils: "The entire history of the *Vollzugsrat* has been a series of mistakes, confusion, adventures, hasty decrees, withdrawal of decrees, . . . [all in all] a chain of distressing incidents."[45] (2) The councils were often separatist and anarchic, interfering with the efficient operation of the provisional government. (3) Parallels drawn between the councils in Germany and Russia could only work to the disadvantage of the SPD, which was now trying to transform itself into a mass party by seeking the support of the middle class as well as that of the proletariat. (4) The SPD could count on the support of industrial labor in a normal parliamentary democratic election, while the outcome of a council election would be much less certain. (5) The SPD could not tolerate the opposition which would have arisen in the trade unions and in the army to the kinds of reforms that the councils proposed. In short, after the revolution the councils could best serve the interests of the party if they were eliminated. As this was not politically feasible, the SPD did the next best thing, which was to transform the councils into relatively innocuous factory grievance committees.[46]

Although workers' councils did continue to exist in both Germany and Russia after the war, creating the impression of "industrial democracy," actually in both countries the councils were shorn of their political powers and reduced to performing economic and administrative functions for the parties in power. In the final analysis, the council system must be seen as a *transitional* form—rather than the final institutional expression—of the revolutions that struck down the German and Russian empires.

[45] Quoted by Henry Egon Friedlander, "Conflict of Revolutionary Authority: Provisional Government versus Berlin Soviet, November-December, 1918," *International Review of Social History*, VII (1962), 174.

[46] Comfort, *Revolutionary Hamburg*, pp. 98-99.

English Economic Thought in Spain, 1776-1848

Robert S. Smith

The man who gives Spain free trade will have conferred on his country a greater benefit than Columbus showing it the way to America.

ALVARO FLÓREZ ESTRADA (1846)

Although the first unexpurgated Spanish translation of the *Wealth of Nations* was not published until 1956, it took much less than 180 years for Spaniards to become acquainted with Adam Smith and other British economists. Some scholars read English and imported books from London. Others relied on French translations or on Spanish versions of French translations from the English. A Spanish digest of Condorcet's synopsis of the *Wealth of Nations* appeared in 1792, two years before the Inquisition approved a direct translation of the English text. But it was not until the middle of the twentieth century that Spanish-speaking economists discovered that what passed for a Spanish edition of Smith's work was mutilated, garbled, and poorly translated.[1]

From the publication of the *Wealth of Nations* in 1776 to the appearance of Mill's *Principles of Political Economy* in 1848, English economic thought was dominated by the Classical school. However the period also produced noteworthy dissenters from Classical doctrine and even saw the beginning of British socialist thought. These currents and crosscurrents were mirrored imperfectly in Spanish economic literature. The transmission of ideas may be traced through translations of English writings, original

MR. SMITH *is James B. Duke Professor of Economics and chairman of the department at Duke University. One of his publications is* The Spanish Guild Merchant. *Most of the research for this paper was made possible by grants from the Research Council and the Council on Hispanic Research of Duke University.*

[1] Robert S. Smith, "*The Wealth of Nations* in Spain and Spanish America, 1780-1830," *Journal of Political Economy*, LXV (1957), 104-125; Lucas Beltrán, *Historia de las doctrinas económicas* (Barcelona, 1961), pp. 97-98.

works in Spanish acknowledging the British influence, references to English economists in periodicals and parliamentary papers, and prescribed texts for formal courses in economics.[2]

I

English economics first appeared in Spanish garb with the publication in 1779 of a piece on "Political Arithmetic," extracted from the writings of Charles Davenant;[3] and in 1789, thirty-seven years after its publication in English, Spaniards had a translation of David Hume's *Political Discourses*.[4] By this time, a few writers had referred to Adam Smith, but Carlos Martínez de Irujo formally introduced Spanish readers to the *Wealth of Nations* by publishing an expurgated version of Condorcet's synopsis.[5] Apparently unsure of freedom from censorship, although his work was published at the Royal Press, Irujo never referred to Smith by name. "The author," he said, produced "the best work on political economy which has been written up to now." It was "authoritative, abstract, and profound," and if Spain should apply its "solid principles" to the advancement of national prosperity, Irujo would feel compensated for his trouble.

The translator of the expurgated *Wealth of Nations* was José Alonso Ortiz, a professor of canon law and theology at Valladolid. The edition of 1794 was followed by a "greatly improved and corrected" edition in 1805-1806.[6] Spain, Alonso declared, did not lack for economists, but none had succeeded in constructing a "general system" of economics. The *Wealth of Nations* was "profound" and "highly metaphysical," requiring "repeated reading to

[2] An exhaustive search for English economics in Spanish translation has not been attempted, but the bibliographical aids used for this essay are believed to cover a high percentage of the published material. I have relied heavily on Antonio Palau y Dulcet, *Manual del librero hispanoamericano* (7 vols.; Barcelona, 1923-1927; 2nd ed., Barcelona, 1948—), but in most cases I have verified author, title, and date of publication from a library copy.

[3] "Del uso de la arithmética en el comercio y rentas," in Nicolás Arriquivar, *Recreación política* (Vitoria, 1779), I, 1-24.

[4] *Discursos políticos* (Madrid, 1789).

[5] *Compendio de la obra inglesa intitulada Riqueza de las Naciones, hecho por el Marqués de Condorcet y traducido al castellano con varias adiciones del original* (Madrid, 1792 and 1803; Palma de Mallorca, 1814). Condorcet's book-by-book analysis of the *Wealth of Nations* was published in the *Bibliothèque de l'homme public* (Paris, 1790), III, 108-216, and IV, 3-115.

[6] *Investigación de la naturaleza y causas de la riqueza de las naciones* (4 vols.; Valladolid, 1794; 4 vols.; Valladolid, 1805-1806).

penetrate the spirit of its assertions." It was Smith who discovered "the universal principle of all wealth, which is the productive labor of man."

Alonso admitted the suppression of passages "absolutely irrelevant to our country or hardly in conformity with the sacred religion we profess." The reader had no way of knowing where the expurgations occur; in fact, the omissions, distortions, and inaccuracies were numerous. Some, but not all, of the departures from the original text may be explained by the translator's desire to appease the Supreme Council of the Inquisition, to which he first submitted the manuscript in 1792. His assurances that he had deleted "everything which could induce error or relaxation on religious and moral matters" found favor with the censors, but he did so at the expense of earning for himself an honest reputation as an interpreter of Adam Smith.

Oblivious to the defects of Alonso's translation, Ramón Lázaro de Dou, the rector of the University of Cervera, reproduced much of the second edition in a two-volume commentary on the *Wealth of Nations*.[7] Calling Smith the Newton of political economy, Dou declared that the Scotsman's genius consisted in "having discovered, as from a high watchtower, that Europeans, dazzled by the brilliance of the mercantile system, have strayed far from the path which they had to follow." But Dou was far from accepting Smith in all particulars: Uztáriz, Spain's foremost mercantilist of the eighteenth century, was a better guide than Smith on commercial policy.

Almost incredibly, the Spanish version of the *Wealth of Nations* published in the 1930's was Alonso Ortiz' text with only grammatical and orthographical changes.[8] At long last, in 1956, Amando Lázaro Ros gave the Spanish-speaking world a complete and accurate translation of the *Wealth of Nations*.[9] Two years later Gabriel Franco and Manuel Sánchez Sarto brought out the second

[7] *La Riqueza de las Naciones, nuevamente explicada con la doctrina de su mismo investigador* (2 vols.; Cervera, 1817). Dou refers to Smith in his *Instituciones del derecho público general de España* (9 vols.; Madrid, 1800-1803), but even in 1817 he was unfamiliar with the 1794 edition of Alonso's translation (*Riqueza*, II, 109-110).

[8] *Investigación de la naturaleza y causas de la riqueza de las naciones*, ed. José M. Tallada (3 vols.; Barcelona, 1933-1947).

[9] *Investigación de la naturaleza y causas de la riqueza de las naciones* (Madrid, 1956).

complete Spanish version. Both follow the Cannan edition, and Franco and Sánchez reproduce Cannan's notes.[10]

Much of the credit for making Smith known in Spain belongs to Say, whom some Spaniards called "the French Smith." The first Spanish version of the *Traité* dates from 1807, and later translations of this and other works of Say are numerous.[11] The translators generally applauded Say for clarifying Smithian economics. Agustín Pascual, the translator of the *Cartilla*, said Say avoided the "frequent faults and errors into which all the economists who preceded him had fallen, without excepting in some things the celebrated Smith." Pascual advised young people to master the *Cartilla*, for "anything else would only confuse them." Manuel María Gutiérrez gave Smith credit for teaching economists "the proper method of discovering the truth," but he thought the *Wealth of Nations* contained many errors which later writers, including Say, had fortunately corrected.[12] The translators of the *Epítome* considered Say the true founder of economic science: the "respectable treatises" of his predecessors, Smith and Steuart, lacked "scientific method and language" and, consequently, were no more than "the embryo or heap of formless elements of science, and not science itself." The anonymous translator of the fifth edition of the *Traité* called attention to the revision: "the primacy of Ricardo has led Say to revise and completely rewrite all the chapters on money."

Excerpts from Malthus' *Essay* were available in Spanish long before the publication of the entire text in 1846, and Malthus also was known in Spain through the translation of Say's letters.[13] Ricardo's *Principles* lacked a Spanish translator until the twentieth

[10] *Investigación de la naturaleza y causas de la riqueza de las naciones* (Mexico, 1958).

[11] Juan Bautista Say, *Tratado de economía política* (Madrid, 1807, 1817, 1821; Paris, 1836); *Cartilla de economía política* (Madrid, 1816 and 1822); *Epítome de los principios fundamentales de la economía política* (Madrid, 1816); *Catecismo de economía política* (Madrid, 1822; Zaragosa, 1833); *Introducción a la economía política* (Paris, 1827); *Cartas de M. Jn. Bta. Say a M. Malthus sobre varios puntos de economía política* (Madrid, 1820; Paris, 1827). The *Cartas* are also included in the 1821 edition of the *Tratado*.

[12] *Discurso inaugural y sucinta esposición de los principios de economía política demostrados por Mr. Juan Bta. Say* (Málaga, 1819).

[13] Based on the 1845 French edition, including Rossi's introduction, the *Ensayo sobre el principio de la población* (Madrid, 1846) was translated by José María Noguera and Joaquín Miquel, under the supervision of Eusebio María del Valle. Excerpts from the London edition of 1803 were published in seventeen numbers of the *Gazeta de Madrid*, June 21–August 6, 1808.

century.[14] He, too, was known to Spaniards only through extracts of his work and, indirectly, through translations of McCulloch's *Treatise* and *Principles*.[15] There are four Spanish versions of James Mill's *Elements*.[16] The translator of the 1831 edition stressed the superiority of Mill to Smith and Say: Mill "does not enunciate a truth without proving it and presenting it with exactness and mathematical precision." John Stuart Mill's *Principles* lacked a Spanish translator until 1943.[17] On the other hand, long excerpts from William Paley's *Principles of Moral and Political Philosophy* appeared in a Spanish periodical published in London by Joseph Blanco White,[18] and parts of Miss Martineau's *Illustrations* appeared in Spanish, soon after publication in English.[19]

Judged by the number of works translated, no British social scientist was better known in Spain than Jeremy Bentham. Liberal statesmen in the Cortes of 1820-1823 sought his advice, and Bentham responded with critical observation on proposed legislation. Spanish versions of Bentham's "Social Science" were published in Salamanca, but the eclipse of liberalism in 1823 counseled the publication of *A Defence of Usury* and other pieces in Paris and London.[20]

Translations from the French (in addition to the works of Say) provided a channel for the flow of English ideas, even in cases in which the author's purpose was to question the British economists or deny the validity of their doctrine. Herrenschwand's *De l'économie politique*, first published in London in 1786, appeared in Span-

[14] *Principios de economía política y de tributación* (Madrid, 1936).

[15] J. R. McCulloch, *Tratado de los principios e influencia práctica de la imposición y del sistema de crear fondos* (2nd ed.; Madrid, 1857); the first edition, which Palau places in 1817, could not have appeared before 1845. The *Principios de economía política* was published in Madrid in 1855.

[16] *Elementos de economía política* (Madrid, 1822; Buenos Aires, 1823; Paris, 1827; Madrid, 1831). The 1822 edition is only a fifty-seven-page summary.

[17] *Principios de economía política* (Mexico, 1943).

[18] "Sobre la población y los mantenimientos, y de la agricultura y comercio," *El Español* (London, 1814), pp. 124-146, 222-238.

[19] Harriet Martineau, *Novelas sobre economía política* (2 vols.; Madrid, 1836).

[20] *Sistema de la ciencia social* (Salamanca, 1820) and *Principios de la ciencia social* (Salamanca, 1821), both by Toribio Núñez, are synopses and running commentaries rather than direct translations of Bentham. Brief extracts of Bentham's *Manual of Political Economy* were published in the *Semanario de Agricultura y Artes*, XIII (Madrid, 1803), 284-288, 298-304, and 315-320; and "Principios político-económicos sobre las colonias" appeared in *El Español* (London, 1814), pp. 109-123.

ish in 1800.[21] Comte Destutt de Tracy's *Traité*, originally a part of his *Eléments d'idéologie* and published separately in 1823, had a Spanish translator the following year.[22] A well-annotated translation of Ganilh's *Dictionnaire* acquainted Spanish readers with economic concepts developed in the first quarter of the century. The translator, Mariano José Sicilia, found opportunities to disagree with Ganilh: he did not believe, for instance, that the "immortal work of Adam Smith" had survived all attempts to undermine the *Wealth of Nations* on "essential questions."[23] The translation of Sismondi's *Nouveaux principes* in 1834 furnished an insight into the growing condemnation of Classical economics for its excessive materialism.[24] Blanqui's *Précis élémentaire d'économie politique*, a potpourri of English and French economics, appeared in translation in 1840,[25] simultaneously with the publication of a Spanish version of Rossi's *Cours d'économie politique*. Italian by birth, Rossi emigrated to France and in 1832 occupied Say's chair at the College de France. The Spanish translator quoted Cherbuliez to the effect that Rossi's *Cours* was "the only work which could wrest [economic] science from the lethargy in which the death of Say left it prostrate."[26] Two years later, Manuel Colmeiro translated Droz's *Economie politique*, with Blanqui's assurance that Droz's was the clearest, most elegant, and most methodical elementary treatise available.[27] Some of Bastiat's writings were published in the 1840's;[28] and Joseph Garnier's *Eléments d'économie politique*, reviewing contributions of French and English economists, was translated three years after its publication in France.[29]

[21] *Principios de economía política por Herrenschwand, traducidos del francés al castellano por Juan Smith* (Madrid, 1800).

[22] Conde Destutt de Tracy, *Tratado de economía política* (2 vols.; Madrid, 1824).

[23] Charles Ganilh, *Diccionario analítico de economía política* (3 vols.; Paris, 1827).

[24] J. C. L. Simonde de Sismondi, *Nuevos principios de economía política*, trans. Francisco Xerez y Verona (2 vols.; Granada, 1834).

[25] Adolfo Blanqui, *Compendio elemental de economía política* (Paris, 1840).

[26] P[ellegrino Luigi Edoardo] Rossi, *Curso de economía política*, trans. Pedro de Madrazo (Madrid, 1840).

[27] J[oseph] Droz, *Economía política o principio de la ciencia de las riquezas* (Madrid, 1842).

[28] *Sofismos económicos* (Madrid, 1847). I have located *Armonias economicas* (La Paz, Bolivia, 1859), but not the 1848 (Madrid) edition cited by Palau.

[29] José Garnier, *Elementos de economía política* (Madrid, 1848 and 1853), trans. Eugenio de Ochoa.

II

Turning to Spanish economic literature of native origin, I would argue that its volume, variety, and quality belie the caricature of a priest-ridden and intellectually impoverished country. There is often a lag between the development of ideas in England and their recognition in Spain, but the evolution of Spanish economic thought under the influence of the Classical writers is unquestionably a major part of the history of Spanish economics in the first half of the nineteenth century.

Smith lived long enough to see his name in Spanish type, although he might have been distressed, or amused, to see it turn up sometimes as "Smit" or "Smitch." I do not know who first spoke his name; clearly, at least three writers were familiar with Smith's work before his death in 1790.[30]

Vicente Alcalá Galiano, secretary of the Economic Society of Segovia, contributed numerous essays to the society's publications.[31] His early pieces show no familiarity with English writers, but in 1788 he composed a long essay on taxation which, Colmeiro claimed, "follows Smith's book step by step."[32] This is an exaggeration; but Alcalá did lean heavily on Smith, paraphrasing among other things the canons of taxation. In 1810 he recalled that the "doctrines of Smith were the thread that happily guided me in this labyrinth of political economy. Following the footsteps of this great master, in the matter of taxes I arrived at some consequences, or principles, all very brilliant and some new." He praised Smith's criticism of Physiocracy, a system, Alcalá said, which "would not and could not be adopted by any European kingdom."[33] Alcalá

---

[30] Fabian Estapé has spared me the trouble of disputing Colmeiro's claim that *Lecciones de economía civil*, a textbook published in 1779, drew anything from the *Wealth of Nations*. The author, Bernardo Danvila, was a plagiarist of Cantillon ("Algunos comentarios a la publicación del *Ensayo sobre la naturaleza del comercio en general*, de Cantillon," *Moneda y Crédito*, No. 39 [Madrid, 1951], pp. 60-70.)

[31] *Actas y memorias de la Real Sociedad Económica de los Amigos del Pais de la Provincia de Segovia* (4 vols.; Segovia, 1785-1793).

[32] Manuel Colmeiro, *Biblioteca de los economistas españoles de los siglos xvi, xvii, y xviii* (Madrid, 1880), p. 16.

[33] "Sobre la necesidad y justicia de los tributos, fondos de donde deben sacarse, y medios de recaudarlos," *Actas y memorias de la Real Sociedad Económica*, IV, 269-359; *Informe de Don Vicente Alcalá Galiano sobre el decreto de 11 de agosto de 1809 en que se mandaron suprimir las rentas provinciales, luego que se subrogasen en otras equivalentes* (Valencia, 1810).

Galiano became treasurer general of Spain in the early years of the century.

Valentín de Foronda, a prominent member of the Basque Economic Society, was influenced in his youth by Baron von Bielfeld; but in 1788 he acknowledged that he had been misled in his efforts to understand economics. In articles published in 1788-1789 he indicated that Quesnay, Mirabeau, and Smith, among others, had guided him toward the acceptance of laissez faire. Tariffs, he said, violate the "natural" rights of liberty and property; and he challenged those who, accepting free trade in principle, insisted on making an exception of grain trade. This was as absurd as to argue that the earth, unlike other planets, does not revolve around the sun. Foronda came to the United States as consul-general in 1802 and in 1807-1809 served as Spain's chargé d'affaires.[34]

In breadth of vision, catholicity of interests, and respect for scientific method, Gaspar Melchor Jovellanos had few peers among Spanish economists and statesmen. His unpublished papers include an "Extract from the work of Mr. Smith" and a translation of parts of the *Wealth of Nations*, which by 1796 he had read four times, in French and English. Jovellanos wrote extensively on questions of economic policy, but his fame as an economist rests largely on his treatise on agrarian reform. Sponsored by the Economic Society of Madrid, this celebrated work attacked the privileges of the sheepherders' guild, which impeded the enclosure of arable land, denounced entail and mortmain, and advocated the expropriation of the real property of religious foundations. Jovellanos cited Smith, as well as other foreign authors, in advocating small-scale peasant ownership, improved farming, and a free market for agricultural produce. Within two years of its publication in 1795 the *Informe en el expediente de ley agraria* was denounced as anticlerical, but it did not get on the honor roll of prohibited books until after the author's death.[35]

Gradually, the "new" economics made its way into the schools. In 1784 Lorenzo Normante y Carcavilla inaugurated the chair of economics in the School of Economics and Commerce founded by

[34] Robert S. Smith, "Valentín de Foronda, diplomático y economista," *Revista de economía política*, X, No. 2 (Madrid, 1959), 425-464.

[35] Edith F. Helman, "Some Consequences of the Publication of the *Informe de ley agraria* by Jovellanos," *Estudios Hispanicos* (Wellesley, Mass., 1952), pp. 253-273.

the Aragonese Economic Society in Zaragoza. Lecturing on the "usefulness of politico-economic knowledge and the need for its methodical study," Normante relied heavily on Genovesi; and in 1786 he introduced his students to the writings of Melon. The local clergy attacked Normante for his "audacious doctrines" on free trade in grain, interest, and sacerdotal celibacy; but the government in Madrid upheld him, and he continued to occupy his chair until 1801. Previously, perhaps in 1792, Martínez de Irujo's *Compendio* was added to the list of readings in his course.[36] Other economic societies followed Zaragoza's example in setting up courses in economics for a nondescript student body; none pretended to be of university caliber.

In 1807 Charles IV restricted higher education in Spain to eleven universities and prescribed for each of them the curricula already approved for the University of Salamanca. Political economy was one of the required courses in the law faculty, and the *Wealth of Nations* (probably Alonso Ortiz' translation) was designated as a text, "until the work of Juan Bautista Say, which will be preferred, has been published in Spanish translation."[37] In 1808 a Spanish version of Germain Garnier's "Method of Facilitating the Study of Dr. Smith's Work" appeared; it was described as a key to "whatever was missing in Smith's work for teaching [his doctrine] in all the universities and public schools."[38] When the *Gazeta de Madrid* commenced (for the second time) to publish extracts of Malthus' *Essay*, the editor observed that this was one of the few works whose importance made them "worthy of being known in all nations." But why, he asked, "among so many useless [academic] chairs, was there none in which the principles of social happiness are taught?"[39]

The Cortes of 1813 decreed that every university should es-

[36] Lorenzo Normante y Carcavilla, *Pruebas del espíritu del Sr. Melon y de las proposiciones de economía civil y comercio* (Madrid, 1787); Félix Correa Pero, *La cátedra de economía y comercio de la Real Sociedad Económica Aragonesa de Amigos del Pais* (Zaragoza, n.d.). Correa's belief that this was the first *cátedra de economía* in Spain appears erroneous. Danvila's *Lecciones de economía civil* (1779) was prepared as a text for a course the author was teaching in the Royal Seminary for Noblemen in Madrid.

[37] *Real cédula . . . por la qual se reduce el número de las universidades literarias del Reyno . . . y se manda observar en ellas el plan de estudios aprobado para la de Salamanca* (Madrid, 1807).

[38] *Gazeta de Madrid*, No. 15 (Feb. 19, 1808), p. 186.

[39] *Ibid.*, No. 15 (Jan. 15, 1811), p. 60.

tablish a chair of economics "as soon as possible." By this time Say's *Traité* had been translated; and in 1814 the faculty of the University of Salamanca decided to continue using Say, "while the teachers, collecting the observations of our economists, patriotic societies, and all the knowledge in this science, prepare a national work."[40] The proposed "national work" never materialized, but in 1817 the Salamanca faculty was called on to advise the Kingdom of Navarre on grain-trade policy. Four professors drew up a forty-page brief, citing Smith and other economists to support their recommendation of complete freedom in grain trade within the kingdom.[41]

Knowledge of the contributions of foreign economists was not confined to literary and academic circles. In every legislature, beginning with the Cortes of Cadiz, which gave birth to the Constitution of 1812, debate on economic questions repeatedly evoked references to British and French writers. The Cortes of 1820-1823, which the king dissolved before it accomplished its reforming mission, was exceptional for the quality of its leadership. "Almost everything that has been done in that legislature for [the nation's] prosperity," said one observer, "is the result of the understanding various deputies have of the difficult and subtle theories of political economy." All the laws enacted were "founded on the enlightened ideas of Say, Smith, Ricardo, Steward [*sic*], Filangieri, Beccaria, and other famous writers who have dedicated their talents to elucidate this essential part of human knowledge."[42] With somewhat less reason the journal of the 1810-1814 legislatures was called a repository of "very learned reports and speeches on the most delicate points in economics."[43]

Taxation, commercial policy, and land reform were salient economic issues in both periods of constitutional government. The

[40] *Informe de la Universidad de Salamanca sobre plan de estudios o sobre su fundacion, altura y decadencia, y sobre las mejoras de que es susceptible* (Salamanca, 1820); *Colección de los decretos y órdenes que han expedido las Cortes Generales y Extraordinarias*, IV (Madrid, 1820), 84-85.

[41] *Dictamen del gremio y claustro de la Universidad de Salamanca, sobre la consulta hecha por los tres Estados del Reyno de Navarra acerca del comercio de granos* (Pamplona, 1817). José María de Zuaznavar y Francia, *Discurso sobre el comercio exterior de granos del reyno de Navarra* (Pamplona, 1818), denounced the *Dictamen*.

[42] Juan Sánchez Rivera, in the prologue of J. B. Say, *Tratado de economía política* (Madrid, 1821), p. vii.

[43] *Ocios de Españoles Emigrados*, I (London, 1824), 113.

penury of the treasury and the size of the public debt made revenue
an overriding consideration, as a result of which neither agrarian
legislation nor tariffs could be considered without reference to fiscal
repercussions. Thus, the provision for the alienation of idle public
lands (1813) was designed to improve farming by encouraging enclosure; but it was also conceived as a means of compensating
veterans of the Peninsular War.[44]

On land reform most legislators regarded Jovellanos as the
surest guide. Indeed, on his death in 1811 the Cortes eulogized the
author of the *Ley agraria* and proposed to have his work read in
the public schools. Jovellanos stopped short of demanding the
breaking up of large entailed estates (*mayorazgos*), but he did
propose long-term leases, which would quicken the farmer's interest
in improving the land and increasing yields. Smith, Jovellanos said,
attributed the flourishing condition of English agriculture to leases
which protected the tenant from dispossession on the death of the
landlord or the transfer of ownership. Count Toreno, who ridiculed
the "so-called economists," Quesnay and Mercier, for teaching
that land is "the only true source of wealth," also cited Smith in advocating tenancy under long-term leases, although he had probably
picked up the idea second-hand from Jovellanos. Ramón Lázaro
de Dou, who was the first president of the Cortes of 1810, doubted
the wisdom of dividing entailed estates into smallholdings and argued that peasant proprietors would generally lack the means to
introduce capital improvements. In the legislature and in tracts
published in 1829 and 1831, "based principally on the authority of
Dr. Adam Smith," Dou proposed the wider use of the hereditary
lease (emphyteusis), a practice already common in his native
Catalonia.[45]

It was the backward state of Spanish agriculture which led a
majority of the legislators, even those who professed to accept free
trade in principle, to make agricultural products a special case in
tariff legislation. With the example of England's Corn Law of 1815

[44] *Colección de los decretos y órdenes que han expedido las Cortes Generales y Extraordinarias*, III (Cadiz, 1813), 174-178.

[45] *Diario de las discusiones y actas de las Cortes*, XVIII (Cadiz, 1813), 380-381, and XXI (1813), 260; Ramón Lázaro de Dou, *Conciliación económica y legal de pareceres opuestos en cuanto a laudemios y derechos enfiteúticos* (Cervera, 1829); *Pronta y fácil egecución del proyecto sobre laudemios fundada principalmente en una autoridad del Dr. Adam Smith* (Cervera, 1831).

before them, the Cortes of 1820 prohibited the importation of grain and flour, except when the domestic price of wheat exceeded 80 reales (about 10 shillings) per *fanega* (about one-fifth of an English quarter) and the price of wheat flour, 120 reales per hundredweight.[46] Very few of his colleagues agreed with Alvaro Flórez Estrada who, although a member of the legislative tariff commission, said it was "shameful" to debate the arguments in favor of prohibition. One deputy, who accepted in principle "the doctrine of the best economists," declared that their theories (of free trade) were not "applicable to the present situation of our Spain." Count Toreno saw in the Spanish corn law a compromise comparable to the English legislation: in England grain producers wanted to prohibit imports entirely; industrial interests wanted duty-free imports; and Parliament took a middle course. The English practice of paying bounties on grain exports also was applauded as a measure "sufficient (according to the economists) to raise agriculture to the highest state of prosperity."[47]

In 1820 Flórez Estrada expressed the hope that he could "persuade Congress from this very day to abolish all tariffs." There was no prohibition, he said, which did not injure more people than it helped: and another congressman, citing Hume, argued that the prohibition of imports always impoverishes a nation. José Canga Argüelles, who was treasury secretary in 1811 and again in 1820, condemned "the eagerness to domesticate on our soil all the foreign crafts," quoting from the *Wealth of Nations* a passage in which Smith pointed out that "moderate taxes" on imports, adjusted to maximize revenue, would still leave "our own workmen . . . a considerable advantage in the home market."[48] But the finance commission of the Cortes reasoned that a few prohibitions, together with moderate duties on permitted imports, were required to put Spain on an equal footing with countries that protected domestic industry. England, several legislators remarked, owed its industrial growth to protective tariffs on imports, combined in some cases

[46] *Colección de los decretos y órdenes generales de la Primera Legislatura, 1820-1821*, VI (Madrid, 1821), 28-29.
[47] *Diario de las actas y discusiones de las Cortes: Legislatura de los años de 1820 y 1821*, I (Madrid, 1820), 61-62, 165, 314-318, 367-376.
[48] *Diario de las sesiones de Cortes: Legislatura de 1820*, II, (Madrid, 1871), 1064.

(wool, for instance) with the prohibition of exports. Congressman Oliver recalled that Smith was a customs-house official when he died: "scarcely would he have obtained or retained that post if his principles had been in conflict with his duties." The finance commission acknowledged, however, that "the principles of economic science and the general opinion of the public demand [the] absolute abolition" of tariffs.[49]

José Canga Argüelles was the leading figure among those who, in the first quarter of the century, aspired to reform Spain's archaic tax structure and inefficient treasury administration. Canga became acquainted with Classical economics long before his exile in England in the 1820's, and his official memoranda and speeches on finance are sprinkled with references to Smith. In the 1811 legislature he asserted that Spaniards discovered that labor is the source of wealth "centuries before the English proclaimed this truth, which we have now considered new because the maxims of our elders are unknown to us."[50]

The great congressional debate, begun in 1810 and resumed in the Cortes of 1820, centered on the subrogation of the so-called provincial contributions into a single tax (*única contribución*). The provincial levies consisted of an assortment of sales, transfer, and excise taxes whose regressive effect was clearly understood and generally deplored. Ramón Lázaro de Dou, in papers submitted to the Cortes of 1812 and in a tract published in 1822, argued that Catalonia, which was exempted from the provincial contributions, had prospered under a tax system (*catastro*) which in effect imposed a single tax on owners of real property and industrial and mercantile enterprises.[51]

In 1811 the Cortes approved Canga Argüelles' progressive income tax, modeled on Pitt's wartime tax bill of 1799, and two years later adopted direct taxes to replace numerous indirect levies. In the 1820 legislature Canga presented a thorough review of government finance and proposed to apply the confiscated properties

[49] *Diario de las discusiones y actas de las Cortes*, XVIII (1813), 20; *Diario de las sesiones de Cortes: Legislatura de 1820*, I, (Madrid, 1871), 110; II, 831 and 1522-1523; and III, (1873), 1873-1874 and 2102.
[50] *Diario de las discusiones y actas de las Cortes*, X (1811), 377-378.
[51] *Equivalencia del catastro de Cataluña con las rentas provinciales de Castilla* (Cervera, 1822).

of the Inquisition to the reduction of the public debt, totaling (according to Canga's estimates) 14,388,000,000 reales.[52]

Opponents of Canga's fiscal reforms included Vicente Alcalá Galiano, who maintained that a single tax on agriculture, industry, and trade would deter capital formation. This, he said, he had learned from reading the *Wealth of Nations*. Vicente's brother Antonio, a member of the Cortes of 1813, took a similar position: although the existing system was "complicated and monstrous," the "principles" of Smith and other economists taught that "the surest way to encourage industry and trade in every society was not to subject their capital to any kind of direct tax." Count Toreno challenged this point of view: Smith, the "holy father of political economy," neither "approves nor disapproves of direct and indirect taxes, but rather discusses the evils of all." In the Cortes of 1820 the legislators were still undecided whether direct or indirect taxes were contrary to the precepts of Smith, Say, and Destutt de Tracy. One congressman thought that Spaniards had failed to learn anything about finance: "from the time we began to talk of the Smiths, the Says, the Sismondis, the revenue from our taxes has declined [and] the costs of collection have increased from 12 to 30."[53]

III

Many of Spain's intellectuals improved their appreciation of foreign scholarship by studying abroad. It was Ferdinand VII who twice provided "traveling fellowships" in the shape of orders of arrest and exile for those who, in 1808-1814 and 1820-1823, had said or written anything derogatory of the absolute authority of the monarchy or the church. Many left the country one step ahead of the police; but some, like Valentín de Foronda and Canga Argüelles languished in jail before their apostasy and "crimes" were brought to trial. London had the best-known, if not the largest, colony of Spanish émigrés. To earn a living many exiles engaged in a variety of lowly occupations, from peddling candy to curing

[52] *Colección de los decretos y órdenes que han expedido las Cortes Generales y Extraordinairas*, I, 116-118; II, 159; IV, 229-230; V, 23-24 and 137; VI, 31-32 and 375-376; J. Canga Argüelles, *Memoria sobre el crédito público* (Madrid, 1820).

[53] *Diario de las discusiones y actas de las Cortes*, XXI (1813), 92-93, 108-116, 176-177, 203-204, 214, 253-254; *Diario de las sesiones de Cortes: Legislatura de 1820*, II, 1307-1312; and *Legislatura de 1821*, III, 1807.

corns; but some professionals lived by the pen, supplemented by British patronage. Llorens identifies seven Spanish-language newspapers published in London in 1824-1829, and the British capital rivaled Paris as a publishing center for Spanish books which could not be published in Spain.[54]

Canga Argüelles was associated with Alvaro Flórez Estrada in editing *Tribuno del Pueblo Español*, a Cadiz newspaper founded by Flórez Estrada to defend constitutional government. When the Constitution was repudiated, Canga was jailed and Flórez escaped a death sentence by sailing precipitately for England. In 1823 the two were united in exile and for three years contributed to *Ocios de Españoles Emigrados*, a London periodical which found its way into Spain and which Ferdinand VII branded "alarming and subversive" because its editors were "liberals by conviction."

Leisure (*ocio*) for Canga Argüelles was only figurative. Within three years he published his four-hundred-page "Elements of Finance" and a five-volume "Dictionary of Finance."[55] The former he wrote in response to a friend's complaint that Smith, Say, Ricardo, and Storch were too abstract to be helpful in comprehending current economic problems. Dedicated to President Guadalupe Vitoria of Mexico, the *Elementos* examines the obstacles to increasing the wealth of nations and analyzes the relation between public and private consumption. Canga estimated that public expenditures in Spain amounted to nearly half of the national income, a proportion which could be reduced to one-quarter if the tax system were reformed. Smith is quoted with approval several times, but Canga

[54] Vicente Llorens Castillo, *Liberales y románticos: una emigración española en Inglaterra* (Mexico, 1954). From 1824 to 1830 an estimated one thousand refugee families were living in the British Isles, chiefly in London. Said *El Emigrado Observador* in 1828: "Except for a very reduced number whose families or friends maintain or help them, the rest live on the 500, 400, 300, and 200 reales monthly which English charity affords them." An advertisement of "Spanish works published by Sr. Ackermann" in the *Museo Universal de Ciencias y Artes*, VIII (London, 1826) lists dozens of books written by Spanish émigrés.

[55] *Elementos de la ciencia de hacienda* (London, 1825) includes the *Cartilla de hacienda* (a sort of catechism) with a separate title page but paged continuously with *Elementos*. Despite the title, the *Elementos de la ciencia de hacienda* (Madrid, 1833), edited by Felipe Canga Argüelles, reproduced the *Cartilla* but not the *Elementos* of the 1825 edition. There were two editions of the "Dictionary": *Diccionario de hacienda para el uso de los encargados de la suprema dirección de ella* (5 vols.; London, 1826-1827) and *Diccionario de hacienda con aplicación a España* (2 vols.; Madrid, 1833-1834), followed by a *Suplemento al diccionario de hacienda* (Madrid, 1840).

dismissed as impractical his proposal to finance the administration of justice through assessments on the litigants.

The *Diccionario*, begun while Canga was in prison, is an encyclopedic repository of economic and historical data, drawn in part from papers (including his own official reports) which Canga brought with him from Spain. He was no slavish disciple of Classical economics. He favored unlimited free trade in agricultural products, especially grain, believing with Smith that the scarcity of food in some places would be compensated by abundance in others. Otherwise, Canga's acceptance of the doctrine was qualified, as he noted with approval Say's recommendation that a nation with a long-standing protective tariff should move toward free trade gradually. The author of numerous memoranda on commercial treaties, he argued that the relaxation of protection should be reciprocal and equitable. England, he declared, had always taken advantage of Spain: the embargo on silk and woolen goods was an example of how this "astute" nation had managed to give fewer concessions than it received from its trading partners. But, in the 1820's he was impressed by Huskisson's attack on protectionism. It is not quite clear, however, why he thought "the maxims so wisely and correctly developed in the year 1825 by the profound Huskisson" should have been "gratifying . . . to the Spaniards who revere the glories of their nation."

Ignoring Malthus, Canga Argüelles adopted Destutt de Tracy's position that population is always proportional to the means of subsistence. This, he said, is the "luminous and unique principle which government desirous of furthering the country's prosperity should consult." Citing Arthur Young, he marveled at the ability of the English farmer to overcome the handicap of an adverse climate and increase agricultural output threefold in the seventeenth century. Canga accepted Say's dictum that money is only part of the wealth of nations, but he disputed the Frenchman's view that paper money must be supported by a 100 per cent metallic reserve. Experience had shown that a reserve as low as 20 per cent would maintain the value of the paper, if the issuer's credit was good. As an appendix to the second edition of the "Dictionary" he published Alexander Hamilton's "Report on the Mint."[56]

[56] "Memoria sobre el establecimiento de una casa de moneda, por Alejandro Hamilton," *Diccionario de hacienda* (2nd ed.), II, 641-657. The other references

After the suspension of *Ocios*, Canga Argüelles became political editor of a periodical which, according to Llorens, was an apologist for the "defectors"—those who, owing their exile to the Spanish king, now supported him.[57] The evidence of Canga's defection is only circumstantial. In a signed article Canga attacked the London *Times* for publishing letters discrediting the "honor of the Spanish nation." England, he charged, was urging Spanish recognition of the independence of the American colonies to improve the British merchant's opportunities for profitable trade.[58] *El Emigrado Observador* survived twelve issues (1828-1829) but did not advance far toward its announced goal of explaining Spain's backwardness as compared with England and France. An unsigned article praised in vague terms an eighteenth-century Spanish book, "full of luminous ideas," which anticipated Smith, Say, and Storch;[59] and an article by "R. Z." adopted the liberal position of denouncing ecclesiastical mortmain, asserting that 15 per cent of Spain's arable land was inalienable on this account.

An Impartial Examination of the Dispute between Spain and Her American Colonies, first published in London in 1811,[60] may be thought of as the commencement of Flórez Estrada's career as an economist. Despite the title, more than half of the 283-page book is devoted to a "brief exposition" of the "principles" of political economy. "My whole system," Flórez declared, "reduces to a single principle: the prosperity of nations always depends on employing the greatest possible number of workers in agriculture, industry, and trade." Throughout Spanish history monopoly and inflation were the major forces restricting employment and output. Because it induced a rise in prices and curbed consumption, the influx of precious metals was the root of Spain's decline. For the same reason, paper money was an iniquitous invention: even if as

---

(above) are to the first edition, specifically: I, 36 and 113; II, 64-74, 285-292; III, 196-202, 395-415; IV, 87-113, 117-124; and V, 104-117.

[57] Llorens Castillo, *Liberales y románticos*, p. 283.

[58] *El Emigrado Observador, periódico mensual, por una sociedad de españoles refugiados en Inglaterra y Francia*, Nos. 1-12 (London, 1828-1829).

[59] Marqués de Santa Cruz de Marcenado, *Rapsodia económico-política monárquica* (Madrid, 1732).

[60] The English edition (London, 1812) followed the Spanish, *Examen imparcial de las disensiones de la América con la España* (London, 1811), of which an enlarged and corrected edition was published in Spain (Cadiz, 1812). The latter is reproduced in *Biblioteca de autores españoles*, CXIII (Madrid, 1958), 1-161.

good as gold, the depreciation of paper in terms of other goods could not be avoided. Free trade, to Flórez Estrada, was an immutable truth: "even if tariffs were abolished by only one country, very considerable advantages would redound to it, especially to Spain, whose principal source of wealth must be reckoned in the perfection of its agriculture." It is doubtless true, as one of his biographers notes, that Flórez Estrada profited from his proximity to the "brilliant flowering of economists" in the London of 1810-1811; but none is mentioned by name in the *Impartial Examination*. Quoting Smith to the effect that if revenues fall short of expenditures, it is better to raise taxes than to borrow, Flórez identifies the author only as "a learned Englishman."[61]

In England for the second time (1814-1820), Flórez Estrada renewed his study of constitutional government and in 1818 published his *Representation to H.C.M. Ferdinand VII, King of Spain, in Defense of the Cortes.*[62] The *Representation*, which censures the royal advisers more than it blames the king personally for Spain's distress, concludes with a seven-point proposal for remedying the problems created by the dissolution of the Cortes in 1814. It was not too late, he thought, to effect a reconciliation which would make the Americas a part of the Spanish nation. One step in this direction would be a declaration of complete free trade between Spain and her overseas possessions and between them and the rest of the world. Martínez Cachero has accumulated evidence to show that the *Representation* made its way into Spain and influenced those who staged the revolt which caused Ferdinand in 1820 to renew his promise to uphold the Constitution of 1812.[63]

The end of constitutional government in 1823 saw Flórez Estrada, again under sentence of death, escape once more to England.

[61] In addition to the writings of Flórez Estrada, I have consulted these recent studies of the man and his work: Luis Alfaro Martínez Cachero, *Alvaro Flórez Estrada, su vida, su obra política y sus ideas económicas* (Oviedo, 1961); the same author's "Prólogo" to the *Obras de Alvaro Flórez Estrada*, Vol. II (*Biblioteca de autores españoles*, CXIII, Madrid, 1958); the "Introducción" by Miguel Artola Gallego, in *ibid.*, Vol. I; and, above all, the unpublished Ph.D. dissertation of Marcia Dell Davidson, "Three Spanish Economists of the Enlightenment: Campomanes, Jovellanos, Flórez Estrada" (Duke University, 1962).

[62] The English edition (London, 1819) followed the Spanish "Representación a S.M.C. el señor don Fernando VII en defensa de las Cortes," in *El Español Constitucional*, I (London, 1818), 26-51 and 65-91. Spanish editions also were published in Madrid and Mexico in 1820.

[63] *Alvaro Flórez Estrada*, pp. 60-62.

By this time there was little hope of preserving the Spanish empire in America, a situation which inspired Flórez to speculate on the consequences of the cessation of the flow of American gold and silver into Europe. His *Reflections on the Present Mercantile Distress Experienced in Great Britain and More or Less Afflicting Other Nations on the Continent of Europe,*[64] signalizes his pessimistic conclusion that "the origin of this unknown ailment is none other than the result of the diminution of the quantity of coin which annually used to be imported into Europe, a diminution which could not fail to follow the important crisis of the independence of the country 'harvesting' the gold and silver." He denied the possibility of restoring Europe's favorable balance of trade with the New World: with independence, the new nations would be less dependent on Europe. Scoffing at the idea of reversing deflation through paper money issues, Flórez recommended increased (private) capital outlays to discover and exploit gold and silver mines in Europe.[65]

Flórez Estrada's major work, "Course in Political Economy," was published in London in 1828. Including a French translation, the *Curso* went through seven editions before the author's death in 1853.[66] For over a quarter of a century it remained the standard text in Spanish universities; and the author, who re-entered political life on his return to Spain in 1834, was the nation's best-known economist, although there was no dearth of dissenters from his extremely liberal views.

In the *Curso* Flórez Estrada makes amends for his earlier failure to credit the economists from whom he had drawn inspiration. He had not hesitated, he said, to appropriate the ideas of others and even quote them literally "when I considered them expressed with clarity and precision." His main purpose was to disseminate the recent discoveries in the science of economics, especially for

[64] London, 1826. This was a translation of *Efectos producidos en Europa por la baja en el producto de las minas de plata* (London, 1824), of which two different editions were published in 1827 under the title *Reflexiones acerca del mal extraordinario que en el día aflige a la Inglaterra y que más o menos incomoda ya a las naciones más industriosas de la Europa.*

[65] The 1827 edition of *Reflexiones*, including the author's reply to his critics (who are not named) is reproduced in *Biblioteca de autores españoles,* CXII, 333-357.

[66] *Curso de economía política* (London, 1828; Paris, 1831; Madrid, 1835, 1840, 1848, and 1852); *Cours eclectique d'économie politique* (3 vols.; Paris, 1833). The 1852 edition is reproduced in *Biblioteca de autores españoles,* CXII, 1-332.

the benefit of Spaniards and South Americans, who lacked a "complete" economic treatise in their own language. Having said this much by way of acknowledging his intellectual debts, Flórez Estrada proceeded to point out the errors of his predecessors and to develop his own ideas. On several points he was convinced that his was a "new theory."

In discussing the "industrial system" Flórez observed that Smith was not the first to find fallacies in both the "mercantile system" and the "agricultural system." Beccaria, Ortes, and Verri—all Italians—anticipated Smith; inexplicably, Flórez ignores Hume completely. Throughout the *Curso* Smith is quoted more often than any other writer, despite the fact that the *Wealth of Nations* "contains not only notable defects but errors of immense transcendency." The preliminary list of faults includes the lack of method and irrelevant digressions; the claim that domestic trade is more advantageous than foreign trade; the assertion that labor is productive only if it results in a salable product; the belief that individual interest may not always be consistent with public interest; the statement that the price of wheat is most stable; and, most regrettably, the belief that the burden of a tax on land always falls on the landlord. Nevertheless, Smith was the founder of the system of economic thought adopted by Europe's foremost economists. The *Wealth of Nations*, "for the liberalness as well as the solidness of the principles expounded in it, must be placed among those books which had most influence in the progress of nations and which have produced the most good for humanity."

Running through the list of the principal writers in the first three decades of the nineteenth century, Flórez Estrada rendered the following judgments: Say, whose chief merit was to make Smith better known on the Continent, also made two contributions: the first was to prove that "market demand depends exclusively on production" (Say's law); the second was to show that gluts result not from an increase of productive facilities but from the poor allocation of labor. Say's error was to consider rent an element of the cost of production. Malthus' population theory was one of "incalculable" value, and the bitter criticism of the *Essay* only proved that "there is no new theory which may not be resisted in the ratio of its significance." Townsend [*sic*], Steward [*sic*], Ricci, and others anticipated Malthus' population doctrine, but his contribution to the theory of rent was original. Ricardo discovered the error in Smith's wage theory, but the Ricardian analysis of rent, tithes, and public credit was erroneous. Sismondi was the first economist who, "not fearing the wrath which the upper and opulent classes might display," defended the interests of the laboring classes. McCulloch and James Mills rectified many "errors and inaccuracies" in the *Wealth of Nations*. McCulloch, in Flórez' opinion, was second only to Smith among British economists; but there were "substantial faults" in his *Encyclopaedia Britannica* article on taxation.[67] Finally, Richard Jones was singled out as the writer who corrected "capital errors" committed by Ricardo, Malthus, Mill, and McCulloch. It was Jones who demonstrated that rent can arise before the second-best land is brought under cultivation.

In Flórez Estrada's scheme political economy has four major divisions: Production, Distribution, Exchange, and Consumption. The analysis (in the *Curso*) of each of these draws on the work of the economists mentioned above, sometimes approving but often clarifying, amending, or refuting their doctrines. As on earlier (and later) occasions, he advocated free trade without admitting any of the exceptions Smith and other Classical writers recognized.[68] He also advocated free trade in ideas, for knowledge makes a man a contemporary of all ages and a citizen of all countries. On questions of money, prices, and public finance his views were substantially those expressed in *Reflections* (1824), although in the 1852 edition of the *Curso* he speculated on the probable effects of the discovery of gold in Siberia, California, and Australia. He deplored what had happened: "the abundance of gold will only produce evils and upheavals in society . . . such a discovery does not yield any lasting advantage."

While the *Curso* represents much the same sort of Classical eclecticism found in McCulloch's *Principles*, in one important re-

[67] McCulloch spoke of "some speculative individuals" who "think that it would be good policy for the governments of countries like the United States, which possess large tracts of fertile and unappropriated land, to retain it in property, letting it by public auction." This, to McCulloch, was a "very questionable position . . . a right of private property in land is the best stimulus to its improvement" (*An Article Practical and Theoretical on Taxation* [2nd ed.; Edinburgh, 1860], p. 10).

[68] When Richard Cobden visited Madrid in 1846, Flórez Estrada delivered an after-dinner speech in which he declared, "The man who gives Spain free trade will have conferred on his country a greater advantage than Columbus showing it the way to America" (*Biblioteca de autores españoles*, CXIII, xiv).

spect Flórez Estarda was a maverick, anticipating Henry George by half a century but attracting even fewer followers than the American dissenter. From the premise (which he traced to the Book of Genesis) that labor is the source of all appropriable wealth, Flórez deduced that land, whose existence required no human effort, ought not to be privately owned: "there exist no solid grounds for opposing its distribution by the head of the state, in accordance with the laws of Creation in which the right of property is established." He translated and inserted in the *Curso* an excerpt from Comte and the *Encyclopaedia Britannica* article on "Property." Like George, Flórez found the man-made arrangements for renting land the major cause of humanity's ills: "Without fear of contradiction, with a single exception, it can be asserted that 99 out of 100 individuals committed to wrest their subsistence from land belonging to someone else form everywhere a class destined never to escape from misery, degradation, and corruption."

Essentially, Flórez Estrada proposed the nationalization of all agricultural land, although he would carry out expropriation gradually and indemnify the owners. In February, 1836, in a desperate move to reduce the national debt, the government decreed the sale of public lands, including Church estates seized under the desamortization laws. In a newspaper article Flórez urged the government to keep the land in the public domain and parcel it out to landless farmers on long-term leases. In the *Social Question*, written in 1839, he broadened his proposal to recommend systematic government purchases of land to increase the number of farmers who would become tenants of the state, the only way, he said, "to improve the lot of the unfortunate proletarian class."[69]

The conservative press and most of his fellow economists ridiculed Flórez' proposals; some branded him a socialist. His severest critic was Ramón de la Sagra, who called his ideas "even more ab-

[69] The articles, "Del Uso que debe hacerse de los bienes nacionales," "Contestación . . . a las impugnaciones hechas a su escrito sobre el uso que deba hacerse de los bienes nacionales," and "Contestación . . . al artículo publicado en el número 194 de 'El Corresponsal' en se impugna por el Sr. D. Ramón La Sagra su escrito la cüestión social," are reproduced in the *Biblioteca de autores españoles*, CXII, 359-406. *La cüestión social, o sea origen, latitud y efectos del derecho de propiedad* (Madrid, 1839) was incorporated into the 1840, 1848, and 1852 editions of the *Curso*. On the desamortization legislation, see Alfonso García Tejero, *Historia político-administrativa de Mendizábal, dedicada al pueblo liberal español* (Madrid, 1858).

surd than those of the Sansimonians"; but in 1848 Sagra praised Proudhon and advocated "pacific" land reform via expropriation with compensation. Elected in 1851, Flórez Estrada joined Sagra as a member of the Academie des Sciences Morales et Politiques.[70]

IV

The thirty-year "reign" of Flórez Estrada's *Curso* diverted attention from other Spanish texts which, with varying success, expounded the new economics in the early 1800's. These runners-up were numerous, and some influenced the teaching of economics before the appearance of Flórez' *Curso*.

In 1797 Ramón Campos, a physics professor, published a slender volume in which he "reduced" economics to a few "exact, clear, and simple principles."[71] In eight short chapters Campos presented a reasonably accurate digest of Smithian theories of value, wages, profit, capital, and taxation; but it may be doubted that he fulfilled his declared purpose of making economics "universally accepted among the number of exact sciences." Smith, he said, "made himself immortal by the brilliance with which he presented the substance of Steuart's work."

The author of a "principles" text published in 1812, who signed himself A.D.P., lamented his inability to complete the general treatise he had planned. His 111-page duodecimo volume teaches little, although the author did denounce bullionism. Revealing his identity, Antonio Domingo de Porlier translated a major portion of Cantillon's *Essai*, believing however that the work was that of the "famous English economist" David Hume. The translation was "cleansed of ideas and expressions which might conflict with our opinions, usages, and customs."[72]

In 1816 Fray Eudaldo Jaumeandreu published his "rudiments" of political economy, a 354-page text in the form of a catechism, which he used for many years in the "free school" supported by the

[70] Joaquín Costa, *Colectivismo agrario en España* (Madrid, 1915), pp. 13-26; Ramón de la Sagra, "Sur la propriété," *Representant du Peuple*, June 13-14, 1848; *Séances et travaux de l'Academie des Sciences Morales et Politiques: Compte Rendu*, XII (1847), 470.

[71] *La economía reducida a principios exactos, claros y sencillos* (Madrid, 1797).

[72] Antonio Domingo Porlier Saenz de Astequieta, *Principios de la economía general y de la estadística de España* (Madrid, 1812) and *Fuentes de la riqueza pública* (Madrid, 1833).

Barcelona Board of Trade.[73] The professor's questions and answers were based on Smith and Say, but Jaumeandreu considered the *Wealth of Nations* and the *Traité* too difficult for beginners. He departed from the Classical position principally on commercial policy. Free trade, he thought, was only advantageous to countries in the same stage of industrial development; and in this argument he may have been the first of several Spaniards who anticipated List. Employed as a consultant to Catalan industrialists, Jaumeandreu, in his second book (1836), elaborated his vigorous defense of protective tariffs for underdeveloped countries.[74]

José Joaquín de Mora's "Catechism of Political Economy," published during his exile in London, owes its inspiration to Smith, "the father of political economy," and the English "liberal politico-economic school." Mora refers to conversations with McCulloch, whom he regarded as "the greatest economist living." Reflecting on the Malthusian controversy, he doubted the possibility of "explaining in one word enigmas so obscure and involved." Richly endowed and sparsely settled, Spain dispelled the fear of overpopulation, while poor and overcrowded Ireland vindicated those who considered human fertility the enemy of happiness and wealth. The appendix of the *Catecismo* is devoted to the teaching of economics. Mora dwelt on the practical usefulness of economic knowledge, noting with satisfaction that "the profound economist Ricardo" had made a half-million pounds in the stock market.[75]

Mora spent ten years (1828-1838) in South America. In Chile he edited the liberal newspaper, *El Mercurio Chileno*, and founded the Liceo de Chile, for which he planned to write an economics text based on Smith, Say, Ricardo, Storch, and McCulloch. He returned to Spain in the 1840's and published *De la libertad del comercio*, an uncompromising defense of free trade. To prohibit trade among nations was not only uneconomical but immoral.[76]

[73] *Rudimentos de economía política* (Barcelona, 1816). In 1814 Jaumeandreu spoke at the inauguration of an economics course in Mallorca. He praised Say and declared (among other *obiter dicta*) that all taxation should be direct (*Oración inaugural . . . en la abertura de la cátedra de economía civil establecida en la ciudad de Palma por la Diputación Provincial de Mallorca* (Palma, 1814).

[74] *Curso elemental de economía política con aplicación a la legislación económica de España* (Barcelona, 1836). See also L. Beltrán, *Historia de las doctrinas economicas* (Barcelona, 1961), pp. 100-103.

[75] *Catecismo de economía política* (London and Mexico City, n.d.).

[76] *De la libertad del comercio* (Sevilla, 1843; Mexico City, 1853).

He predicted (1843) the repeal of the Corn Law and declared that the "immortal Huskisson" ought to be counted "among the most illustrious benefactors of mankind."

The Marquis de Valle Santoro wrote a principles text which went through three editions (1829-1840).[77] Like many Spaniards, Valle Santoro thought the works of Smith and Say were too voluminous, abstract, and diffuse for the average reader; in his *Elementos* their ideas were transformed into "ordinary and simple language, free from all scientific jargon." The result, of course, was oversimplification. In the third edition Valle Santoro criticized Flórez Estrada's "Social Question," arousing Flórez to reply that although Valle Santoro appreciated the soundness of Smith's precepts, he was "ignorant of all their implications."

José Espinosa de los Monteros, who identified himself as an infantry colonel, composed a lengthy "Treatise of Political Economy Applied to Spain."[78] The "applications" are acknowledged to be mainly drawn from Say's *Cartilla*. Despite the fame of Smith and Say, it was significant, Espinosa thought, that England and France adopted free trade only with respect to commodities in which they had an obvious comparative advantage. Tariffs and import restrictions were necessary to create a favorable milieu for industry to develop; but "great caution" should be exercised, lest protection last beyond the time industry required to achieve a competitive position. Espinosa thought the essence of many modern ideas could be found in the neglected writings of early Spanish economists.

Eusebio María del Valle's *Curso*, published in 1842, was the product of twenty-four years of teaching at the University of Madrid.[79] He acknowledged his indebtedness to Flórez Estrada but also quoted freely (abjuring plagiarism) from Sismondi, Ganilh, Destutt de Tracy, Malthus, Ricardo, Storch, and Jean Baptiste and Louis Say. Del Valle followed Jaumeandreu in regarding commercial policy as a relative matter: beginning with England ("the industrial history of nations is the history of [trade] restrictions"), he went on to say that if underdeveloped countries did not adopt

[77] Marqués de Valle Santoro (Barón de Claret), *Elementos de economía polí tica con aplicación particular a España* (Madrid, 1829, 1833, and 1840). Valle Santoro also wrote a *Memoria sobre la balanza del comercio y examen del estado actual de la riqueza de España* (Madrid, 1830).

[78] *Tratado de economía política aplicada a España* (Madrid, 1831).

[79] *Curso de economía política* (Madrid, 1842).

protective tariffs, they would never escape the hopeless stagnation of a people "merely and abjectly agricultural." The rise of the United States showed that Americans had been "faithful to the doctrine which they learned under English domination."

Andrés Borrego, an exile in England from 1823 to 1833 and finance minister of Spain in 1840, published his "Principles of Political Economy" in 1844.[80] He praised the Spanish economists who followed Smith, Malthus, and McCulloch, although he felt that none except Valle Santoro had made "the economic conditions peculiar to our country the object of research directed to applying to our state the scientific remedies which it demands." Flórez Estrada in particular "follows the purely crematistic tendency of Smith, Ricardo, Malthus" and "only incidentally touches on the special questions which science will be called on to resolve in Spain." The central task of economics was to find that combination of all the productive powers of society which would maximize general welfare. In this he found Sismondi the best guide.

Manuel Colmeiro, whose most important writing falls in the two decades after 1850, produced a two-volume text in 1845.[81] Calling his work "eclectic," Colmeiro said an economist ought not to be either too "spiritualistic" or too materialistic. He should reject the mysticism of De Maistre, the skepticism of Ferrier, the dogmatism of Ricardo, the crematistic tendencies of Smith and the English school, and the radical doctrines of Bentham, San Simon, and Pecquer. Colmeiro developed the infant-industry argument for protection, a position taken by many "liberal" writers in Spain, going back to Alonso Ortiz.

In addition to these "principles" texts, Spanish writers produced an extensive literature, much of it polemical, inspired by current economic issues. No question was more persistently and vehemently debated than commercial policy. While, as Tallada put it, "a Pleiade of brilliant orators and writers" argued the merits of "Manchesterian liberalism," those who rejected free trade as the appropriate policy for Spain were at least as articulate as the so-called Pleiade. Protectionism, nevertheless, lost ground between 1841 and 1869,

[80] *Principios de economía política con aplicación a la reforma de aranceles de aduana, a la situación de la industria fabril en Cataluña, y al mayor y más rápido incremento de la riqueza nacional* (Madrid, 1844); Palau lists a second edition, 1877.
[81] *Tratado elemental de economía política ecléctica* (Madrid, 1845).

and in the latter year the Spanish tariff as well as Britain's appeared
to justify Disraeli's observation that protectionism was not only
dead but damned.[82]

Two prolific writers, Manuel María Gutiérrez and Juan Güell
y Ferrer, were the most vigorous leaders of the attack on the liberal
drift in Spanish trade policy. A translator of Say's *Traité* and Mill's
Elements, Gutiérrez in 1818 inaugurated courses in economics in
Málaga with a stirring address praising Smith and the Classical
writers. Two decades later he "confessed" that in his youth he had
been too unfamiliar with the "practical world" to realize that free
trade would not work. His detractors claimed that he was on the
payroll of the Catalan textile manufacturers' association, a charge
which Gutiérrez denied, although he said he would not be ashamed
if it were true. The economics of Gutiérrez' position practically
reduces to the argument for equalizing the selling price of foreign
and domestic goods: by virtue of a tariff the latter would acquire
"an artificial power . . . to compete."[83]

Güell was perhaps Spain's best-known economist in the second
half of the nineteenth century—that is, in the period in which
academicians as well as legislators increasingly doubted the wisdom of free trade and saw Spain re-enter the protectionist camp.[84]
Although Güell, like Gutiérrez, defended the interests of the Catalan
textile industry, he also advocated a protective tariff for Spain's
infant machinery industry. Textile manufacturers, accustomed to
importing British machinery, discounted the prospects of develop-

[82] J. M. Tallada, *Historia de las finanzas españolas en el siglo xix* (Madrid,
1946), pp. 242-248.

[83] Gutiérrez' bibliography consists of numerous periodical pieces in addition
to the following pamphlets and books: *Discurso inaugural y sucinta esposición
de los principios de economía política demostrados por Mr. Juan Bta. Say* (Málaga, 1819); *Comercio libre o funesta teoría de la libertad absoluta* (Madrid,
1834); *Nuevas consideraciones sobre libertad absoluta de comercio y puertos
francos* (Madrid, 1839); *Impugnación a las cinco proposiciones de Pebrer sobre
los grandes males que causa la ley de aranceles a la nación en general, a la Cataluña en particular, y a las mismas fábricas catalanas* (Madrid, 1837); *Contestación a un artículo sobre libertad de comercio del Excmo. Sr. D. Antonio Alcalá Galiano* (Madrid, 1843).
José Arias de Miranda's *Breves reflexiones sobre algunos puntos de la cüestión
de el comercio libre en España que pueden servir de contestación a todos los im-
pugnadores de este doctrina* (Madrid, 1844) is one of several rebuttals of Gutiérrez' arguments.

[84] On this transition, see Manuel Pugés, *Como triunfó el protectionismo en
España* (Barcelona, 1913) and Mariano Sebastián, *El fracaso del intento de una
economía cosmopólita* (Madrid, 1957), pp. 87-99.

ing at home efficient machinery manufactures; Güell believed that the industry could in a short time become competitive with English imports. In general, Güell's theory is similar to that of List's *National System*: he said he would favor reducing or removing protective duties "as soon as [Spain's] circumstances are equal to England's in its present condition." Even Cobden, he claimed, admitted that free trade was a relative matter.[85]

The debate over taxes and public debts continued unabated, as one finance minister after another wrestled unsuccessfully with the country's fiscal problems. While an anonymous Friend of the Farmers was denouncing the "monstrosity" of direct taxation, García de la Madrid argued that Say's principles of taxation recognized both the advantages and disadvantages of direct taxes; and Pastor found in the "natural law" of political economy, discovered by Smith and Say, a safe guide to fiscal legislation.[86] In an essay approved for publication by the Madrid Economic Society, Aurrecoechea declared that direct taxation was theoretically the best, but that not even England, "the wisest nation in the world in the science of economics," employed predominantly direct taxes. He quoted Smith's explanation of the "impossibility of taxing the people, in proportion to their revenue. . . ."[87] In 1824 Pablo Pebrer, writing in London, warned of the bankruptcy of Spain if the proposed British loan were consumated: with the new loan Spain's foreign debt would rise to £13.5 million. A few years later Pebrer published a book on English finance in which he proposed paying off the public debt with a capital levy of 9.25 per cent. He did not explicitly recommend this remedy for Spain, but in dedicating his work to the Queen he observed that "Spanish credit has already experienced the good effects of your Majesty's policy."[88] This was

[85] Most of Güell's writings are collected in *Escritos económicos del Excmo. Sr. D. Juan Güell y Ferrer, con una introducción por D. Adolfo Blanch* (Barcelona, 1880).

[86] Amigo de los Labradores, *Observaciones sobre las perjuicios y monstruosidad de la contribución general directa* (Madrid, 1820); Miguel García de la Madrid, *Principios o máximas sobre los impuestos deducidas de las obras del Say* (Barcelona, 1820); Estevan Pastor, *Moral filosófica aplicada a las leyes de contribuciones* (Madrid, 1822).

[87] José María Aurrecoechea, "Observaciones político-económicas sobre la hacienda pública de España," *El Amigo del País: Periódico de la Sociedad Económica Matritense*, II (Madrid, 1844), 156-172, 217-224, and 254-256.

[88] "Exposición a la nación española y al Congreso por el ciudano A. P. Pebrer," *El Español Constitucional*, IV, No. 31 (London, 1824), 616-632, and *Taxation,*

an excess of optimism. Recognizing the need for a better understanding of fiscal problems, in 1841 Canga Argüelles, Flórez Estrada, and five other economists drafted the statutes of a National Society for Finance and Public Credit; but government opposition seems to have killed the proposal.[89]

Worth at least brief mention are a half-dozen other writers who drew inspiration from British authors and adopted their ideas to the Spanish scene. Estevan Boutelou, the royal gardener, was one of several Spaniards who admired Arthur Young. He deduced from Young's description of English agriculture that the four- to five-thousand-acre estates of Andalucía were inefficient: their division into small farms would increase output and encourage population growth.[90] Cambronero demanded the reform of the system of entailed estates: Smith, Say, Sismondi, as well as Jovellanos, had shown that entail was the cause of low agricultural yields.[91] Luyando, "captain of a frigate," was one of several voices clamoring for the dissolution of the tobacco monopoly.[92] Sacasa challenged the legislation fixing the maximum rate of interest: economists from Hume to Bentham had demonstrated the futility of interfering with the market forces which determine "the price for the use of capital."[93] Another author described Bentham as the "ingenious creator" of savings banks: "like almost everything useful," the institution was born in Britain.[94]

Juan López Peñalver (apparently a pseudonym) may deserve

Revenue, Expenditure, Power Statistics, and Debt of the Whole British Empire (London, 1833).

[89] *El Amigo del País*, I (Madrid, 1841), 108.

[90] "Observaciones sobre las grandes labores de Andalucia e ideas sobre las utilidades y perjuicios que resultan al estado y a la agricultura de la excesiva extensión de los grandes cortijos," *Semanario de Agricultura y Artes*, XXIII, No. 590 (Madrid, 1808), 214-252.

[91] Manuel María Cambronero, *La institucion de mayorazgos examinada histórica y filosóficamente con un proyecto de ley para su reforma* (Madrid, 1820).

[92] José Luyando, *Examen de las ventajas que producirá el desestanco del tobaco y ensayo de única contribución* (Cádiz, 1813). There was also an *Apéndice a el ensayo de única contribución* (Cádiz, 1813) and a reply to Luyando in Rafael Gómez Roubaud, *Manifesto documentado en respuesta a los hechos que se sientan en el papel del capitán de fragata Don José Luyando* (Cádiz, 1813).

[93] José Sacasa, *Disertación contra las leyes que tasan el uso del dinero* (Madrid, 1821).

[94] Francisco Quevedo y San Cristóbal, "Memoria sobre el modo de establecer y generalizar en España las cajas de ahorros y sociedades de socorros mutuos," *El Amigo del País*, I (1844), 27-36.

a unique place in the history of Spanish economic thought. López learned from Classical economists the subsistence theory of wages and sought to find empirical proof of it. Observing that the laborer's family spent 70 per cent of its income for bread, he established a positive correlation between the market price of wheat and the death rate. With the price of wheat and the wage rate as variables, he devised an equation for estimating changes in the level of living from "comfort" to "starvation." Professor Estapé, practically the only one who has noticed López' work, regards him as a precursor of Jevons.[95]

V

To trace the migration of thought is to show how ideas surmount the barriers of language, geography, and intolerance. In Spain, as late as the 1840's a few lonely voices were advocating the return to *Colbertismo*; but most writers accepted as profound and irreversible the revolution in economics which, beginning with the Physiocrats, had its greatest impact with Smith and the Classical school.

Clearly, English economic thought flowed into Spain; but it may be argued that it came in intermittent rivulets rather than in a steady stream. For this there are several explanations. Civil and European wars created political and social conditions which impeded, without completely throttling, the flow of ideas. English is not an easy language for the Spaniard; and his greater familiarity with another Romance language explains the many French translations (or Spanish translations of French translations) of English books, which were imperfect substitutes for Spanish versions based on the original English. One may ask why, if a Spaniard was encouraged to translate the *Wealth of Nations*, no one turned his hand to translating the *Principles* of Malthus or Ricardo. There is no satisfactory answer which does not involve the element of chance in the Spaniard's becoming acquainted with the work and having the desire, skill, and means to undertake the task.

Chance also played a part in the accessibility of the products of English presses. Men of means and those who had personal con-

[95] *Reflexiones sobre la variación del precio del trigo* (Madrid, 1812), and Fabián Estapé, "Las 'Reflexiones sobre la variacion del precio del trigo' de Juan López de Peñalver," *Anales de Economía*, XIII-XIV (1953-1955), 173-205.

tacts abroad could depend on receiving foreign publications regularly. Jovellanos, for instance, relied on Lord Holland to send him British publications through diplomatic channels. But there was no library or learned society whose acquisition practice could assure Spaniards of prompt or even eventual receipt of books from England. Incidentally, I would be interested to know how Alonso Ortiz acquired his copy of the *Wealth of Nations*, which he incorrectly identified as the eighth edition.

The role of official and clerical censorship in barring foreign literature is important, although it may easily be exaggerated. Only the 1788 French translation of the *Wealth of Nations* was proscribed by the Inquisition; the English text was never on the *Index*. The *Defensa de la usura* was published in Paris, or so it appears from the title page, but the work of Bentham was not prohibited in Spain. Yet even after the dissolution of the Inquisition, censorship was not uncommon; and the prospect that a book might be banned could have been a deterrent to authors and translators. Probably a greater deterrent was the limited market, given the low level of income and literacy. Some "practical" foreign books, such as those dealing with new crops and farming methods, appeared in Spanish translation, thanks to a government subsidy. This avenue of financial support was rarely open to prospective translators of theoretical treatises. The University of Salamanca, however, may have supported Toribio Nuñez' digests of the work of Bentham.

A few Spaniards had a comprehensive view of English economic literature by virtue of living in England and in some cases talking with British economists. They also had an opportunity to judge the consistency of economic thought with the contemporaneous development of the British economy. British writers, on the other hand, knew little of Spain and afforded small comfort to Spaniards who wondered whether the policy implications of Classical theory should not be modified to suit their relatively backward country. Cobden, who visited Spain in 1846, proclaimed the universal blessings of free trade; and in this he was seconded by his host, Flórez Estrada. But the suspicion that the recommendations of economic liberalism, if adopted by Spain, would redound largely to the advantage of England was frequently expressed; and it may not have been wholly unfounded.

At each step in the reception of foreign economic thought in Spain there were writers to proclaim the finality of what Smith or Say or Ricardo had said. Ramón Campos in 1797 presumed to "reduce" Smithian economics to a few scientific principles, and a generation later the editors of *El Censor* (1820) thought that economics had progressed so far that "hardly a single fact remains that may not be explained by its fundamental principles with almost the same confidence and certainty as . . . the explanation of mathematical sciences." Although, in the course of a half-century, debate among economists had demonstrated the inconclusiveness of many economic "principles," in 1849 Antonio Cervera asserted that the "liberal principle" and laissez faire provided the only

anchor of salvation for modern societies. . . . The principles of economic science, like those of other sciences, do not admit of any exception. Natural laws in the moral order, as in the physical order, are eternal, invariable. All principles are absolute or they are not principles; it is therefore a grievous error to maintain that there is no absolute principle in economics. . . . It is lamentable that eclecticism has been injected into all the moral sciences, because it has disfigured them and reduced them to nullity. It has also caused immense harm to economic science, giving some people an occasion for establishing the absurd theory of non-absolute principles.[96]

An otherwise obscure writer, Cervera had this to say in *El Amigo del Pais*, the journal of the Madrid Economic Society. It is curious but surely coincidental that *El Amigo* suspended publication the following year. It is certainly not true that Spanish economists were closing up shop because, as Cervera implies, the "absolute principle" had been discovered.

[96] "Economía Política: Principios absolutos y no absolutos," *El Amigo del País,* VII (1849), 17-18.

Economic Ideas in the Development of Jamaica

Craufurd D. W. Goodwin

By the end of the eighteenth century Jamaica had become one of Great Britain's most valuable colonies.[1] It produced large quantities of sugar and lesser amounts of other staples, and it provided excellent harbor for the navy in the Caribbean.[2] During the nineteenth century, however, the island underwent periods of serious economic, political, and social upheaval. First, the old "mercantile system" of close economic integration with the mother country began to deteriorate and expose the colony to the uncertainties of world markets; then, in 1807, abolition of the slave trade eliminated the principal source of new manual labor; finally, emancipation in 1833 forced the white colonists to shift from compulsion to incentives and to accept former slaves as equal participants in the economy. In this paper I shall outline against the background of economic and social change the transfer to Jamaica of British economic ideas during the critical hundred years from roughly the last quarter of the eighteenth century to the beginning of the last quarter of the nineteenth century. This period was significant for the development of the ideas which were transferred as well as for Jamaica; it saw British political economy move from the polemics of the later mercantilists through Adam Smith and Ricardo to the completed Classical system of John Stuart Mill, Sr., and Cairnes.

MR. GOODWIN *is assistant provost and director of international studies at Duke University, where he is associate professor of economics. Two of his books are* Canadian Economic Thought *and* Economic Enquiry in Australia.

[1] It may even be argued that Jamaica and the other tropical possessions were central to Britain's rise to commercial prominence. See Phyllis Deane, *The First Industrial Revolution* (Cambridge, 1965), p. 53.

[2] For general background to this paper, see particularly, Gisela Eisner, *Jamaica, 1830-1930* (Manchester, 1961); Douglas Hall, *Free Jamaica, 1838-1865, An Economic History* (New Haven, 1959); Philip D. Curtin, *Two Jamaicas: The Role of Ideas in a Tropical Colony, 1838-1865* (Cambridge, Mass., 1955); and Sir Alan Burns, *History of the British West Indies* (2nd ed.; New York, 1965).

The materials cited in the paper are books, pamphlets, periodicals, and government reports written by residents of Jamaica and published either on the island or elsewhere. Little effort has been made to canvas manuscript sources or newspapers. The special character of works preserved in libraries may give bias to the account, but it is hoped that if the items consulted were not always the most significant, they were at least representative.[3]

The first section of the paper deals briefly with the source of economic ideas in Great Britain and then more extensively with media for their transmission from the metropolis to the colony. Later sections cover use and modification of the ideas in Jamaica.

The Source of Economic Ideas and the Media for Their Transfer

Economic analysis fascinated British thinkers as early as the Middle Ages, and many of the most significant writings of the mercantilist period came from Britain.[4] But the flowering of British political economy occurred in the late eighteenth century during the years when the present study begins. The outstanding single work of the period is, of course, Adam Smith's *Wealth of Nations*. This book and other attractions quickly brought to the subject numerous able, industrious, and articulate writers.[5]

Several factors account for the ready transferability of the economic doctrine which was developed by the Classical economists of Great Britain. First, a wide spectrum of writers with varying levels of sophistication, ranging from rigorous mathematicians and logicians to the rankest popularizers, took up the subject. Readers could find their political economy in the form which suited them best. Second, the close relationship between theory and policy in political economy, made clear by most writers, gave an urgency to

---

[3] Works cited are, with a few exceptions, contained in the libraries of one or more of the following institutions: The Institute of Jamaica, Kingston; The Royal Commonwealth Society, London; and the British Museum, London.

[4] See, for example, Jacob Viner, *Studies in the Theory of International Trade* (New York, 1937).

[5] Accounts of the development of economic thought during this crucial period can be found in most of the standard histories, e.g., J. A. Schumpeter, *History of Economic Analysis* (New York, 1954), pp. 379-750; Overton H. Taylor, *A History of Economic Thought* (New York, 1960), pp. 49-270; and Joseph J. Spengler and William R. Allen, *Essays in Economic Thought: Aristotle to Marshall* (Chicago, 1960), pp. 259-453.

the subject, particularly for British emigrants to the extent that it was related to international trade and colonization.[6] Finally, Classical economics developed what was almost a religious fascination for many of its proponents; "schools" of disciples grew up around major figures such as David Ricardo, while practically all converts to political economy saw in the subject lessons for personal morality and even divine injunctions. These converts went forth not merely as sympathizers but as true believers and missionaries.[7] The success of British economic evangelists in transferring their doctrine to numerous foreign countries is well known.[8] This paper examines the peculiarities of the transfer of economic thought to a tropical colony.

Jamaica's culture during the period under examination was derived almost entirely from Great Britain. The indigenous inhabitants had been obliterated by the Spanish conquerors, and most traces of the Spaniards were destroyed in turn by the British. The African slaves were actively discouraged from retaining or developing their native culture, their religion, and their social customs.[9]

The most effective media for the transfer of ideas were visitors to Jamaica and the island's white inhabitants themselves, most of whom identified their interests closely with the imperial metropolis from which they came and to which they often returned. The flow of ideas took place through personal travel and the importation of publications, and by late in the eighteenth century works written by Jamaican residents were numerous enough to strengthen the direct impact of literature from abroad. Local newspapers and pamphlets contained extensive excerpts from the British press, while quarterlies and monthlies reproduced imported ideas intact and suggested applications to domestic surroundings. At first, coverage of economic matters, and particularly of theoretical topics, was not

[6] See Bert F. Hoselitz, ed., *Theories of Economic Growth* (Glencoe, Ill., 1960), chaps. ii-iv; and Lionel Robbins, *Robert Torrens and the Evolution of Classical Economics* (London, 1958).

[7] See Mark Blaug, *Ricardian Economics: A Historical Study* (New Haven, 1958).

[8] See, for example, Joseph Dorfman, *The Economic Mind in American Civilization* (5 vols.; New York, 1946-1959).

[9] Features of African tribal culture which survived in Jamaica are described in Madeline Kerr, *Personality and Conflict in Jamaica* (London, 1963), esp. pp. 137-155; Joseph J. Williams, *Psychic Phenomena in Jamaica* (New York, 1934), pp. 23-49; and Martha W. Beckwith, *Black Roadways: A Study of Jamaican Folk Life* (Chapel Hill, 1929).

extensive; most publishers may have felt with the editors of the *Jamaica Quarterly Journal and Literary Gazette* that they were "too inexperienced in the responsible undertaking of Editorship, to trust themselves in the selection of the various and dangerous subjects of political economy which may be offered; and too modest in the estimation of their own abilities, or their claim upon public attention, to conceive that their notice of such writings would add one tittle to the importance or elucidation of the subject they discussed."[10] Nevertheless, a beginning was made, and economic discussion became a significant part of colonial intellectual life.[11]

Political economy was brought to the colony first for use in contemporary debate. The agrarian bias of some eighteenth-century economic writings appealed particularly to the reading public of the colony, because all suggestions that land was the primary source of wealth were closely in accord with the planters' own preconceptions.[12] Colonists speculated also that the free-trade policies advocated by Adam Smith might benefit Jamaica. In 1818 one writer cited Smith at length to support an argument that unrestricted commerce would make the island the Caribbean entrepôt for sale of European goods, especially Irish textiles. He appealed for sympathetic attention from colonists to the writings of economists: "men who have reduced the affairs of commerce to fixed principles—whose ideas upon the subject are, as it were, methodically arranged, and who agree in opinion with the great writer on Political Economy, formed upon bases, which sophistry cannot shake, nor partial effects disprove—that *'all Trade ought to be left to itself.'* "[13] This writer singled out Smith for high praise: "It is difficult to withhold assent to the opinions of so acute a reasoner as that celebrated writer—who may, indeed, be looked upon as 'The Reformer of the Commercial Policy of Europe.' "[14]

[10] "Index Indicatorius," July, 1818, p. xix.

[11] The *New Jamaica Magazine*, published at the old capital city of Saint Jago de la Vega, was particularly interested in scientific agriculture; see "West India Agriculture," I (Jan., 1798), 23-29. The *Jamaica Magazine* and the *Jamaica Quarterly Journal and Literary Gazette*, published at Kingston during 1812 and 1818 respectively, reviewed and reprinted from British books and periodicals.

[12] A long serial article, translated from Spanish, entitled "Of the Honour and Profit of Agriculture" and distinctly Physiocratic in tone, was carried in the *Columbian Magazine*, Kingston, from October, 1796, to February, 1797.

[13] "Letter XVII. On the Best Means of Promoting the Trade of Ireland," *Jamaica Quarterly Journal and Literary Gazette*, II (1819), 371.

[14] *Ibid.*, II, 872.

Adam Smith's strictures on slavery and on the colonial system, however, soon raised alarm in the West Indies and led to condemnation more frequent and vigorous than admiration for his work. The increasing acceptance in Britain of Smithian economics and the rejection of mercantilist views on which, many Jamaicans believed, colonial prosperity rested, were seen as a threat to the continued fostering hand of the mother country.[15] Unambiguous interpretations of the "new" economic theory for colonial policy, such as the writings of William Spence, did not quiet the colonists' fears. In response to Caribbean appeals for assistance during the Napoleonic Wars, Spence had replied that, as prescribed by political economy, the colonies must be left for nature to take its course. "On every sound principle of mercantile policy, their disease does not admit of being cured by the applications of any medicine:— it is one of those cases which must be left to the *vis medicatrix naturae*, as the sole agent capable of effecting a radical cure."[16] Spence rejected all relief proposals as "wholly at variance with every rational principle of political economy," and he even went to the extent of suggesting that had Adam Smith been alive he would have recommended "the abandonment, forthwith, of all those plantations which are most unprofitable, by those Planters who are possessed of the smallest capital."[17] This was cold comfort for the Jamaicans.

John Rippingham, a local Jamaican literary figure, expressed in 1817 the anxiety of many colonists about the trend of political economy:

> The theory of national wealth has long been a favourite subject among political philosophers. The great principles in which those writers have concurred are sufficiently known; and the application of them to the various circumstances of state exigence has brought the practice and the theory into immediate opposition. It is, however, far from

[15] The *Columbian Magazine*, published at Kingston, condemned Smith both for suggesting that free labor could be as economical as slaves and for having expressed criticism of the character of Dr. Samuel Johnson. X. Y., "Comments on Dr. Adam Smith's History of Slavery," Nov., 1798, pp. 346-347; and Verax, "Defence of Dr. Johnson Against the Contemptuous Strictures of Dr. Adam Smith," June, 1800, pp. 663-667.

[16] William Spence, *The Radical Cause of the Present Distresses of the West-India Planters Pointed Out; and the Inefficiency of the Measures which Have Been Hitherto Proposed for Relieving Them, Demonstrated* (London, 1807), p. 3.

[17] *Ibid.*, pp. 4, 19-20, 63.

being clear, that either those elements or experience can greatly assist in the advancement of colonial interests.[18]

George Bridges, a vociferous spokesman for planter interests, took a less cautious position eighteen years later. He called for total rejection of political economy as a guide to colonial policy.

> Artful and selfish individuals, professing to instruct their fellow subjects in the mysteries of political economy, have lately declared our colonies to be a burden on the country!— It is high time, therefore, that the destinies of England should cease to be confided to heartless theorists and false economists, who have made every possible effort, within the last few years, to destroy our colonial commerce.[19]

During the British debates over Corn Law protection in the 1840's, the *Jamaica Monthly Magazine* was explicit in stating what had become the general colonial view that free trade, and with it political economy, would mean an end to prosperity in the islands. The periodical warned—"let the West Indies be sacrificed to the mania of new fangled political economy and the greediness of Brummagem tinkers, and ere many years have passed away the British people will find that like their Reform Bill, free trade has been a fallacy, and that Britain's chief glory, so long as she was glorious, arose from her devotion to 'SHIPS, COLONIES, and COMMERCE.' "[20] Jamaicans remained passionately concerned with economic questions, but after they recognized that their own case could not be defended easily through appeals to accepted theory, they lost confidence in the scientific approach and avoided discussion of principles. Economic homilies about thrift and industrious behavior continued to be repeated as often in the colony as in Britain, but usually without the customary deference to political economy.[21]

Not until after the final demise of the mercantile system in the 1840's and 1850's did some leading Jamaicans conclude that little

---

[18] *Jamaica, Considered in its Present State, Political, Financial, and Philosophical* (Kingston, 1817), p. 138.

[19] *Emancipation Unmask'd, in a Letter to the Right Honourable the Earl of Aberdeen* (London, 1835), p. 9.

[20] "The Brazils—the Late Debate," I (May, 1844), 190.

[21] A column by "The Economist" in the *Gossip*, published in Falmouth, Jamaica, during the 1820's, was reminiscent of Mrs. Marcet's works; the *Jamaica Journal of Arts, Sciences, and Literature*, Kingston, ran articles on such subjects as the importance of the division of labor, e.g., "On Agriculture," Oct., 1837, p. 119.

more could be gained from continued rejection of political economy, and cautiously they began to advocate dissemination of economic principles in the hope that answers could be provided for
the island's mounting problems. Around mid-century several amateur literary and scientific societies, of a type which became popular
throughout the Empire at this time, illustrated the change of outlook toward economic ideas by beginning to examine relatively
theoretical questions. The president of the Kingston Literary and
Philosophical Society, W. Arnold, explained the reasons for the
new reflective turn of mind: "Assuredly, a great deal of the apathy
or aversion which recently pervaded every rank in society, in applying the mind to serious, calm, and deliberate study, may mainly
be attributed to the late sudden alteration to which our social and
political relations had been subjected."[22] Another member of the
society saw in economic analysis the only hope for Jamaica's relief
from depression; he complained that "The problem of political
economy remains yet to be solved, and industry itself partakes of
the general disorder. The equilibrium between production and consumption, is everywhere lost; endless catastrophes in industry every
day take place."[23] The Jamaica Society of Arts (designated "Royal"
in 1856) was established in 1854 to plan for and encourage agricultural and industrial diversification, in accord with "principles of
political economy." Despite this society's intention to avoid "all
discussion of Polemical or Political subjects," its *Transactions*
touched increasingly upon such matters as causes of depression,
optimum scale in agricultural production, and methods of stimulating manufacturing development.[24] The Jamaica Institute, which
grew out of the Royal Society of Arts in 1879, continued the practice of making available public lectures and non-technical articles
illustrative of economic principles.[25]

[22] "Inaugural Address," *Transactions of the Kingston Literary and Philosophical Society* (1843), p. 12.
[23] A. Henriques, "Lecture on Anthropology," *ibid.*, p. 31.
[24] E.G., "The Lesser Staples and Other Articles of Commerce," *Transactions
of the Jamaica Society of Arts*, I (1854-1855), 72-75; "The Sugar Planter and
the Staple Agriculture of the Colony," *ibid.*, II (1856), 45-48; and J. Watson,
"Labour and its Advantages," *ibid.*, III (1857), 27-32. Papers presented to the
Royal Society were published also in the *Pioneer, and Jamaica Miscellany*, a
journal started apparently by the Kingston Mutual Improvement Society. See
Pioneer (1858), pp. 23-25.
[25] See *Report of the Governors of the Jamaica Institute, together with Reports from the Librarian and Curator, 1879-80* (Kingston, 1881); and similar

In addition to these quasi-adult education societies, several periodicals after mid-century began to express a new enthusiasm for economic study. The *Jamaica Quarterly Journal* in 1861 set out to attract "original and communicated articles in social science" (with only slight success), while the *West India Quarterly Magazine* in the same year established a section headed "Literature; Political and Social Science."[26] Public libraries also began to acquire works on economics, particularly by such standard authorities as Adam Smith, John Stuart Mill, Harriet Martineau, and Herbert Spencer.[27] The rapid growth of interest was illustrated by the Library of the House of Assembly. In 1852 this collection contained no more than two works which could be classified as economics; by 1865 it had sections both on "Political and Social Science and Legislation" and "Political Economy, Commerce, and Statistics" with a wide range of the major economic writings of the period, including books by Bentham, Brougham, Cairnes, Mill, Alison, Bastiat, Gilbart, McCulloch, Ricardo, Adam Smith, Dugald Stewart, Thornton, Tooke, and Arthur Young.[28]

Proposals were put forward repeatedly during the nineteenth century for the formal teaching of political economy in Jamaica. John Rippingham, even though fearful that acceptance of contemporary economic principles would lead to cessation of assistance to the colonies, cited Malthus on the value of political economy in the education of colonial public servants, and he advocated economic teaching and research as prerequisites for any form of self-government.[29] A "Plan of a College in Jamaica," circulated during 1838, contained a provision for lectures on political economy with the following caveat: "The Course of political economy might be

---

Reports in later years. See also Rev. John Radcliffe, *Objects of the Jamaica Institute* (Kingston, 1881).

[26] *Jamaica Quarterly Journal of Literature, Science and Art*, Kingston (July, 1861); and *West India Quarterly Magazine*, Kingston, I (1861-1862), 474.

[27] See *Catalogue of Books, the Property of the Colonial Literary and Reading Society to the 1st of June, 1864* (Kingston, 1864), pp. 32-33; and Public Library of Jamaica, *A Catalogue of Works Arranged According to Subjects* (Kingston, 1896).

[28] *An Alphabetical Catalogue of the Books in the Library of the Honble. House of Assembly of Jamaica* (St. Jago de la Vega, 1852); and *Catalogue of the Library of the Assembly of Jamaica* (Spanish Town, 1865).

[29] *Mr. Rippingham's Tract upon Education in General, Including a Statement of the Principles and Modes of Education in England and Scotland with Especial Considerations upon the Present State on Education in Jamaica* (Kingston, 1818), pp. 17, 25-26.

confined to the readings of a simple elementary volume of moderate extent, such as for example, the admirable 'conversation,' by Mrs. Marcet. . . ."[30] James M. Phillippo appended a similar plan for "A College in Jamaica" to his book *Jamaica: Its Past and Present State* (1843). He aimed at education of the "respectable youth of all colours" from the "intermediate portion of the community" in an institution modeled on the University of Glasgow. One of the three initial professors would have as part of his charge "the principles of political economy," although he added quickly, "The course of Political Economy might be confined to the reading of a simple elementary volume."[31]

The first actual instruction in political economy in Jamaica probably took place at the short-lived Queen's College, founded at Spanish Town in 1873. Grant Allen, a devoted disciple of Herbert Spencer, was "Second Master" in charge of mental and moral philosophy as well as a handful of other subjects.[32] The college collapsed after only two years from lack of students and problems associated with an unrealistic structure. Another abortive effort at higher education was a University College to prepare candidates for the University of London B.A. and M.A. examinations established in connection with the Jamaica High School at Kingston.[33] A college building was opened in 1890, but the predictable problems of extreme paucity both of students and funds quickly appeared. Political economy was offered in the senior portion of the school and in the college at least as early as 1892; the examiner reported in 1893 that "The various points of the paper were discussed with much clearness."[34] The required texts each year varied among elementary books by Jevons, Marshall, and Fawcett. The University College gradually expired during the early years of the

[30] The plan is reproduced in the *Morning Journal*, Kingston, July 12, 1838. This proposal, and the history of Jamaican higher education in general, are discussed in Lloyd Braithwaite, "The Development of Higher Education in the British West Indies," *Social and Economic Studies*, VII (1958), 1-64.

[31] James M. Phillippo, *Jamaica: Its Past and Present State* (London, 1843), pp. 477-487. See also Edward Bean Underhill, *James Mursell Phillippo* (London, 1881), p. 136.

[32] Braithwaite, "The Development of Higher Education," pp. 15-20, and see below.

[33] See *Proposals by the Jamaica Schools Commission for the Extension of University Teaching to Jamaica, Adopted by the Commission, October 29th, 1886* (n.p., n.d.).

[34] *Jamaica High School Calendar, Midsummer, 1893*, Kingston, pp. 3, 5, 26, and Braithwaite, "The Development of Higher Education," pp. 20-22.

twentieth century. Various other avenues of extension higher education were opened to Jamaicans, but it is doubtful that at any time substantial knowledge of economics was transmitted by them.[35]

Beginnings of Indigenous Analysis-Adaptation of Mercantilist Doctrine

Jamaica developed during the eighteenth century as an integral part of the British "mercantile" system, within which colonies had clearly defined functions as suppliers of raw materials, as consumers of manufactured goods, and as strategic bases for military forces. Colonies were restrained from trading with foreigners, but at the same time they were granted favored treatment in the metropolitan home market. Jamaican residents and their spokesmen in Britain believed from an early date that their continued prosperity depended on perpetuation of the mercantile system, and as a result they took pains first to describe the colony and its economic potential in glowing terms, and second to remind the mother country of mercantilist theory and of the mutual responsibility in the familial relationship. The volume of mercantilist propaganda from Jamaica was related directly to the level of economic crisis in the colony, reaching peaks of intensity around Napoleonic Wars, the abolition of the slave trade, and emancipation. Writings predominately mercantilist in tone ceased by the middle of the nineteenth century.

With few exceptions, the earliest mercantilist tracts emanating from Jamaicans were little more than brief reminders of the island's alleged virtues and importance.[36] However, toward the end

[35] E.g., Students at the Jamaica Church Theological College were able to enroll for extension work in political economy at the University of Durham (*Statutes and Calendar of the Jamaica Church Theological College*, 1894, p. 11). A recent general indictment of the higher education system initiated by the British in the West Indies is contained in Eric Williams, *Education in the British West Indies* (Port-of-Spain, 1950).

[36] E.g., *The Trade Granted to the South-Sea-Company: Considered with Relation to Jamaica. In a Letter to One of the Directors of the South-Sea-Company; by a Gentleman Who Has Resided Several Years in Jamaica* (London, 1714); *The Importance of Jamaica to Great Britain, Considered . . . In a Letter to a Gentleman* (London, 1740); and *A Letter to a Member of Parliament, Concerning the Importance of Our Sugar Colonies to Great Britain, by a Gentleman, Who Resided Many Years in the Island of Jamaica* (London, 1745). One early Jamaican mercantilist tract, entitled *An Inquiry Concerning the Trade Commerce and Policy of Jamaica*, was of exceptional quality. The author, who may have been Charles White of the Government Printing Office, made estimates

of the eighteenth century, as the specter of imminent freer trade loomed large, they assumed a more urgent tone, and more elaborate works were produced to put the case.[37] One author took the trouble to collect public documents designed to provide "abundant proof of that grand system of reciprocal interchange of benefits, and of privileges and restraints, under which the mother-country has drawn to herself, and continues to draw advantages so various, and so important to her navy, her manufactures, trade, commerce and active industry, of every species (to say nothing of revenue), as surpass all the powers of calculation. . . ." He hoped to "demonstrate beyond contradiction, that the ancestors and predecessors of the present colonists were allured, prompted, and assisted, to cultivate the soil, by every possible means which government could devise."[38]

Characteristic assumptions of early Jamaican mercantilist writings were, first, that maximization of staple export production should be the primary objective of an economic system; and, second, that the Negro population could be treated as a productive factor whose costs should be minimized and not as consumers whose satisfaction should be maximized.[39] Authors were usually either plaintive or on the defensive, appealing for protection and special assistance or opposing changes in legislation. Extensive attention was given to the institution of slavery, and the case was developed repeatedly that Africans were congenitally unfit or currently unprepared for freedom.[40] Frequently this argument was masked by

---

of aggregate national expenditures, income, and capital assets. He proposed formation of a "public bank" to maintain employment and stimulate growth. I examine this work in greater detail elsewhere.

[37] A particularly good work, mainly descriptive and stimulated apparently by a talk of abolition, was "A Gentleman Lately Resident on a Plantation" [Peter Marsden], *An Account of the Island of Jamaica* (Newcastle, 1788).

[38] *Colonization of the Island of Jamaica* (n.p., 1792), pp. 1-2.

[39] One author complained in 1809 that too little attention had been devoted by economists to the technical question of how the highest level of production could be obtained from slaves with a given expenditure, whether by compulsion, piece work incentives, or other methods (*An Essay on Task-Work, Its Practicability, and the Modes to be Adopted for its Application to Different Kinds of Agricultural Labour* [Jamaica, 1809]). Douglas Hall, "Slaves and Slavery in the British West Indies," *Social and Economic Studies*, XI (1962), 305-318, argues cogently that planters thought of slaves merely as pieces of capital equipment.

[40] E.g., G. Francklyn, *An Answer to the Rev. Mr. Clarkson's Essay on the Slavery and Commerce of the Human Species, Particularly the African; in a Series of Letters from a Gentleman in Jamaica to his Friend in London* (London, 1789); and Dennis Reid, *An Address to the Right Hon. Geo. Canning, on the Present State of this Island, and Other Matters* (Jamaica, 1823).

descriptive accounts of the island, which portrayed the dissolute character of the Negroes and efforts allegedly being undertaken by the whites for their improvement.[41] Charges from emancipationists that cruelty was causing a decline in the slave population led colonists to a search for other explanations for fluctuations in the numbers of slaves.[42] It was emphasized that humanitarian advances could never be undertaken successfully by Britain without clear agreements from other countries to do likewise; otherwise the Empire would lose its competitive advantage in the production of staple commodities and the economic strength on which all permanent improvements had to rest.[43]

The Jamaica House of Assembly, which represented the more prosperous segments of the community, maintained a steady outflow of mercantilist argument through memorials, addresses, and committee reports. These writings included the familiar accounts of distress, pleas for "a return to the system established by the wisdom of our ancestors," and appeals for such farfetched assistance measures as substitution of West Indian coffee for cocoa in the diet of the British military forces. ("The unpleasant part of the change would be soon forgotten, whilst the advantages would be permanent, by assisting to give the national taste a direction favourable to the public interest, and assuredly not inimical to the health or comfort of the people."[44] The Assembly was capable also of produc-

[41] E.g., A Gentleman long resident in the West Indies [James Stewart], *An Account of Jamaica and its Inhabitants* (Kingston, 1809); James Stewart, *A View of the Past and Present State of the Island of Jamaica* (Edinburgh, 1823); Britannicus, *State of Society and Slavery in Jamaica* (London, 1824); and H. T. De La Beche, *Notes on the Present Condition of the Negroes in Jamaica* (London, 1825).

[42] See *Report of a Committee of the House of Assembly of Jamaica on the Slave Trade, 23rd November, 1804* (Kingston, 1804), and Alexander Barclay, *A Practical View of the Present State of Slavery in the West Indies* (London, 1826). An extensive discussion of population characteristics of slaves was "A West Indian," *Notes in Defence of the Colonies: On the Increase and Decrease of the Slave Population of the British West Indies* (2 parts; Jamaica, 1826).

[43] Bryan Edwards, *A Speech Delivered at a Free Conference Between the Honourable the Council and Assembly of Jamaica . . .* (Kingston, 1789).

[44] *Copy of the Representation and Petition of the Assembly of Jamaica, to His Royal Highness the Prince Regent* (n.p., 1811), p. 3; *Report from a Committee of the Honourable House of Assembly, Appointed to Inquire into Various Matters Relative to the State of Commerce and Agriculture of the Island . . .* (Jamaica, 1813), p. 11; also *Report of a Committee of the House of Assembly of Jamaica, 20th December, 1799* (London, 1800), and *A Report of a Committee of the Honourable House of Assembly of Jamaica, Presented to the House, December 10, 1817, Relative to the Present State of the Island, with Respect to its Population, Agriculture, and Commerce . . .* (London, 1818).

ing sophisticated analyses of the island's economy and of its place in the imperial economic system. A committee of the House in 1804 attempted to estimate the net costs of ending both the slave trade and "that system of reciprocal monopoly, so long and happily established between the mother-country and her colonies." It concluded that Jamaica might prosper either under the pure mercantile system, or under absolute free trade; during the gradual breakdown of mercantilism, however, the colonies would suffer the disadvantage of both arrangements. "The prominent grievance of the sugar planter is, that this natural tendency of commerce to an equitable level is, in his particular case, obstructed by positive regulations, which prevent feeding the market in proportion to the demand, and compel him to bring and land his goods in Great Britain, however much the mart be glutted, and re-exportation obstructed, by causes over which he has no controul."[45] This committee was able to argue that the Jamaican economy was valuable to Britain both according to mercantilist criteria—achievement of a positive foreign trade balance—and according to Smithian objectives, an increase in the division of labor and total production:

Whether tried on the principles of the mercantile system, or on those of the economists, as developed to the English reader in the writings of Mr. Hume and doctor Adam Smith, this important commerce will be found equally beneficial.

Applying the test of the former, the immense advantage of giving encouragement to the agriculture and manufactures of the kingdom is not diminished by what the advocates for that system most dreaded, an unfavourable balance, for, adding to the actual exports to Africa and the West-Indian islands our surplus produce, re-exported and entering into the general balance with other nations, a considerable direct balance will be found in favour of Great Britain; and it must now be admitted by the most rigid advocates for the old system, that what is retained for the expences of the proprietors resident in Great Britain, and the interest of the capitalist, whose funds are lent to the planters, must be added to that balance, and is as much a part of the general revenue of the kingdom as if dug from a mine in Cornwall.

On the principles of the economists this commerce is no less beneficial, and superior to any other possessed by the mother-country, her home trade excepted. None affords so extensive encouragement to the productions of her land and labour, or furnishes such a surplus of valu-

[45] *Report of a Committee of the House of Assembly of Jamaica on the Slave Trade, 23rd November, 1804* (n.p., n.d.), p. 24.

able commodities to be exchanged for foreign equivalents, whether these shall consist of merchandise, of naval stores, or raw materials for manufactures, of corn in times of scarcity, or military services in the hour of danger.[46]

During the nineteenth century the property owners of Jamaica came increasingly to depend upon a few public spokesmen to articulate their local and increasingly pragmatic brand of mercantilist argument; the Reverend George W. Bridges and A. A. Lindo were particularly vocal advocates. Bridges, a clergyman trained at Oxford University, maintained from the pulpit, through works of local history, and through the press a subtle defense of such fundamental colonial economic institutions as the plantation system and slavery.[47] He called repeatedly for gradual rather than revolutionary social change, and, like many of his colleagues, he pointed to Santo Domingo as an example of the disastrous conditions which could follow radicalism. Lindo, a merchant, expounded the planters' position on a variety of economic questions from immigration to tariff protection. He reacted irritably to the Smithian economic arguments of his critics, saying in 1828: "if we are in the schools we may expatiate on enlarged principles and abstract notions; we may scale the heavens in imagination; but if we step into the senate-house, we must descend to earth, and consider that the wants of a nation cannot be subsisted on the aerial food of abstract principles."[48] A variety of social and community organizations helped

[46] *Ibid.*, p. 36. Similar arguments are presented in *Addresses and Memorials to His Majesty, from the House of Assembly at Jamaica. Voted in the Years 1821 to 1826 Inclusive; and Which Have been Presented to His Majesty by the Island Agent* (London, ca. 1828), pp. 10-11.

[47] Principal works of Bridges were *The Annals of Jamaica* (2 vols.; London, 1828); *A Voice from Jamaica in Reply to William Wilberforce, Esq. M.P.* (London, 1823); *Dreams of Dulocracy* (London, 1824); *The Statistical History of the Parish of Manchester, in the Island of Jamaica* (Jamaica, 1824); *Emancipation Unmask'd* . . . (London, 1835). Bridges reported in an autobiographical work that the Jamaica House of Assembly frequently sent him funds in recognition of past "services" (*1834-1862. Outlines and Notes of Twenty-Nine Years* [n.p., 1862]).

[48] A. A. Lindo, *The Injurious Tendency of the Modifying of our Navigation Laws Made Manifest* (London, 1828), unpaged. See also *Letters to the Proprietors and Mortgagees of Estates in the Island of Jamaica, on Promoting Immigration into that Colony* (London, 1836); *Dr. Underhill's Testimony on the Wrongs of the Negro in Jamaica, Examined in a Letter to the Editor of the Times* (Falmouth, 1866); *A Letter Addressed to the Editor of the "Times"* (Jamaica, 1877). A similar work of propaganda is Alexander Barclay, *Effects of the Late Colonial Policy of Great Britain Described, in a Letter to the Right Hon. Sir George Murray* (London, 1830).

to perpetuate the mercantilist gospel, especially the notions of mutual responsibility between metropolis and colony and judgment of colonial economic performance according to the level of raw material exports.[49]

Advent of Classical Economics: The Question of Immigration

A revolution in economic thought began to accompany social change in Jamaica during the nineteenth century, bringing application to local problems of Classical rather than mercantilist principles. The fundamental novelty in approach, which like the social change itself came slowly, was acceptance of the position that the welfare of all inhabitants, and particularly the satisfaction of their wants, should be the objective of the economy rather than merely production of staple export commodities. In Britain a similar shift away from the mercantilist viewpoint had been associated with industrial change, growth in per capita income, and enlargement of the franchise; in Jamaica it was a product of emancipation and the establishment of an independent peasantry. The essential distinction was between the mercantilist producer orientation and Classical consumer orientation described so succinctly by Adam Smith from the Classical viewpoint in 1776:

Consumption is the sole end and purpose of all production; and the interest of the producer ought to be attended to, only so far as it may be necessary for promoting that of the consumer. The maxim is so perfectly self-evident, that it would be absurd to attempt to prove it. But in the mercantile system, the interest of the consumer is almost constantly sacrificed to that of the producer; and it seems to consider production, and not consumption, as the ultimate end and object of all industry and commerce.[50]

The first writers to examine Jamaican problems from the viewpoint of aggregate welfare maximization were spokesmen for the

[49] E.g., *Report to the Jamaica Chamber of Commerce on the Sugar Duties Question in England* (Kingston, 1846); *Report of the Standing Committee of the Chamber of Commerce, Jamaica, upon the Present Condition of that Colony; the Causes of its Depression; and the Remedial Measures Necessary to Restore its Prosperity* (London, 1847); a school history text by James O. Clark, *An Abridged History of Jamaica* (Falmouth, 1859); and publications of the Jamaica Association, which was dedicated to "the promotion of every object tending to promote the political, social and religious interests of the people of this Island" (*The Rules of "The Jamaica Association"* [Kingston, 1874], p. 3).

[50] *An Inquiry into the Nature and Causes of the Wealth of Nations* (New York: Modern Library, 1937), p. 625.

freed slaves, mainly missionaries from Britain who judged local issues in terms of the well-being of their congregations. Few missionaries were acquainted with the details of analytical tools, and their innovations were largely in approach. The Baptists were the most articulate spokesmen. James M. Phillippo, an energetic and influential pioneer in social thought, gathered substantial quantities of economic data about the lower classes, and he sought in practical terms means of raising the incomes of his parishioners.[51] Edward Bean Underhill, who presented the Baptist case in Great Britain, pleaded repeatedly for "searching inquiry into the legislation of the Island since emancipation, its taxation, its economical and material condition" and also for "just laws and light taxation" in the interest of the "emancipated peasantry."[52] Missionaries and other sympathizers worked hard to place freed slaves on the land, and they were led naturally to consider such matters as incentives to settlement and alternative systems of land tenure.[53] The experience of the United States with free homesteads was described repeatedly, by some who yearned specifically for a landed peasantry and by others who in desperation would try any road to prosperity.[54] Efforts at agricultural reform typically brought the bitter enmity of planters who wished to retain the Negroes as dependent and docile labor not aroused by ambitious hopes or thoughts of economic independence.[55]

The economic motivation of the freed slaves was of special in-

[51] James M. Phillippo, *Jamaica: Its Past and Present State* (London, 1843).

[52] Edward B. Underhill, *A Letter Addressed to the Rt. Honourable E. Cardwell, with Illustrative Documents on the Condition of Jamaica and an Explanatory Statement* (London, 1865), pp. 14-16, 66-70.

[53] E.g., Joseph John Gurney, *To the Planters of Jamaica* (Kingston, 1840), p. 12.

[54] E.g., William Wemyss Anderson, *A Description and History of the Island of Jamaica* (Kingston, 1851), and by the same author, *Jamaica and the Americans* (New York, 1851), p. 15. Anderson looked to the American "home in the woods" to eliminate the master-slave relationship and bring out the "hardy industry" of the Jamaicans. See also a description of the "politico-economical condition" of Jamaica by a correspondent from the New York *Evening Post*, John Bigelow, *Jamaica in 1850: or, the Effects of Sixteen Years of Freedom on a Slave Colony* (New York, 1851). Like Anderson, Bigelow rejected Carlyle's suggestion of forced labor, and he advocated homesteads as the way to create a middle class.

[55] Early persecution of the missionaries is described in [William Knibb], *Facts and Documents Connected with the Late Insurrection in Jamaica, and the Violations of Civil and Religious Liberty Arising Out of It* (London, 1832); and Edward Bean Underhill, *The Jamaica Mission, in its Relations with the Baptist Missionary Society, from 1838 to 1879* (London, 1879).

terest to the missionaries, who came to believe that ambition and acquisitiveness were the high roads to moral as well as to material success in Jamaica. Unlike the island's mercantilist writers who saw low and stable wages as the long-run fate of workers, missionaries injected the notion of economic progress. The Reverend Samuel Oughton stated as a general principle that "man is a being formed for education, progression, and improvement," and "the cultivation of artificial wants tends to the development of these faculties." He set out "to prove that such cultivation is *beneficial in its tendency*, and that by it *the interest, and happiness, of all classes* of the human family are promoted; and *more particularly* to show that it tends in an especial manner to *advance the prosperity and well being of the poorer classes*, to raise the mechanic and labourer in the social scale, as well as to increase their comfort and wealth."[56] Oughton and his brother ministers were not so radical as to advocate immediate equality as an objective of Negro enterprise. Rather they wished Negroes to be placed on the ladder of economic advancement with full opportunities open to them to obtain through competition with whites both middle-class comforts and spiritual redemption.[57]

The single issue which illustrated most clearly the difference in mode of thought between the mercantilist planters and the missionaries who were oriented toward the Classical viewpoint was the question of whether large-scale immigration should be encouraged to the colony. As proprietors of a heavily labor-intensive industry, the planters from the earliest days viewed an adequate flow of immigration as central to their prosperity. Only when an end to the slave trade seemed imminent, however, did they find it necessary to present elaborate arguments to defend their need. A select committee of the House of Assembly in 1804 prepared a summary of

[56] Samuel Oughton, *Jamaica: Why it is Poor, and How it May Become Rich* (Kingston, 1866), p. 10. This pamphlet originated as a lecture "delivered in the Mico Institution before, and on behalf of, the Kingston Young Men's Mutual Improvement Society," entitled "Artificial Wants, and their Influence in Promoting the Commercial Prosperity, Intellectual Improvement, Social Happiness, and Religious Advancement of a Country and People." It was reprinted in the *West India Quarterly Magazine*, I (1861-1862), 474-483.

[57] Detailed statements of missionary objectives are contained in John Clark, W. Dendy, and J. M. Phillippo, *The Voice of Jubilee: A Narrative of the Baptist Mission, Jamaica* (London, 1865), particularly a section by D. J. East, p. 14; and Leonard Tucker, "*Glorious Liberty*": *The Story of a Hundred Years Work of the Jamaica Baptist Mission* (London, 1914).

the case for uninterrupted labor inflow, stressing the role of colonies as factories for the production of staple commodities. The committee developed an argument for continuation of the slave trade which was remarkably similar to the rationale offered thirty years later for the Wakefield system. Their report said that unless a guaranteed supply of manual labor was provided for the colonies the more respectable and enterprising class of settlers could never be persuaded to migrate, a balanced colonial society could not be achieved, and rapid economic growth would not take place. In contrast to Wakefield's device for assuring an effective supply of labor in the colonies, which was a land price "sufficient" to prevent workers without substantial capital from obtaining property, the committee advocated an uninterrupted trade in slaves. It explained:

The only means by which that most useful body of men, the overseers and bookkeepers on plantations, can acquire a competence, is by purchasing a few negroes (at first generally hired by their employers on liberal terms), and gradually adding to the number, until equal to commencing a settlement. Take away this sole mode of commending an establishment, and you drive from the country the most enterprising and intelligent. In future you would expect in vain adventurers of the description who have lately resorted to the island and superintend plantations—young men of decent families, of good morals, and in many instances of liberal educations.[58]

After abolition, similar arguments were repeated in hopes that the slave trade might be restored.[59]

By the 1820's when it seemed likely that, after all, the slave trade would never be renewed, and what was even worse, that emancipation might be a strong possibility, Jamaicans joined spokesmen elsewhere in the Empire in praise of proposals for assisted migration of Britain's own "superabundant" population. Arguments that had been used in support of importing bond labor were applied easily to the attraction of free labor. Planters quickly saw an alternative to slavery in the "shovelling out of paupers" from the old world.[60]

[58] *Report of a Committee of the House of Assembly of Jamaica on the Slave Trade, 23rd November, 1804*, p. 10.
[59] E.g., *A Report of a Committee of the Honourable House of Assembly of Jamaica, Presented to the House, December 10, 1817, Relative to the Present State of the Island.* . . .
[60] The usefulness of Britain's excess population for Jamaica was described in detail in Alexander Macdonnell, *Colonial Commerce; Comprising an Inquiry into*

A major impetus was given to British colonial theory when in 1829 Edward Gibbon Wakefield proposed a "system" of emigration to the colonies which would include movement of capital and persons from the middle classes as well as paupers. Wakefield recommended land sales in new countries at prices "sufficient" to provide funds for assisted passages and public works, and to keep labor available for hire by preventing it from acquiring property. An underlying assumption of the Wakefield theory was that economic development would take place in the new world most effectively against a social background as much as possible like that of the old. Coming just before emancipation, Wakefield's notions were endorsed enthusiastically in Jamaica, although seldom with attention to detail or with specific acknowledgment of Wakefield himself. Generally, Jamaicans favored a stringent variant of the scheme wherein indentured settlers of any color would make up for the loss of the freed slaves. John Neilson proposed in 1833 that laborers be brought to the island "bound for three or five years as may be fixed upon, and at the end of their apprenticeship, have a grant of ten acres of land to them and their heirs for ever without any restriction." He argued in the same vein as Wakefield that only in civilized circumstances, which would include such economic institutions as banks and a working class, would incentives operate and development take place.[61] Another commentator on the Wakefield schemes believed that "Such a mode of proceeding would establish a permanent increasing class of labourers, producing an agricultural population, and eventually a tenantry, drawing ample measures from a country where riches are unrivalled."[62]

Immigration schemes on the Wakefield model found natural adherents in the West Indies, more in fact than in Australasia or Can-

---

the Principles upon Which Discriminating Duties Should be Levied on Sugar, the Growth Respectively of the West India British Possessions, of the East Indies, and of Foreign Countries (London, 1828).

[61] John Neilson, *The Present and Future Prospects of Jamaica Considered . . .* (Kingston, 1833), pp. 11, 13, 17, 19-24.

[62] Bridges, *Emancipation Unmask'd*, p. 21. Bridges called Jamaica "the finest poor-man's country in the world." An appeal for colored immigrants from the United States is Alexander Barclay, *Remarks on Emigration to Jamaica: Addressed to the Colored Class of the United States* (London, 1840). A plea for "willing immigration from the African Coast" is contained in *Report of the Standing Committee of the Chamber of Commerce, Jamaica, upon the Present Condition of that Colony; the Causes of its Depression; and the Remedial Measures Necessary to Restore its Prosperity* (London, 1847), p. 12.

ada for which the model had been devised. Principal gainers under Wakefield's system were owners of extensive colonial estates who were dependent on hired labor, and the only near equivalents in the Empire to the island planters in this respect were the Australian squatters, who also were enthusiastic supporters of Wakefield.[63] But the Jamaica planters found additional reasons to those proposed by Wakefield for favoring his system. They saw in both the immigration of Europeans and land restriction not only a ready supply of new workers but also an essential weapon of discipline for the freed slaves who were already employed. Most whites in Jamaica viewed with genuine alarm an increase in wages and the movement of Negroes after emancipation to small farms; they feared their own increased costs and loss of labor, but they also believed that a genuine retrogression in the human condition was the result. Even though economic historians today agree that the development of peasant agriculture led to valuable diversification of the economy and contributed substantially to national income,[64] the unsatisfactory performance of the sugar sector and the evident decline of some large estates convinced most contemporary observers that Negro settlement had brought only depression to the economy and sloth and dissolution to society. Planters and merchants both held to the mercantilist notion, expounded effectively by Sir James Steuart, that workers aimed at a certain target income and could not be persuaded to labor beyond achievement of this goal. Few Jamaicans accepted the contrary Smithian argument, developed during a period of rapid economic growth in Britain, that labor productivity rose rather than declined with increasing wages.[65] Planter skepticism about the desirability of rising wages was strengthened by Thomas Carlyle's famous diatribe on the Negro character, his "Occasional Discourse on the Nigger Question" (1849).[66] H. B. Evans gave a typical interpretation à la Carlyle of the impact of emancipation upon incentives:

The Negro . . . soon found that one or two days' work would supply him with what luxuries he might require, and that the bounteous earth

[63] See my *Economic Enquiry in Australia* (Durham, 1966), pp. 72-83.

[64] Hall, *Free Jamaica, 1838-1865*, pp. 157-181; and Eisner, *Jamaica, 1830-1930*, pp. 210-217.

[65] For discussion of the relationship between this conflict of views and the condition of economic development see Deane, *Ind. Rev.*, p. 141.

[66] *Fraser's Magazine*, Dec., 1849.

would give him the rest; consequently he resigned himself to a state of semi-barbarism, and each succeeding year saw him less inclined to perform the duties of his station; he had pumpkins and bread-fruit, and Indian corn, and herbage for his cow and goat,—then, why need he work? Not he.[67]

Robert Emery, "for thirty years resident in the island," stated the case thus in 1859: "The Europeans, as a body, are in the van of civilisation; the Africans, as a body, are but laggards in the rear." Possession of property, he claimed, had made the Negro incurably lazy. "The earth provides almost spontaneously for his wants. Necessity, the spur to exertion, has no existence. As slaves, the negroes were compelled to work, and they worked. Emancipated, they had a right to be idle, and they certainly took a liberal advantage of this pleasant privilege of freedom."[68] Although all of these conclusions rested on a combination of inadequate data, prejudice, and xenophobia, they were firmly held and influential.

Jamaicans used their prejudice as a basis for two novel arguments to support their special variant of the Wakefield system. The first was the educational example which would be presented to the former slaves by "a white labouring population whose habits of order and industry and their happy effects to themselves, might lead the negro to fall into them likewise."[69] The second argument was based on the old principle that all men required hardship as a spur to labor; where nature was bountiful, as in the tropics, hardship had to be created artificially through land restriction. As A. A. Lindo reminded Jamaicans, it was through a happy combination of circumstances that "the natural aversion of man to hard labour . . . in Europe is overcome by the privation of land."[70]

James Maxwell, a physician and civic leader, proposed in 1848 "a well-arranged and systematic scheme of European and African immigration" in a pamphlet which embodied in relatively sophisticated form most of the arguments for the local biracial version of

[67] H. B. Evans (Late Surgeon Superintendent of Immigrants, Lucea, Jamaica), *Our West Indian Colonies: Jamaica a Source of National Wealth and Honour* (London, 1855), p. 21.

[68] *About Jamaica: Its Past, Its Present, and Its Future* (London, 1859), pp. 9-10.

[69] A. A. Lindo, *Letters to the Proprietors and Mortgagees of Estates in the Island of Jamaica, on Promoting Immigration into that Colony* (London, 1836), p. 2.

[70] *Ibid.*, p. 8.

the Wakefield system. He said that balanced rates of increase of the two races were essential for maximum economic growth in the islands. Persons of European origin should remain at least 10 per cent of the population to

infuse a portion of their superior skill and ingenuity, and excite a commendable emulation among their coloured fellow-labourers, *which is the paramount object of European immigration.* . . . The introduction and permanent residence of such persons are as necessary for the moral and intellectual improvement of the negroes as the ebbing and flowing of the tide to preserve its physical constitution.[71]

Maxwell believed that an appropriate combination of white and black immigrants would asure optimum economic and social development in the colonies—the same objectives Wakefield hoped to achieve through the immigration of all social classes from Britain to the future dominions. Maxwell wrote:

European immigration must be viewed more as a prospective than an immediate measure. Its main objects are to strengthen and consolidate our social system, to advance civilization, to give a tone to morality, and to diffuse a knowledge of the arts and the improvements of modern agriculture, by the superior skill and intelligence of properly selected immigrants. African immigration, on the other hand, to which the country looks with extreme solicitude, will be a prompt and certain remedy for agricultural difficulties. . . .[72]

Like Wakefield, Maxwell expected to see in future years advancement in the "civilization" of the Negro residents, and he even predicted that educated West Indians might assume leadership in other tropical portions of the Empire.[73]

Using the approach taken by Maxwell, it was possible to present a relatively liberal and humanitarian case for immigration rather than the conservative and cynical position of the planters. In 1859 George Solomon, a Kingston merchant, argued that immigrants should be a necessary economic complement to the freed slaves who had moved from the sugar estates to small mixed farms.

[71] *Remarks on the Present State of Jamaica* . . . (London, 1848), pp. 4, 16, 19, 21. Similar statements are contained in Leonard Rowe Valpy, *Jamaica: Its Existing Condition, With a Few Suggestions for its Amelioration* (Kingston, n.d., ca. 1856-1860).

[72] *Remarks on the Present State of Jamaica* . . . , p. 12.

[73] *Ibid.*, pp. 27-41. A later statement of the importance of systematic colonization to Jamaica, by an American journalist, is W. G. Sewell, *The Ordeal of Free Labor in the British West Indies* (New York, 1863).

Markets for the products of these farms could come only from re-
suscitated plantations worked by immigrants. He stated categorically, "We do not desire cheaper labor, *but more of it. . . .*"[74] The
only way in which free labor could compete internationally with
slave colonies of other nations was for economies of scale to be
achieved. "Free Labor, on a *small* scale, cannot compete, under the
same auspices, with cultivation upon extended principles. No better example than this could be desired to prove our assumption, that
it is *magnitude*, rather than other intrinsic superiority, which makes
slave productions cheaper than free productions."[75] Solomon saw
immigration, by making possible continued plantation agriculture
in addition to small-scale cultivation, as the only key to self-sus-
taining colonial growth: "we can discover no other absolute draw-
back to our progress—for labour is certain to bring confidence—
confidence, capital—capital, improved machinery—improved machinery, greater economy of time and expense."[76] He envisioned
freed slaves living happily on their small holdings, providing food-
stuffs to new immigrant laborers, and thus sharing fully in the fruits
of progress.

It can be argued that proposals for systematic immigration to
Jamaica were merely clever propaganda, or at best rationalizations,
for schemes which were predominantly in the writers' own self-in-
terest. It may be said further that writers about immigration cared
not about the long-term economic and social development of the
island, as they argued, but only about their own need to obtain
adequate cheap labor. Identical charges may easily be laid, however, against proponents elsewhere of the pure Wakefield system, in
which the principal difference from the Jamaican version was the
distinction between laborers and employers on the basis of social
class and possession of property rather than race. In any event,
arguments for systematic immigration were probably influential in
gaining support for actual immigration schemes which flourished
after emancipation.[77]

Immigration was the single most clear-cut economic issue over

[74] George Solomon, *Population and Prosperity; or, Free vs. Slave Production*
(Kingston, 1859), p. 43.
[75] *Ibid.*, p. 6.
[76] *Ibid.*, pp. 36-37.
[77] Ronald V. Sires, "Sir Henry Barkly and the Labor Problem in Jamaica,
1853-1856," *Journal of Negro History*, XXV (1940), 216-235.

which the planters could disagree with spokesmen for the freed slaves. The conflict in viewpoints rested on differences in personal interest as well as in social philosophy. On the one hand, the planters saw immigration as a steady flow of labor which would replenish the supply of a major input and help to minimize unit costs. So long as maximum and most efficient output of the principal staple products was accepted as the legitimate objective of the economy, this position could be defended consistently. Missionaries and other defenders of the Negroes, however, argued that the welfare of the mass of the Jamaicans was the correct end of economic activity and that this would not be improved by immigration.[78] Over the question of immigration the conflict between Benthamite and mercantilist methods and goals became most apparent. In reply to a critique of immigration schemes by the Baptist minister, J. M. Phillippo, a spokesman for the planting interests wrote: "the question of immigration viewed in the light of philanthropy so far from being considered as impeding the progress of civilization, is to be maintained on the ground of its greatly extending the field of civilization."[79] Phillippo might legitimately have asked "civilization for whom?" The churchmen usually took the position that subsidized immigration was an unwarranted infringement of the free-market economy; one class was asked to subsidize another to distort the natural allocation of resources and income. The North Cornwall Baptist Association passed the following resolution in opposing all appropriations for immigration:

This meeting earnestly protests against any part of the Public money being thus appropriated.

First. Because it is contrary to the sound principles of Political Economy that the Taxpayers at large should be compelled to contribute to the expense of conducting any branch of industry whatsoever, and it

[78] Representative critiques of immigration to Jamaica, written in the island and in Britain, are Thomas Clarkson, *Not a Labourer Wanted for Jamaica* (London, 1842); *The British West India Colonies in Connection with Slavery, Emancipation, etc., by a Resident in the West Indies for Thirteen Years* [Mrs. Campbell, née Bourne] *with an Introduction and Concluding Remarks by a Late Stipendiary Magistrate in Jamaica* [Stephen Bourne] (London, 1853); Reverend William Garland Barrett, *Immigration to the British West Indies. Is it the Slave-Trade Revived or Not?* (London, 1859); Hall Pringle, *The Fall of the Sugar Planters of Jamaica, with Remarks on their Agricultural Management and on the Labour Question in that Island* (London, 1869), esp. p. 39.

[79] "Jamaica—Its Past and Present State," *Jamaica Monthly Magazine*, I (April, 1844), 68-69.

is especially unjust that the labouring class which forms a majority of the population should help to pay for the introduction of foreign labourers to compete with or supplant themselves.

Secondly. Because (though the adequacy or inadequacy of the labour supply in no way affects the question) this meeting is convinced that had wages been allowed to rise or fall in this as in other countries according to demand, and fairly and regularly paid, there would have been everywhere an abundant supply of labour and the people would not have had to turn their attention to other industries; it is also the belief of those assembled that even now, with reasonable inducements, thousands otherwise employed would be willing to labour regularly upon sugar properties.[80]

An insurrection at Morant Bay in 1865, and the controversy which surrounded repressive measures used by Governor Eyre for its termination, gave a new tone of bitterness to discussions of immigration.[81] In the face of open rebellion, planters became only more certain of the need to import fresh labor, while spokesmen for the Negroes, some of whom were accused unjustly of seditious activities, became increasingly defensive. Charges by distinguished defenders of Eyre in England, such as Carlyle and Ruskin, of laziness and untrustworthiness among Negroes strengthened the planters' old arguments for artificial stimuli to labor and the salutary pressure of immigration.[82] Even a Royal Commission, which in 1866 rendered an ambivalent report on Eyre's conduct, observed that the insurrection was rooted in the characteristic wish of Jamaican workers to avoid wage labor—"a principal object of the disturbers of order was the obtaining of land free from the payment of rent."[83] Charles Roundell, secretary of the commission, stated publicly that much more stringent measures should be introduced to strengthen labor discipline:

[80] W. Bancroft Espeut, *The Labour Question in and the Condition of Jamaica* (Kingston, 1876), p. 37.

[81] An account of the controversy over the Eyre affair, and its wider implications, is Bernard Semmel, *Jamaican Blood and Victorian Conscience: The Governor Eyre Controversy* (Boston, 1963).

[82] *Ibid.*, pp. 102-127. Examples of planter tirades are *Jamaica; Who Is to Blame? by a Thirty Years Resident* (London, 1865); and *Jamaica: Its State and Prospects* (London, 1867). Ironically one writer used Adam Smith's language, aimed originally at Anglo-Saxon landowners, to describe the economic character of the Negroes. They had, he said, "a desire to reap where they have never sown, to become rich where they have never laboured" (D. B. Panton, *The Present Crisis! and How to Meet It* [Kingston, 1866], p. 7).

[83] *Report of the Jamaica Royal Commission, 1866* (London, 1866), p. 40.

The reasons which induce the governments of Europe to lighten the burden of taxation on the working classes, with whom subsistence is difficult, and the motive to exertion urgent, fail of application in the case of the semi-civilized people of a tropical country, whose standard of physical comfort is low and easily satisfied. In a word, in such a community direct taxation, which presses upon the means of subsistence, is proved to be at once the most productive source of revenue, and incidentally an instrument of high value in the work of civilization.[84]

Roundell repeated the familiar Wakefield argument that because the prime colonial need was for capital, an adequate and obedient labor supply through regular immigration should be held out as an attraction to potential capitalists.[85] In the later years of the century, arguments of this kind became a standard refrain.[86]

The Birth of Nationalist Economics

The Morant Bay crisis led to abolition of the Jamaica Legislature and suspension of representative government; but it also opened the way to a broadening analysis of the Jamaican economy. Prior to 1865 a few missionaries had been almost the only persons who thought and wrote in terms of the entire island economy; planter society viewed sugar production as the only legitimate objective of economic activity, and as analysts they were interested at most in a rudimentary application of mercantilist doctrine to local conditions. Colonization theory was the only significant feature of nineteenth-century economic science which fell on fertile ground in Jamaica. The whole apparatus of a modern price economy had little meaning so long as feudal ties of bondage were regarded nostalgically as the legitimate relationships of society.

At least three factors contributed to a change in attitude toward economic problems after Morant Bay: sharp pangs of conscience experienced by British intellectuals who became concerned with the island, an increase in the size and responsiveness of the

[84] Charles S. Roundell, *England and Her Subject-Races with Special Reference to Jamaica* (London, 1866), p. 34.
[85] *Ibid.*, p. 39.
[86] E.g., Will Ewen, *Labour, Pauperism, Crime; A Short Review of the Present State of Things in Jamaica* (Kingston, 1877); and George Levy, *The Land the True Source of Jamaica's Prosperity. Suggestions for the Permanent Resuscitation of her Decayed Agriculture* (Kingston, 1895), p. 4.

domestic audience for nationalist discussions, and growing appreciation of the relatively impressive economic performance of peasant proprietors during their first thirty years of freedom, particularly as compared with the disappointing achievements of the planters. Growth of the nationalist economic viewpoint is beyond the scope of this paper.[87] However, it is useful in closing to demonstrate the revolution in attitude by contrasting the pronouncements on economic questions of governors before and after the rebellion.

Sir Charles Metcalfe may be taken as representative of the more enlightened colonial governors who, during the years after emancipation, were sympathetic to "the peasantry," yet nevertheless followed the planters' lead and "turned with anxiety towards immigration, as the only perceptible mode of alleviating the existing defects."[88] Metcalfe did not question the fundamental assumptions of the planters or the legitimacy of maximum sugar production as the goal of his administration, and for this reason he categorized the Baptist missionaries as "pretended ministers of religion, but really wolves in sheeps' clothing, who foment discontent and disaffection among the negro population."[89] Metcalfe viewed low wages as a major objective of public policy, and he endorsed any proposal which could be expected to strengthen the dependence of labor on capital. He complained thus of the effects of emancipation in Jamaica:

The wages of labor had been settled more at the will of the laborer than at that of the employer. And this must continue to be the case until a great increase of the laboring population shall make labor cheaper; until laborers shall be made dependent on labor; or until such a number of properties shall be thrown out of cultivation by the impossibility of meeting the expense as may produce the same effect as an increase of the laboring population.[90]

[87] I shall examine Jamaican nationalist thought in a later article.

[88] *The Speech of His Excellency the Right Honourable Sir C. T. Metcalfe, Bart., G. C. B., The Governor of Jamaica, on Opening the Jamaica Legislature, on the 27th of October, 1840* (London, 1840), p. 16. See also *The Speech of His Excellency the Right Honourable Sir C. T. Metcalfe, Bart., G. C. B., Governor of Jamaica, on Proroguing the Jamaica Legislature, on the 11th of April, 1840* (Kingston, 1840).

[89] Letter from Metcalfe to his aunt, June 10, 1840, in John William Kaye, *The Life and Correspondence of Charles, Lord Metcalfe* (London, 1854), II, 428.

[90] Unidentified citation of Metcalfe in Kaye, *ibid.*, II, 375-376.

Even the noted liberal, Lord Elgin, who was also governor in the 1840's, had little more to suggest than adult education as a spur to Jamaican development.[91]

Beginning in the late 1860's a new spirit of questioning was evident in the attitude of colonial governors toward the Jamaican economy. John Peter Grant, who succeeded Governor Eyre, made strenuous efforts for the first time to achieve broad-based economic development through programs of public works, widespread education, and subsidized innovation.[92] The outstanding example of a change in official viewpoint was Sir Anthony Musgrave, governor of Jamaica from 1877 to 1883. Musgrave was a competent amateur economist as well as an experienced colonial administrator.[93] He was accustomed to judging economics according to their effectiveness at producing goods and services, and undoubtedly he was familiar with the sympathy expressed by J. S. Mill and other liberals for Jamaican Negroes as a result of the Eyre affair.

Musgrave made his first important public pronouncements concerning West Indian development in a paper to the Royal Colonial Institute in 1880 on the topic, "Jamaica: Now, and Fifteen Years Since." At the beginning he stated openly his belief that by retaining an antiquated mercantilist frame of reference, analysts of the Jamaican economy had seriously misrepresented the island's condition and potential for growth. Instead of the foreign trade statistics of a few staple commodities, "the exchangeable value of products" of all types should be the criterion of economic performance.[94] The sugar sector had received far too much emphasis and peasant agriculture practically none at all. According to all available "tests of prosperity" the peasants had been quite successful economically,[95]

[91] Theodore Walrond, *Letters and Journals of James, Eighth Earl of Elgin* (London, 1872), pp. 19-22.

[92] Walter Scott Seton-Karr, *Grant of Rothiemurchus* (London, 1899), p. 92. Concerning Grant's plans for a compendium of Jamaican economic statistics, see Sidney Levien, *Jamaica as a Field for Immigration* (Kingston, 1879), p. 3.

[93] See my *Economic Enquiry in Australia*, pp. 518-543.

[94] *Jamaica: Now, and Fifteen Years Since* (London, 1880), pp. 10, 18. Musgrave's paper was printed as a pamphlet and was also included in the *Proceedings of the Royal Colonial Institute*. Musgrave may have written the paper in direct response to a gloomy account of the Jamaican economy presented to the Institute several years before by Nevile Lubbock, "The Present Position of the West India Colonies," *Proceedings of the Royal Colonial Institute*, VIII (1876-1877), 261-303. Sir Anthony was in the audience at the time.

[95] *Jamaica: Now, and Fifteen Years Since*, pp. 7, 10. The tests included the "amount of public indebtedness, the faith which is kept with the public creditors,

while planters went ever deeper into debt and pleaded constantly for government assistance. Peasant prosperity, moreover, had been achieved in the face of inequitable taxation: "property is scarcely taxed at all, the revenue for general purposes of government being raised entirely from indirect taxation on the consumption of the mass of the residents, and chiefly of the negro population—the absent proprietors of sugar estates or other property escaping altogether."[96] The decline in sugar production, Musgrave argued, had resulted from a foolish labor policy whereby workers had been effectively driven from the estates after emancipation. "The planters cannot get labour enough now because their predecessors carefully taught the peasantry to do without the sugar estates."[97] If the Jamaican planters had shown as much imagination in dealing with problems of seasonal labor as had their counterparts elsewhere in the Empire, such as the station owners of Australia with their need for seasonal shearing, other economic problems could have been overcome. Planters seemed handicapped by a social philosophy inherited from slavery which prevented them from viewing their former slaves dispassionately and from performing the entrepreneurial role effectively. In their revulsion at the notion of the normal employer-employee relationship, planters had fallen upon the chimera of immigration. Musgrave said: "I cannot help thinking that if half as much trouble had been taken to organise supplies of labour from native sources as has been taken to obtain it from India, the wants of the community could have been satisfied without foreign immigration."[98]

Musgrave wished above all to point up the need for a new economic outlook, and he did not attempt to suggest detailed solutions for immediate Jamaican problems. His principal policy proposal was for government support of innovation. "The object is to show by trial, at the expense of public subscription for the purpose, what new products may be introduced with profit to the community.[99] He advocated with excellent prescience experiments with exports

---

and the care which is taken to reduce the burden of the liability" as well as the "extended area both of cultivated and of grass lands . . . the demand for such imported articles of comfort and convenience as clothing, boots and shoes, furniture . . . books," and "the number of depositors in the Savings Bank. . . ."

[96] *Ibid.*, p. 9.
[97] *Ibid.*, p. 15.
[98] *Ibid.*, p. 16.
[99] *Ibid.*, p. 21.

of bananas and cattle,[100] and he arranged for a distinguished botanist to move to the island from Kew Gardens.[101] He recommended in general that government provide the environment wherein private enterprise could flourish; this should include "the ready administration of justice, the diffusion of education among the people," and "those means of communication and transport which in all countries have so important an influence in stimulating industry by giving value to its products."[102] His advocacy of government activity was always pragmatic rather than doctrinaire. "Most of these have been done or must be undertaken by the Government. I wish that more were within the power or the will of private enterprise."[103]

Sir Anthony's views evoked vigorous criticism from some islanders,[104] but his paper was seen by others as a significant new interpretation of Jamaica's growth, and it was used in 1884 in support of a formal request for a return to representative government.[105] In 1888, in response to an attack in a Colonial Office memorandum, Musgrave restated his case for a broad view of Jamaican development, this time with more complete statistics and citations from Adam Smith. He summarized thus the distinctive characteristic of his own thought and of his own administration: "I willingly avow that my desire has been to improve Jamaica for the Jamaicans, for those who dwell in the colony, rather than to regard it, as was formerly the case, as a place to be squeezed for the benefit of a comparatively few absentee proprietors and West India sugar merchants who cannot, if they would, afford employment to more than about five per cent. of the great mass of the taxpaying peasantry of this colony. . . ."[106]

---

[100] *Ibid.*, pp. 21-22. Musgrave complained of public apathy as a bar to all innovation in Jamaica. "It is not the custom in Jamaica to admit that anything is profitable" (*ibid.*, p. 22).

[101] The Duke of Manchester described Sir Anthony's role in this move during discussion of a paper presented to the Royal Colonial Institute by the new Botanist, D. Morris, "Planting Enterprise in the West Indies," *Proceedings of the Royal Colonial Institute*, XIV (1882-1883), 264-265.

[102] *Jamaica: Now, and Fifteen Years Since*, p. 23.

[103] *Ibid.*, p. 26.

[104] E.g., *Review of the Paper Entitled "Jamaica: Now, and Fifteen Years Since"* (Kingston, 1880).

[105] *Jamaica. Papers Relating to Proposed Change in the Form of Government* (London, 1884).

[106] *West Indies. Memoranda on Certain Points of Inquiry Concerning the Finances of the Island of Jamaica* (Kingston, 1883), p. 12.

Summary and Conclusion

Economic ideas moved to Jamaica with immigrants, travelers, and the flow of goods. However, the acceptance, use, and modification of these ideas on the island depended upon an assessment of their usefulness and applicability by the local population. During the first part of the period examined by this paper, the ruling economic philosophy in Britain of mercantilism was transferred with ease to the West Indies. Under the mercantile system, the colonies were seen to have a central role in maintaining the prosperity of the mother country and they, in turn, were promised encouragement and protection. Sugar planters and merchants found that mercantilist theory justified their own existence and provided a rationale for their receiving assistance in times of trouble. Therefore, they endorsed, adopted, and popularized these principles.

The new body of economic doctrine which stemmed from the writings of Adam Smith had far less appeal to the planters than did mercantilism. It rested on principles of free choice, free trade, and a free citizenry; and its advocates looked with skepticism upon most forms of coercion and upon special favors to any segments of the economic system, even colonies. Ample media existed for the transfer of Classical economic thought to the colony, but in the absence of a hospitable reception the flow did not take place.

The single feature of the evolving body of classical doctrine which appealed especially to Jamaican leaders during the first half of the nineteenth century was the theory of colonization, perfected by Edward Gibbon Wakefield, which provided an excuse for immigration and an apparent solution to the mounting labor problems resulting from emancipation. The immigration issue, however, illustrated clearly the strong survival of mercantilist notions and the failure of most members of the Jamaican ruling class to accept the concept of mass welfare as an economic goal. Sponsored migration was viewed as a means of obtaining cheap labor for the propertied classes, and seldom as a technique of national development. The few missionaries and others who viewed community objectives in wider terms made little intellectual impact.

A turning point in the general outlook on society in Jamaica was the rebellion of 1865. This event pointed up in stark terms, to observers in Britain as well as to a growing number of local residents, that feudal attitudes had become an anachronism in Jamaica and that major economic difficulties lay ahead. The writings of Sir Anthony Musgrave were the first major attempt to demonstrate the need for a new point of view and the application of modern economic analysis to the Jamaican economy. In a few brief critical works, Musgrave revealed the faults of the old approach and signaled the start of a new.

Toward a Theory of the Intercultural Transfer of Ideas

C. D. W. Goodwin and I. B. Holley, Jr.

What can we learn from the foregoing papers? Can these studies be used to enlarge our understanding of how formulated bodies of thought have passed from one cultural orbit to another in significant periods of history? We shall attempt to place insights gathered from them within the larger context of the work of scholars of the communication process. Section one contains suggestions of the contributions to an understanding of the transfer of ideas which may come from communications theory. In section two we present a tentative model, or framework of analysis, as a guide for future investigators in the history of transfer.

I

When the members of this symposium first began to give serious consideration to their specific topics, they were immediately impressed with the multiplicity of approaches which may be taken to the general subject. One has only to consult a standard reference tool such as the Library of Congress compilation of the subject headings to discover the great variety of approaches which have been taken toward the question, and consequently, the wide range of literature which is relevant to its examination. "Intercultural transfer" leads to "communication," which in turn leads to "information theory," "language," "mass media," and so on. In addition to works on the process of transfer there are also innumerable studies of the transfer of specific ideas and institutions—economic, social, political, and cultural. However, it became evident in the discussions of the symposium that research on the transfer of ideas has been relatively unco-ordinated among disciplines, and barriers have remained to interdisciplinary co-operation. An important ob-

MR. HOLLEY *is professor of history at Duke. For* MR. GOODWIN, *see p. 338.*

jective of this paper is to suggest how advances in certain fields, and particularly in communications theory, can be useful to the historian. A by-product of the symposium may be to indicate that the historian can stimulate some theoretical advance on his own.

The phenomenon of cross-cultural transfer of ideas falls within the general scope of "communications science," no matter which definition one accepts for this term.[1] For example, Warren Weaver's definition of communication as "all the procedures by which one mind can affect another" obviously includes the flow of ideas.[2] Similarly, the definition of Wilbur Schramm applies, that communication is "when two corresponding systems, coupled together through one or more non-corresponding systems, assume identical states as a result of signal transfer along the chain."[3] Even the most general definition of communication as the transfer of information by signals through space covers the subjects examined by this symposium. If there is a difference in the meaning of such terms as information and idea when used by communications theorists and contributors to this collection, it is one of complexity only and not of kind.

Most progress in understanding the communications process has come in three disciplines: mathematics, linguistics, and psychology. Mathematicians in the last few decades have made great headway in explaining the physical aspects of communication and have provided the theoretical tools needed to advance such devices as the telephone, television, and the electronic computer. Linguists and linguistic anthropologists have explored the character of, and relationships among, messages in communication. Social psychologists have investigated human participation in communication through the study of group dynamics. The question must arise, then, of the place of the historian in the study of communications. The answer is that the historian may contribute as an expert in handling types of data unfamiliar to the other students of the subject. A common characteristic of the three disciplines in which the greatest advances have been made is the search for technical and social be-

[1] A recent collection of readings, ranging over "the heart and core of human communication," is Afred G. Smith, *Communication and Culture* (New York, 1966).

[2] Claude E. Shannon and Warren Weaver, *The Mathematical Theory of Communication* (Urbana, Ill., 1949), p. 95.

[3] Smith, *Communication and Culture*, p. 522.

havior patterns of communication through analysis of empirical data. Hypotheses are formulated and tested either by direct laboratory experiment or by their conformity to social data which can be readily collected and easily measured.

Where this symposium differs from the mainstream of research in communications is in its focus on historical experiences selected because they are of special significance in the course of human development rather than solely as evidence to confirm or disprove a hypothesis, and some of the data examined are not easily susceptible to rigorous empirical treatment. The true historian is not concerned with historical incidents exclusively for their own sake (for then he becomes a mere antiquarian), nor does he abandon the scientific method and ignore the insights gained from scientific progress (for then he is a poor craftsman). Nevertheless, the task of the historian is different from that of a pure physical or social scientist because the materials he studies encompass the full range of recorded experience and therefore are more diffuse; his approach must be compounded both of science and of art. In a sense, this symposium, and more particularly this article, is an attempt to bridge parts of the proverbial two cultures and to indicate the potential usefulness of each one to the other—to achieve idea transfers of its own. On the one hand, it is possible that the communications theorist may gain from the historian, who is trained in the handling of complex documentary evidence, suggesting new hypotheses which then can be submitted to rigorous tests. On the other hand, it is certain that the historian will acquire from the communications theorist analytical techniques and insights which will give order to the material he studies. It seems likely even that the theory of communication could bring about a revolution in some areas of historical interpretation comparable to the revolution it has wrought in communications technology.

The most spectacular progress in the study of communications has come in the area of pure information theory, the examination of physical message transfers from point to point.[4] Embedded in the terminology and analytical apparatus of this subject are concepts which are especially valuable in the more restricted study of the intercultural transfer of ideas. The most fundamental concept

[4] See, for example, John R. Pierce, *Symbols, Signals and Noise: The Nature and Process of Communication* (New York, 1961).

in information science is the simple notion of a communications system in which there is a linear flow of information from a source, through a transmitter, down a channel to a receiver and thence to an ultimate destination. A significant modification of this linear model for the process of the flows of intercultural ideas as well as for the flows of other messages is the concept of cybernetics developed by Norbert Wiener and associates.[5] Here a communications system is pictured as circular, with feedback from the destination affecting the continued flow from the source. The technical device called a servomechanism, which amplifies and transmits the cybernetic effect, has obvious analogies in social institutions. The concepts of entropy, meaning the degree of randomness or disorganization in a flow of information, and of noise, meaning the communication of useless information, are both directly applicable to the type of material which has been examined in the chapters above. The capacity of a noiseless channel, meaning the maximum rate at which useful information can be transmitted over a channel, the coding process, the disturbing effects of noise, and the use of redundancy to overcome uncertainty in communication are all factors which the historian in the same way as a communications technician should examine in any system he studies. The historian must be attentive to the equality of, and relationships among, the varieties of expression at the source in a transfer, the effectiveness of the channel, and the intelligibility and fidelity of the message. He may find it useful to make an estimate of the total quantity of "information" passed through a transfer system, meaning the potential volume of communication, contrasted with the actual meaningful signals communicated. No attempt can be made here to describe the full range of analytical tools in information theory which strike the present writers as valuable to the historian. Nor is a universal prescription proposed for historiography. Rather the general usefulness of information theory is suggested as a guide to historical understanding.

Social psychologists have viewed communication as one aspect of the process of social interaction, and consequently they have focused their studies on human rather than physical codes and net-

[5] Norbert Wiener, *Cybernetics, or Control and Communication in the Animal and the Machine* (New York, 1948).

works.[6] They have drawn heavily on the mathematical theory of communication, especially the concepts of noise and feedback and control, substituting psychological barriers and distances for physical ones. But the psychologists have also introduced to the analysis of communication such distinctly novel and human considerations as environmental relationships and expectations. They have distinguished among the participants in communications by their type of role perception, task orientation, or other determinants of behavior. Special attention is given to two-person or small group interaction as a key to understanding the communication process, and networks among individuals in personal contact are found to be analogous to physical networks. Human characteristics are stressed by psychologists as vital determinants of communications networks, and the networks in turn are seen as determinants of social organization and performance. Psychologists have been specially interested in the concept of noise in human communications channels, both white noise or irrelevant information and coding noise or ambiguity of signals. The ability of human networks to filter out or compensate for noise and information distortion through redundancy and other techniques is found to be critical to their effectiveness and survival. Psychologists have not derived their concepts fully from the mathematical theory of communication, but they have gained valuable framework for analysis from a substantial degree of dependence. Their experience in this respect, as well as their discoveries, should be instructive to the historian.[7]

The linguistic approach to the study of communications has particular relevance to examinations of intercultural transfers. Analysis of speech is always important to an understanding of communications among articulate human beings, but it is crucial where two languages interact. Linguistics is concerned both with the signal system which lies at the base of the technology of communication and the human and social context in which the exchanges occur. The two basic divisions of linguistics, historical and descriptive, are relevant to the student of idea transfers. The first division may cast light on a special case under study; the second, in which is in-

[6] See, for example, Jurgen Ruesch and Gregory Bateson, *Communication: The Social Matrix of Psychology* (New York, 1951).
[7] See, for example, Fred Attneque, *Applications of Information Theory to Psychology* (New York, 1959), and Henry Quaster, *Information Theory in Psychology: Problems and Methods* (Glencoe, Ill., 1955).

cluded linguistic geography, may lead to greater understanding of the transfer process itself. Modern linguists have been moving from the study of linguistic units and syntax to analyses of meaning or semantics. The study of non-verbal symbols, or more specifically kinesics—communication through body movements—may even be relevant to the historian of ideas. The crucial importance of linguistics to an understanding of culture contact is expressed in most extreme form in the so-called Whorfian hypothesis that patterns of language are fundamental determinants of culture, social forms, and personal behavior.[8]

The theory of communications has had a powerful impact upon a number of disciplines other than the three mentioned here, all of which may contribute to an understanding of intercultural transfers. In political science, Karl W. Deutsch and others have shown that communication is central to the formation of political units and that social and political problems can stem from communication difficulties such as "overload."[9] Economists concerned with economic development have focused specifically on the transfer of educational methods and technological thought.[10] Sociologists have looked at communications from a variety of perspectives;[11] for example, they have examined coding systems for their impact on social relations, and the effect of social stratification on the flow of messages. Cultural anthropologists have analyzed the impact of such factors as differences in perception on the success of cultural contact.[12] Students of journalism and mass media have made effec-

[8] Joshua A. Fishman, "A Systematization of the Whorfian Hypothesis," in *Communication and Culture*, pp. 505-516. For a general treatment, see George A. Miller, *Language and Communication* (New York, 1951). See also John B. Carroll, "Communication Theory, Linguistics, and Psycholinguistics," *Review of Educational Research*, XXVIII (1958), 79-88.

[9] Karl W. Deutsch, *The Nerves of Government: Models of Political Communication and Control* (London, 1963). See also L. W. Pye, ed., *Communications and Political Development* (Princeton, 1963), and Robert T. Oliver, *Culture and Communication* (Springfield, Ill., 1962).

[10] For example, see C. A. Anderson and M. J. Bowman, eds., *Education and Economic Development* (Chicago, 1965); and Zvi Griliches, "Hybrid Corn: An Exploration in the Economics of Technological Change," *Econometrica*, XXV (1957), 501-522.

[11] See Pitrim A. Sorokin, *Sociological Theories of Today* (New York, 1966), esp. parts i and ii.

[12] See, for example, Donald T. Campbell, "Distinguishing Differences of Perception from Failures of Communication in Cross-cultural Studies," in F. S. C. Northrop and Helen H. Livingston, eds., *Cross-cultural Understanding: Epistemology in Anthropology* (New York, 1964). See also Leonard W. Doob, *Communication in Africa* (New Haven, 1961).

tive use of the theory of communication for a number of purposes which closely approach the tasks of the historian of ideas. In addition to using the concepts of entropy, channel capacity, redundancy, and noise, they have developed analogues in social theory to the physical notions of "systems coupling" through chain relationships, and "gatekeepers" as transmitters of messages.[13]

II

A Conceptual Framework for the Historical Analysis of Idea Transfer

From the brief survey of the various applications of communications presented in Section I, it should be clear that a complete theory of the intercultural transfer of ideas, susceptible to test and trustworthy for prediction, is still far off. The purpose of this section is to set forth a simple analytical framework which may guide future historical examinations of idea flows. It is hoped that with the approach implied in this framework greater knowledge of the transfer process and of significant historical incidents can be gained. If a single characteristic of idea transfers had to be given, it might well be "complexity." This model framework is designed to enable a historical investigator to see the phenomenon broken into its component parts—as they have been distinguished by communications theorists—and thereby advance toward greater understanding.

The main discrete elements in the process of intercultural transfer are these: (1) the source of an idea in one culture, (2) the agent through which the idea is transferred, and (3) the receiver of the idea in a second culture. These elements may be single individuals, but more often they are complex social institutions. An important objective in the historical analysis should be the discovery of whether the three elements in the transfer (or two, where no intermediary agent is involved) consciously enter into the process. A complication exists where an element is a plural entity, such as an entire community, because then conscious participation may be only partial for this single element. A cybernetic feedback, conscious or unconscious, also may be a characteristic of the transfer process.

[13] See, for example, Wilbur Schramm, "Information Theory and Mass Communication," *Journalism Quarterly*, XXXII (1955), 131-146.

The following diagram illustrates in simple outline form the essence of the conceptual framework needed for historical analysis of the transfer of ideas:

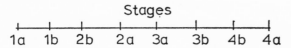

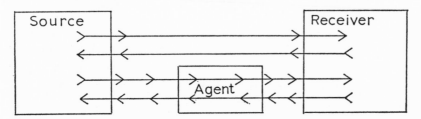

This diagram shows that the stages of transfer in one direction may be either two or four depending upon whether or not an agent or intermediary has an active role in the process. The stages also may occur with the individual elements participating wittingly (stages marked "a") or unwittingly (stages marked "b"). Arrows on the diagram indicate the location of potential stages in the transfer process and also the direction of idea flows. The possibility of cybernetic feedback is portrayed by a flow of ideas back from the receiver to the source.

Once the schematic framework for analysis of the transfer of ideas has been described, it is easier to identify the type of additional factors in the process which deserve the historian's attention. First, the characteristics of behavior of the principal participants must be examined using the tools of the psychologist. The role perceptions, goals, expectations, coding procedures, and interpersonal networks of the source, agent, and receiver should all be investigated for an understanding of the communication. If appropriate, the functions of "gatekeepers" (such as broadcasters or newspaper reporters) as filters of information should be assessed. Second, the historian must explore the flow of messages which make up the intercultural transfer and the channel through which the transfer occurs. He should ask such questions as, what is the channel capacity? what is the amount and type of noise in the system? what is the character of the messages which make up the flow? Here he may look to the linguist for aid.

Finally, the historian must examine the total social, economic, political, and cultural environment in which the transfer of ideas takes place. He must leave the guidance of the communications theorist and venture into grounds where his trained intuition—the historian's art—must be his main guide. In this part of his analysis, the historian may learn much from the economist, the sociologist, and the political scientist, in the same way as he learned from the communications theorist; but his borrowings, his selection of evidence, and his appraisals will remain a measure of his special skill.

For the historian who would venture into the intriguing and challenging field of intercultural transfers, the authors readily concede that the foregoing discussion may seem at once too simple and too complex. It must appear too simple in that it understates the difficulties the investigator is sure to encounter. The suggestions offered give little or no attention to the essential and incredibly intricate task of analyzing the source, the agent or agents along the line of transmission, and the receiver in their appropriate milieu. Nor, for that matter, is any real attention devoted to the problem of time. Transfers may often continue through extended periods, changing in character as the process goes on. This evasion is deliberate. The authors consciously trimmed away all but the barest essentials. It was their intention in doing so to induce more historians to consider their work on intercultural transfers in terms that would most readily lead to fruitful borrowings from the growing literature on the theory of communications. On the other hand, the authors were equally aware of the forbidding character that some of the mathematical studies on communications almost certainly present to many students of intercultural transfers. They will be content if they have managed to steer a middle course, encouraging a wider appreciation of what has already been written in a variety of disciplines without at the same time making these studies appear too formidable.

III

For Further Reading

The starting point for anyone concerned with the theory of information is Claude E. Shannon and Warren Weaver, *The Math-*

ematical Theory of Communication (Urbana, Ill., 1949). Even with the aid of Warren Weaver's chapters, however, non-mathematical readers will find this heavy going. A somewhat more accessible and highly readable introduction to the field is John R. Pierce, *Symbols, Signals and Noise: The Nature and Process of Communication* (New York, 1961). For those wishing a briefer introduction there is George A. Miller, "What is Information Measurement?", *American Psychologist*, VIII (1953), 3-11. For another brief account of information theory and its application to a variety of disciplines, see Brockway McMillan *et al., Current Trends in Information Theory* (Pittsburgh, 1953).

Several stimulating anthologies and collections of readings are available. Perhaps the best all-around volume for illustrating the remarkable range of applications of information theory is Alfred G. Smith, *Communication and Culture* (New York, 1966). Also useful are James H. Campbell and Hal W. Helper, eds., *Dimensions in Communication* (Belmont, Calif., 1965), and Wilbur L. Schramm, ed., *The Process and Effects of Mass Communication* (Urbana, Ill., 1954). Rather more tangential and less thoroughly related to the theory of information but also provocative is F. S. C. Northrop and H. H. Livingston, eds., *Cross-Cultural Understanding: Epistemology in Anthropology* (New York, 1964).

For those interested in pursuing the problem of model building in the transfer of ideas, a useful starting point is F. Craig Johnson and George R. Klave, "General Models of Communication Research: A Survey of Developments of a Decade," *Journal of Communication*, XI (1961), 13-26, 45. Historians and scholars in the social sciences will be particularly interested in two articles by Karl W. Deutsch, "On Communication Models in the Social Sciences," *Public Opinion Quarterly*, XVI (1952), 356-380, and "Communication Theory and Social Science," *American Journal of Orthopsychiatry*, XXII (1952), 469-483. Also helpful is Irwin D. J. Bross, "Models," a chapter in his volume, *Design for Decision* (New York, 1953), reprinted in Campbell and Helper, above. Similarly useful is B. H. Westley and M. S. MacLean, Jr., "A Conceptual Model for Communications Research," *Journalism Quarterly*, XXXIV (1957), 31-38, reprinted in Alfred Smith, above.